11/1/22

To Frank,

Thank you very much for having me on your show.

Sincerely,
Elliot

Movers & Shakers, *Vol. 2*

Movers & Shakers, *Vol. 2*

Sixty More Interviews on Everything from Judaism and Terrorism to Politics and Science

By Elliot Resnick

Brenn Books • • New York

Copyright © 2017 by Brenn Books

www.BrennBooks.com

All rights reserved.

ISBN 10: 0-9886768-4-2

ISBN-13: 978-0-9886768-4-8

PRINTED IN THE UNITED STATES OF AMERICA

To the Klass family,

founders and owners of The Jewish Press,

for decades of friendship with my family,

for believing in me, and for giving me the opportunity to thrive

Table of Contents

Rabbinic Wisdom

Mohammed's Sword

Israeli Mystique

Knesset Outliers

Religion vs. Science?

Hitler's Inferno

God vs. the USSR

Skewering the Left

Anti-Semitic Diversity

Organizational Chiefs

Miscellaneous

Preface

"The debate over quotes stretches from the newsroom to the courtroom. While most agree it's no crime to fix a simple grammatical error, there is wide disagreement over the extent to which journalists should alter quotes.

"If only sources could say it right the first time. If only they didn't ramble, switch tenses, inject 'ummm' or 'ah' into sentences and use 'gonna' instead of going to. If only their subjects agreed with their verbs. Then there wouldn't be the temptation – or necessity – to ever clean up a quote."

— *Fawn Germer, "Are Quotes Sacred?," American Journalism Review*

Editing interviews is a tricky business. Abba Eban is reputed to have answered reporters' questions with perfectly constructed paragraphs in impeccable English. Most humans are not that talented. They ramble, veer off course, and make grammatical errors. Is editing their words permissible? If yes, to what extent?

For nearly a decade, The New York Times Magazine ran a pithy 700-word interview column by Deborah Solomon, condensed from conversations that sometimes ran over 10,000 words. Her interviews were engaging – but did they accurately reflect what had been spoken? Some of her interview subjects thought not. Tim Russert, Ira Glass, and Amy Dickinson all publicly accused Solomon of misrepresenting their conversation and inserting questions into the published interview that she hadn't asked.

The New York Times resolved their Deborah Solomon problem largely by appending the words "condensed and edited" following her columns starting in late 2007. This disclaimer now regularly appears after Q&A's in many publications. But is it necessary? And regardless of whether it appears or not, what can one edit? What are the guidelines?

In 2005, the Columbia Journalism Review asked Solomon to outline the protocol for rearranging elements when preparing an interview for publication. She replied, "There's no Q&A protocol. You can write the manual." She later claimed she was joking, but the fact of the matter is that no agreed-upon rules for editing interviews exist. Nearly everyone will change "wanna" to "want to" and eliminate verbal ticks like "you know." But can you correct an interviewee's grammar? Can you tighten his answers? Can you insert a question you didn't ask to break up a long answer?

When Eugene Lyons of the United Press interviewed Joseph Stalin in 1930, Lyons composed an article immediately afterward and then read it to the Soviet premier. Stalin made a few minor corrections and then wrote: "more or less correct, J. Stalin." Modern interviewers possess a tool that Lyons, at the time, did not – a portable recording device – which allows them to aim higher than "more or less correct." But even with an accurate transcript of a conversation, is fidelity to the record more important than readability? If it isn't, what's the proper balance?

Susan Johnston Taylor – who has written for The Atlantic and Wall Street Journal, among other publications – argues that a "writer's job is to find the most interesting parts of the interview and edit out the fluff, while still accurately capturing what the subject said." She notes: "Most Q&As don't come out of the box perfectly formatted, and most people's speaking habits are full of verbal ticks, colloquialisms, starts and stops, and fractured sentences. Unless you're trying to capture a famous person's speaking habits, it's often better to edit the majority of these out for superior clarity. Just remember to keep any substantive changes in brackets…"

I share these principles. That means if an interviewee repeats the same point twice, I eliminate one of them. If he says "President Trump" repeatedly, I change some of them to "he." If he makes a parenthetical remark that detracts from the flow of the interview, I delete it – unless it changes the tenor of what follows or precedes it. In that case, for the sake of accuracy, the words must stay in or ellipses must take their place.

I try to never omit key elements. For example, if I'm interviewing an author, I believe I have a moral obligation to let him lay out, and defend, the basic thesis of his book. If he is an activist or politician, I must give him the opportunity to defend his cause. Whether I agree with the cause or book is irrelevant. If he is being interviewed, he deserves a chance to make his case.

Selective editing is tempting, but I try my best to avoid it. If an interviewee offers two reasons why he believes something, I personally may find reason #2 more interesting than reason #1, but if he emphasized reason #1 and only spoke about reason #2 briefly, I cannot in good conscience omit the former and focus exclusively on the latter. I can eliminate the entire line of questioning if I wish (assuming the question is not essential), but if I am to leave the question in, I must let reason #1 stand and give it at least somewhat greater prominence than reason #2.

Another item I try to be careful about is editing my own questions. If it's simply a matter of improving the wording of a question, I will do so unhesitatingly. But the improved question cannot differ in any significant way from the one I actually asked. I cannot change the tone or add elements to it. Every answer comes in response to a specific question. Change the question and you change the reader's impression of how the person replied. What may be a perfectly understandable response to one question may sound arrogant or evasive if placed after a different question (or a reworded one).

That's why adding questions to interviews is also generally verboten. The only time I will add a question is if it's essentially a "conversation filler" designed to break up a long answer and thereby improve the flow of the interview. For example, if someone in the middle of an answer says, "I did that because…," I believe it perfectly fine to add the question "Why?" before these words and begin a new answer with the sentence "Because…"

At the end of the day, many of these decisions are judgment calls. And a writer has to be honest with himself. His goal, as I see it, is to make the interview as interesting and engaging as possible without sacrificing accuracy. Occassionally, I find myself desperately wishing to "improve" an answer – from a linguistic standpoint – but I desist, knowing that it would be dishonest to do so without permission. If an answer reads particularly badly, the only solution is to contact the interviewee and get his consent to change it or to insert additional words in brackets.

This last rule is particularly important when it comes to verbs. Adding words such as "the," "a," "them," "because," etc. is generally harmless if it's clear from the transcript that these words were implied. But verbs color one's entire impression of what one is reading. "Denounce" is different than "criticize," which, in turn, is different than "chide." Each of these verbs carries a different shade of meaning, and a writer can't simply insert one into an interview – even if some form of the word was implied – without permission or ensconsing it in brackets.

We are all human. Even when we try our best, we occasionally make mistakes. But those who aim for accuracy are much more likely to achieve it than those who don't really care. I would like to think I belong to the former group and, so far, thank God, no one has accused me of distorting their words. May that never change.

~ ~ ~ ~ ~

As in volume one, the interviews in this book mostly derive from those I've conducted for The Jewish Press. Most interviews appear here exactly as they did in the newspaper aside from some minor editorial changes (along with postscripts informing readers what the interviewee and/or his cause has been up to since the interview's publication date). In several cases, though, I've deleted or added words (based on the original transcript) when I thought doing so would improve the interview.

This volume also includes original interviews with Katie Hopkins, a highly controversial British conservative, and Leo Hohmann, news editor for WorldNetDaily and author of *Stealth Invasion: Muslim Conquest Through Immigration and Resettlement*. Both concern Islamic terrorism, a topic that greatly interests American Jews but which is rarely spoken about honestly in public. I also conducted a third interview – with the controversial Rabbi Natan Slifkin – to round out the "Religion vs. Science?" section.

~ ~ ~ ~ ~

A rabbi from my youth used to respond to questions about his welfare by cheerfully quoting the words of the Psalmist: "Praise the Lord for His kindness is everlasting!" Throughout my life, God has extended His kindness to me in far greater measure than I deserve, and for that, and much else of course, I thank Him dearly. Thirteen years ago, God directed my path to The Jewish Press, where co-publisher Mrs. Naomi Klass Mauer was kind enough to offer me a job. For the opportunity and kindess she and her brother-in-law – managing editor Mr. Jerry Greenwald – have shown me over the years, I am supremely grateful.

I am also grateful to Jewish Press senior editor Jason Maoz, who edits my interviews, and generally selects them too; Shlomo Greenwald, a fellow Jewish Press editor, alongside whom I work; and my numerous other colleagues whose company and good cheer make The Jewish Press a most congenial place to be employed.

Also deserving thanks are Eli Chomsky, who edited some of the older interviews in this book; Sara Lehmann, who kindly gave me permission to reprint her interview with "Donald Trump's dealmaker," Jason Greenblatt; and the many people over the years who have commented on my interviews, especially my mother – both my biggest fan and greatest critic. Unlike teachers or lecturers, writers get no instant feedback. They have no idea if people enjoyed their work or if it made any impression. That's why the occasional "I loved your interview" is most gratifying and greatly appreciated. Thank you all.

Striking Chords

Ben Zion Shenker

The Man Whose Tunes Grace Shabbos Tables Worldwide

You may not know his name, but if you sing *"Eishes Chayil"* on Friday night, you're familiar with his music.

Ben Zion Shenker, 88, has composed roughly 500 songs in his lifetime, including *"Eishes Chayil"* (completed in 1953), *"Mizmor L'David, Hashem Ro'i"* (composed in 1946), and *"Yasis Ala'yich"* (composed in 1965). In addition, he has published several records of Modzitz music, including the very first chassidic record in the United States, "Modzitzer Melave Malke," released in 1956.

Recently dubbed "the greatest living figure of chassidic music" by NPR, Shenker still composes several new pieces every year. He is currently recording an album of some of his *Haggadah* compositions, which he hopes will be out before *Pesach.*

The Jewish Press interviewed him at his home in Flatbush last week.

The Jewish Press: Where were you born?

Shenker: In Williamsburg, Brooklyn, 1925. My parents came to America in 1921. Both of them came from small towns not far from Lublin.

How did you first get involved in music?

Music is something you have to be born with. My early involvement didn't come until I was about 12 years old when I joined a choir led by a fellow by the name of Joshua Weisser. He heard me singing one Shabbos and told my father he'd like me to join his choir. But choirs at that time weren't known for their religiosity, and my father thought I was too young to go away from home.

This was a shul choir accompanying the *chazzan*?

Yes, you don't have too many of them now, but at one time all the big shuls had *chazzanim* and choirs. It was almost a given.

In any event, my father told him he didn't think it was a good idea. But Weisser found out where I lived and went to speak to my mother. My mother told him the same thing, but he was persistent and promised that wherever we went he would put me up at the rabbi's house or the finest *baal habas*....

So I joined and became the alto soloist. He had special solos for me; he even wrote some new ones because I was able to do what they call a coloratura, which is like a *shalsheles*. Most kids couldn't do it, but I had the aptitude because I used to listen to a lot of *chazzanishe* records when I was a kid. In fact, when I was three or four years old, maybe even younger, we had a Victrola player in the house, and my mother would sit me down in front of it for hours with a pack of *chazzanishe* records. So I was pretty well advanced as far as my knowledge of *chazzanus*, and Weisser appreciated that.

Is it true you also had your own radio program at age 13?

I had a 15-minute feature on one of the Jewish radio stations in downtown Brooklyn. When I started off, it was on a Sunday afternoon, around 12:00, so I had to get permission from the yeshiva to leave. My teacher was Rav Pam – it was his first year teaching in Mesivta Torah Vodaath – so I went over to him and told him I have a radio program and have to leave at 11:00. He said, "A radio program?" He couldn't believe what he was hearing.

He said, "I can't give you permission. You have to go to the principal, Rabbi [Shraga Feivel] Mendlowitz. So I went to Rabbi Mendlowitz, and he also looked at me...and had a little hard time giving me permission. But he [eventually agreed]. He said, "Number one, you have to come back to the second *seder*. Secondly, I don't want you to hang around there. Go there, do your job, and leave. Don't make any friends with anybody." Those were the terms.

How did your musical association with Modzitz start?

That happened when I was 15. The Modzitzer Rebbe came here in 1941 as a refugee from Poland. He was invited for a Shabbos in Bed-Stuy, and at the Shabbos meal – to which my father and I had been invited – there was a book on the sofa behind the Rebbe called *LaChassidim Mizmor*, with little biographies of all the *rebbeim* who were known as composers and singers. The book also had a biography of the Modzitzer Rebbe, and in it were some musical notations. I was studying music at the time and knew how to read music, so I started singing to myself. The Rebbe overheard and said, "You can read notes?" I said, "A little bit, yeah." He said, "Let me hear, let me hear."

So I started reading his own *niggunim* and he became very excited. Later, he asked me to sing *Shir Hama'alos* before *bentching*, so I sang one of his own *niggunim* that I had learned from a Lubavitcher friend who had studied in yeshiva in Otwok. The Modzitzer Rebbe was [based in Otwok after WWI] and my friend heard the Rebbe singing his *niggunim* at *Sha'le Seudos*. The Rebbe was so surprised, though, because the *niggun* was made in 1938, I think, and this was 1941. How did it ever get to America so quickly?

[Anyways, to make a long story short, I soon] became his musical secretary. Any time he made a new *niggun*, I was the one who notated it.

How many pieces did you notate?

About 100, but he had many more. In fact, to the present day, they keep discovering compositions by him and his father which were never notated. In Israel they have a *machon* that devotes itself to collecting all of Modzitzer *niggunim*, starting from the first Rebbe.

How many Modzitzer *niggunim* do you know?

About 1,000 at least, including from the Rebbe's father and son. The son was a very prolific composer also.... Some of his *niggunim* became very popular, like the one for *Lecha Dodi*: "Dum di di dum dum, dum di di dum dum, *lo seivoshi...*"

Who wrote the Modzitzer "*Ezkara*" which famously takes almost a half hour to sing?

That was the Rebbe's father, Reb Yisrael. He had a very bad case of diabetes, and he developed sores on his leg until it became gangrenous. So he went to the doctors in Warsaw, and they said, "Something has to be done because you might *chalilah* die." So they advised him to go to Berlin where there was a surgeon who was very well known at that time.

When he was in Berlin, he looked at how beautiful the city was, and the words "*Ezkara Elokim v'ehemaya bir'osi kol ir al tila benuyah...* – I remember you, God, and I tremble when I see every city on its pedestal, but the city of God, Yerushalayim, is down in the depth" came to him. It's a *tefillah* we say in *Ne'ilah.*

The story is told that he asked the doctor not to have anesthesia because at that time anesthesia was still in the early stages, and there was a rumor that it could have an effect on your mind. So he had the surgery without anesthesia, and [he is said to have composed this piece during the surgery].

Did you feel out of place at that first Shabbos meal with the Modzitzer Rebbe? After all, you weren't a Modzitzer *chassid.*

My father was not a Modzitzer *chassid* either, but we were all *chassidim.* My father was a Trisker *chassid,* which comes from Chernobyl *Chassidus.* Trisk and about seven other *chassidusin* – Skver, Tolna, Rachmistrivka... – are all *einiklach* of Chernobyl.

You have to remember that Torah Vodaath was also considered more or less a very chassidic yeshiva because Rav Shraga Feivel was a chassidishe guy.

Your two most famous compositions are probably "*Eishes Chayil*" and "*Mizmor L'David.*" How did you come up with these two pieces?

You never know how these things come to your head. I composed "*Mizmor L'David*" in Palestine in 1946. It came to me while sitting in my uncle's house for *Sha'le Seudos.*

"*Eishes Chayil*" I composed later on when I was married already. I can't say it came to me in one sitting. It was something I worked on. Every Friday night I had thoughts about it until finally I finalized it in 1953.

Your "*Eishes Chayil*" is sung almost everywhere. What tune did people sing before yours?

In my parents' house, we never sang "*Eishes Chayil.*" There are tunes for "*Eishes Chayil*" from the *talmidim* of the Baal Shem Tov, but I don't know them. There is also one from Rav Nachman Breslover, which I once saw notated some place.

What other songs of yours are famous?

Well, there's one that's becoming very popular in Israel now at all the chassidishe weddings. It's called "*Hatov, hatov.*" In fact, about four weeks ago, I got a call from Avraham Fried. He was searching the Internet and heard me singing "*Hatov, hatov*" at a gathering with the present Modzitzer Rebbe this past Chanukah. "I got to have that song," he told me, "I love it." So I invited him over to the house, he recorded it for himself, and he'll get back to me probably.

You've composed something like 500 pieces of music. Do you remember them all?

Well, if you don't sing them, you forget them. In fact, we have a *kumzitz* every *Chol HaMoed* and, beside myself, I usually ask two of my friends to sing something because I want to take a little rest. [This year] one of them started singing a song that was familiar to me, but I wasn't sure what it was. He went through the whole thing, and I said, "What's that song?" It turns out it was one of my own.

If someone wanted to listen to your music, where could he hear it?

Twice a year we have a *kumzitz,* and we also have gatherings in the Modzitz *shtiebel* on Coney Island Ave. on the *yahrzeit* of each of [the Modzitz Rebbes]. And then there are 12 CDs that are being sold now in Judaica stores. Out of the 12, I would say about seven are Modzitz and five are mine.

What's your opinion of the current state of Jewish music?

I'm not a big *chassid* of contemporary Jewish music because what they're trying to do is imitate goyishe music. Sometimes they latch a song onto holy words that have no *shaichus* whatsoever with the *niggun,* and that bothers me a little bit.

Wasn't Eastern European Jewish music also influenced by its environs?

That's true, there were influences, but the songs sounded Jewish – put it that way – whereas some of the songs you hear coming out now don't. There's all these different kinds of styles that they use now – even rap. It's hard to go along with that kind of situation.

You're 88 years old and still composing. Some people your age would retire and take it easy.

Believe me, sometimes I wonder why I'm not doing that. But in a way, it keeps me alive; it keeps me a little young also.

— originally published January 29, 2014

Postscript: *Ben Zion Shenker passed away at age 91 on November 20, 2016. Weeks earlier, he released his last album, "Shiru LaShem Shir Chadash," containing 15 original compositions.*

Cantor Joseph Malovany

The Polish President's *Chazzan*

Born in 1941, Cantor Joseph Malovany serves as rector of the Institute of Jewish Traditional Liturgical Music in Leipzig, Germany; dean of the Academy of Jewish Music in Moscow; professor of Jewish Music at Yeshiva University in New York; and cantor of Manhattan's Fifth Avenue Synagogue.

He's sung with such orchestras as the Israel Philharmonic, the London Classical, the Prague Symphony Orchestra, the Russian State Symphony, and the Sao Paulo Symphony Orchestra and has received numerous honors, including Poland's Cross of Merit – Commander of the Legion of Honor.

He recently spoke with The Jewish Press.

The Jewish Press: Where did you grow up?

Cantor Malovany: I was born and grew up in Tel Aviv and went to the Bilu school. It was famous all over the world because of its shul, which had a choir of 40 boys. When I was eight-and-a-half years old, I was already *davening Kabbalas Shabbos* [for the *amud*] accompanied by the choir.

Except for *Barchu*, I presume.

No, including *Barchu*. At the time, Rav Isser Yehuda Unterman was the chief rabbi of Tel Aviv and he permitted it as a matter of *chinuch*. Later there were some halachic objections, so Rav Unterman said our teacher,

Shlomo Ravitz, should sing *Barchu* and *Kaddish* together with the boy.

When did you know you would become a *chazzan* by profession?

I actually originally wanted to become a conductor and studied classical piano and conducting at the Academy of Music of Tel Aviv. But I found out that in order to get into the world of symphonic conducting, a very important component is entering international conducting competitions. I applied and was accepted to quite a few, but all of them required [conducting] on Shabbos, and I was not prepared to give up an inch in my *frumkeit*. As an *einekel* of Reb Avraham Michael Malovany and Reb Yosef Stein – who learned *b'chavrusa* with the Satmar Rebbe in Europe – it was out of the question. So it was at that crucial moment that I decided to apply my knowledge of music to *chazzanus* and become a *chazzan*.

So you left the world of classical music behind?

No, I still practice every day for 30-45 minutes. I have a huge grand piano at home, and this morning, for example, I played Brahms' sonata in F sharp minor and Bach's chromatic fantasy. In fact, when I have a concert with an orchestra where I am the only one performing, I insist on conducting one symphonic classical music piece for my own pleasure – "The Barber of Seville" by Rossini, for example, or Verde's "The Force of Destiny."

Who were your cantorial "heroes" growing up?

First was my teacher Shlomo Ravitz. Then there was Moshe Koussevitzky and his brother David Koussevitzky, whom I knew very well and loved very much. I knew Moshe too. In fact, I accompanied him on the piano when he gave an outdoor concert for 5,000 Israeli soldiers on a July day in the 1960s.

Of course I also liked Yossele Rosenblatt very much, and Mordechai Hershman too. Hershman was not a composer but he had such a beautiful voice and his interpretation was always so sublime that it got to me.

How do you view your job as a *chazzan*?

A *chazzan* first and foremost has to regard himself as a *shliach tzibbur*.

The prayer *"Hineni"* on Rosh Hashanah and Yom Kippur says a *shliach tzibbur* should have a beard, should have a nice voice, and should be *"me'urav bedaas im habriyos,"* involved in the life of his community. This is extremely important.

Number two, I always tell my students that before you try to be a *chazzan,* you have to be a *baal tefillah.* A *baal tefillah* is someone who is extremely well versed with the *nusach,* with the musical motifs of *davening.* Every *tefillah* – take *Yishtabach* or *Ahavah Rabah* for example – has a musical motif and that's the way to sing it. If you sing a congregational melody, it should be built on this motif; if it isn't, at least come back to it somehow. If you don't, you are breaking a traditional chain that goes back a couple of thousand years.

Sometimes I hear a *shliach tzibbur* sing a pop chassidic melody – which is not pop and not chassidic. It's nothing. It has no quality. It comes from the nightclubs. There is nothing Jewish there. I would even venture to say it's a *chillul hakodesh.* What right do people have to bring the banging of the disco into the synagogue?

In an interview several years ago, you criticized people who study Gemara during *davening*.

Yes, I'm very critical because, I think, they have no *kavanah* in their *tefillah.* They're just saying the words to be *yotzei* and then they're into the learning. What did Shlomo HaMelech say? There is a time for everything. So there is a time for *tefillah* and a time for learning. I learn the *Daf Yomi* every morning at 6:30 in my shul. I love learning, but *tefillah* is *tefillah* and learning is learning.

Which famous personalities have you met in your career?

I've been friendly with Israeli prime ministers beginning with Golda Meir, who was very musical. She liked *chazzanus,* and her son was a cellist. I was also friendly with Yitzhak Rabin, Yitzhak Shamir, and Arik Sharon. Arik loved *chazzanus;* he was not a big maven but he loved it.

The highlight among the prime ministers, though, was of course Menachem Begin. I remember when he turned 65 I was invited to sing at his birthday and he told me what *chazzanus* pieces to sing. I was very close with him.

How about other world leaders?

I've met Gorbachev several times. His English is not so great but whenever I see him, I tell him a couple of jokes about himself – which someone translates for him – and he's on the floor.

I met Putin only once and that was for International Holocaust Day in 2005, 60 years after the liberation of Auschwitz. I was invited to do all the *tefillos*. I remember I asked the president of Poland, "Can you please introduce me to President Putin?" So he says, "Volodya, come here. This is Joseph Malovany. He's my cantor. He sang in my royal castle, and you have to invite him to sing in the Kremlin." After that we went aside and chatted for about 5-7 minutes on all kinds of interesting things.

Can you share anything from that conversation?

I'd rather not.

Until recently you used to travel often to Eastern Europe. Why?

When the Soviet Union began to crumble I felt there was a need to do something for Soviet Jewry. I knew they were musical and I thought *chazzanus* would do a lot for them. So when I received an invitation to come to Moscow, I went and helped establish the Moscow Academy of Jewish Music and the Moscow Jewish Men's Choir. Until today, this choir travels all over the world. It's my creation – all the music they sing, all the arrangements, everything.

What was it like traveling to the Soviet Union before the Cold War ended?

I had a run-in with the KGB because in a speech I referred to "St. Petersburg" when the city's official name was still Leningrad. I remember two guys came Friday night to our hotel room and wanted to give me a hard time. I said to them, "If you arrest me for saying that, within an hour President Reagan is going to be on the phone with Gorbachev and you'll be in trouble for creating an international crisis."

So nothing [happened]. But as they were leaving the room, they noticed that my wife had lit Shabbos candles. One of the KGB officials looked and looked and then said, "I remember my grandmother lighting candles like this and she did something with the hands." I looked at him – I had tears in my eyes – and said, "Was it your mother's mother?" He said, "Yes." I said to him, "I have news for you. You're Jewish. What are you giving me a hard time for?" I gave him a hug and we drank vodka.

Have you had any interactions with famous rabbinic personalities? Chassidic rebbes, for example?

I had three chassidic rebbes. The first was the Lubavitcher Rebbe, with whom I had an unbelievable relationship. The second was the Satmar Rebbe, whom I told you learned *b'chavrusa* with my grandfather in Europe. When I used to go into the Satmar Rebbe, he would stand up. When I objected, he said, "I'm standing up not for you; I'm standing up in honor of your grandfather."

And the third was the old Bobover Rebbe, Reb Shlomo. He was very musical. I once met him in England, and he asked me for my *haskama* on a new melody he had composed. His *meshorerim* sang it for me, and I thought that, musically speaking – for a person who had no knowledge of music to be able to compose such a thing with modulations to different keys – it was genius. When they finished it, the Rebbe said to me, "*Nu*, what do you say?" I said to him, "A *niggun* like this can only be composed *b'ruach hakodesh*."

He became [a bit startled] and said, "Yossele Rosenblatt once spent Shabbos in Bobov and a similar story happened. My father, Rav Bentzion, asked Reb Yossele for his opinion on a *niggun* he composed and he said the very same words: 'Only *b'ruach hakodesh*.'"

— originally published April 20, 2016

Postscript: *The Academy of Jewish Music in Moscow has since closed its doors.*

Abie Rotenberg

Composing Music for the Soul

Trying one's hand at something new is always risky. In the 1990s, Michael Jordan learned the hard way that excellence in one field – basketball – doesn't necessarily translate into even mediocrity in another – baseball.

Abie Rotenberg hopes to have better luck. Arguably the greatest living composer of Jewish music, Rotenberg recently published his first novel, *The Season of Pepsi Meyers* (Audley Street Books). Set 25 years in the future, the novel's plot centers around a promising young Jewish baseball player who discovers the beauty of Torah Judaism midway through his stellar rookie season.

Rotenberg's musical oeuvre includes "D'veykus" (six volumes), "Journeys" (four volumes), "Aish" (two volumes), "The Marvelous Middos Machine" (four volumes), and "The Golden Crown."

The Jewish Press: You're a successful composer. What made you decide to write a novel?

Rotenberg: Well, I've always been writing. As a lyricist you obviously write – even if the form is different. But the plot of the novel came to me one morning on the way to shul three years ago. It started at the end of my block, and by the time I got to shul – it's about a 15-minute walk – I had the outline of the book in my head.

Is the book primarily for *frum* or non-*frum* readers?

I hope the majority of copies go to Jews who really don't know that much about *Yiddishkeit*. At the same time, there are so many *frum* kids today who really don't understand the basics of Judaism. In school, they learn how to read a Rashi and maybe how to understand a line of Gemara but sometimes *hashkafa* is not laid out properly, and if you try to teach it to them in an organized fashion, it's very boring. So a book like this where principles of *emunah* are embedded within a baseball story is something even *frum* kids will hopefully gain from.

Let's turn to music, which is of course the source of your fame. How and when did your musical career begin?

I was musical as a child. I sang in a choir, and my father, who was from Europe, played piano and loved chassidic *niggunim* and *zemiros*, so there was always a lot of singing in my home. Already in high school, I think, I composed a couple of songs.

Then, when I got into Yeshiva Chofetz Chaim in Queens, I was learning *b'chavrusa* with Rabbi Label Sharfman. He was one of The Rabbis' Sons [a music group primarily active in the 1960s and '70s], so naturally we talked about music. He got to hear my compositions and liked them, so we decided to do something together – and that became "D'veykus."

What happened afterward?

Baruch Hashem, my music was accepted and enjoyed by people right away, so I became known as a composer of *niggunim*. It wasn't until the mid-'80s that I started to write English songs, and those were the "Journeys" albums with pieces like "It's Time to Say Good Shabbos," "Mama Rachel," "Memories," "The Ninth Man," "The Atheist Convention," and "Joe DiMaggio's Card."

It's a very different process. When you compose a *niggun*, you try to understand the feeling David HaMelech put into that particular *pasuk*, and, if done successfully, the song can become a kind of *peirush* on the words. When you write an English song, though, you're really thinking of a theme or a message and the song almost becomes secondary.

How do you come up with your English songs? Is it sudden inspiration or dogged perspiration?

I have songs that I wrote in one evening and songs that took me years to finish. For example, I wrote a song for a HASC concert about special children called "Who Am I?" which was composed in a burst of inspiration. I started writing between ten and eleven o'clock at night and finished around three in the morning.

But other songs I've struggled with, and it's taken me a long time to find the right lyric, the right word, and, even musically, the right note. For example, I wrote a song about the Holocaust called "What Will Become of All the Memories?" which took me five years to finish. And I have many songs that have never been published – and may never be published – simply because I haven't been able to finish them.

A recent reviewer of *The Season of Pepsi Meyers* called you "an Orthodox Paul Simon." Your reaction?

Well, I love Paul Simon's music and I was certainly influenced by Simon and Garfunkel growing up in the 1960s. I also loved and was influenced by the Mitchell Trio.

How about Jewish influences?

Shlomo Carlebach, Baruch Chait, Moshe Yess. I also know Modzitz music very well and loved Ben Zion Shenker growing up. I mentioned earlier that my father knew chassidic music, so my musical influences are chassidic, Carlebach, Simon and Garfunkel, the Beatles – I guess, like most people, it's a real *cholent*.

Can you share some memories of your interactions with Shlomo Carlebach and Moshe Yess?

I played guitar once with Shlomo. This was when I was just starting out – I was maybe 19 years old – and Shlomo had hurt his leg and couldn't stand and hold his guitar because he was on crutches. He had a concert at

Queens College and somebody heard that I knew how to play guitar, so they called me up at the last minute and promised that Shlomo was going to come early and rehearse the songs with me.

Well, Shlomo came an hour late – not to the rehearsal, but to the concert itself – and it was like a nightmare because I didn't know what he was singing and he didn't know what I was playing. But we got through the night, *baruch Hashem.*

How about Moshe Yess?

Moshe Yess and I were very close. Not only did he sing on the "Journeys" albums – "The Ninth Man," "There's No Place Like Home," "The Pesach Blues" – but he was also my partner in the first "Marvelous Middos Machine" production. I was teaching in a school in Toronto at the time and every afternoon after *Minchah* I would go over to his house, and for two or three hours we'd write songs and the script together. It was one of the best and most creative periods of my life.

Moshe Yess was an incredibly creative person, and his music had a deep impact upon me. When I heard his great song "My Zaidy" for the first time, it opened my eyes and I said, "There *can* be quality folk Jewish music" – and I was determined to try my hand at it.

What inspired you to write "The Marvelous Middos Machine" for children after writing so many successful compositions for adults?

Having my own children. "The Marvelous Middos Machine" is a series that focuses on trying to get kids to make the correct choices – not to lie, not to be jealous, not to be lazy, not to fight, not to embarrass others, etc. And I wanted to educate children in these *middos* in a creative way.

And honestly, some of the most enjoyable lyrics I have written have been the children's lyrics. For example: "Never Take Kids to a Store" – I love that song. I wrote it myself, but I love it. It was so much fun to write.

I think adults perhaps appreciate the lyrics more than children.

I think that's one of the reasons we were successful with "The

Marvelous Middos Machine" series – because when your kid asks you to play a CD in the car, you're not going to want to play it more than once if it hurts your ears to listen to it.

What's your take on the current state of Jewish music?

I don't follow it that much. I really don't. I'm not a wedding performer, so I don't have to know all the hit songs of today. But music always changes, so whatever is well-accepted and inspires people is good. I have a song on "Journeys 3" called "Yes, We've Got the Music," and the lyrics at the end of the song are "...but one thing we must keep in mind / a Jewish song of any kind / is only precious if and when / it brings us closer to Hashem."

So that's what Jewish music is. Jewish music is something that should help us identify as Jews. And what's being Jewish? It's a connection to *Hakadosh Baruch Hu*. So if music gets us there, it doesn't matter what the rhythm is, it's a beautiful thing.

In the 1990s, Rabbi Emanuel Feldman wrote an article titled "A Ten Coarse Affair" in which he lambasted contemporary *frum* weddings for essentially exhibiting "glatt gluttony" and featuring music "distorted [by] the strident rhythm of the jungle." Do you disagree with him?

Rabbi Feldman was my inspiration for the wedding song on "Journeys 2." On some wedding invitations people write, "Please dress *tznius*" when the wedding itself is anti-*tznius*! *Tznius* doesn't only mean you cover your elbows. It also means you don't show off your money.

As far as the music is concerned, though, I understand what Rabbi Feldman is saying, but I'm wary to criticize anything because music always changes. If you took a *rosh yeshiva* from the 1960s and brought him in a time machine to a contemporary wedding in Lakewood, he would be shocked out of his mind. It could be the *frumest* wedding but this *rosh yeshiva* from the '60s would *platz* and run out of the room in horror because all the music has rock rhythms. So music changes, and if today's kids get closer to *Hakadosh*

Baruch Hu because of these songs, it's wonderful. I know many people feel differently but I hesitate to say anything negative.

What are you working on now?

I'm actually working on a *sefer* in English.

On what topic?

I don't want to say, but I hope to have it finished some time within the next year.

As far as music is concerned, there's nothing really happening at the moment – although my kids say I should release a single. Maybe I'll do that.

— originally published December 30, 2015

Postscript: *In late 2016, Abie Rotenberg published his first work of non-fiction, "Eliyahu HaNavi: The Prophet Through the Prism of Tanach, Talmud and Midrash" (ArtScroll). Rotenberg told me the book "is the culmination of over eight years of work."*

Cantor Bernard Beer

Preserving the Musical *Mesorah*

After a half century at Yeshiva University's Philip and Sarah Belz School of Jewish Music – 30 of those years as its director – Cantor Bernard Beer has retired.

Born and bred in Brooklyn, Beer received his musical training at Yeshiva University, Columbia University, and the Julliard School of Music. He served as a professional cantor in several synagogues from 1965-1989 and is currently editor of the Journal of Jewish Music and Liturgy and executive vice president of the Cantorial Council of America (a position he's held since 1974).

He is also currently recording the traditional liturgy for the entire year as part of the "Nusach Legacy Project." The first volume, "Musaf of Rosh Hashanah," was released earlier this year.

The Jewish Press: Your career in Jewish music dates back quite some time. Apparently you've been singing on key since age three.

Beer: It's true. Both my parents were very musical, and my mother was always singing in the house. My brothers remember that she couldn't get over that when she asked me to repeat a song as a three-year-old boy, I was able to sing it on pitch. I even sang "The Anniversary Waltz" at my oldest brother's bar mitzvah; I was four years old at the time.

How did you wind up entering the field of *chazzanus*?

I was born into it. My father was an outstanding *baal tefillah* and *baal korei*, and we lived in Boro Park in the 1940s where there were large cathedral synagogues, each of which had a *chazzan*. At the time, Boro Park had two of the greatest *chazzanim* who ever lived: Moshe and David Koussevitzky. And prior to Moshe Koussevitzky, there was a *chazzan* by the name of Berele Chagy at Beth El in Boro Park who also was outstanding. So I was brought up with it. It was in the air we breathed.

Did you always know you wanted to pursue *chazzanus*?

I was always into it. I used to listen to all the recordings of the great *chazzanim* – Rosenblatt, Koussevitzky, Hershman, Kwartin – and would try to replicate them. After my bar mitzvah, I *davened* at the *amud* in many shuls in Boro Park.

But then my voice began to mature and I didn't begin singing again until the age of 18. At the time I was going to college and majoring in languages because I wanted to be a teacher. But then I started attending classes at YU's school of Jewish music – which at the time was called CTI, the Cantorial Training Institute – and for the first time encountered music as an academic discipline. I was so impressed that I decided to change my major.

In 1967, I was appointed to the faculty of the school and I also taught in MTA. I taught general music, *nusach*, and cantillation.

When you say "*nusach*," you mean something different from what the average Jew who uses this word does, correct?

Nusach ha'tefillah can refer to the text – Ashkenaz, Sephard, Arizal. But it also can refer to the melody. Every synagogue service has its own unique melody chant. For example, *Kaddish* of *Maariv* on Rosh Hashanah or *Barchu* on the *Shalosh Regalim*.

In reference to *Kol Nidrei*, the Mishnah Berurah quotes the Maharil that you're not allowed to change the custom of the community when it comes to *niggunim*. People, though, are not cognizant of this *halacha*, and even though I've retired I hope to be involved in outreach programs to go to different communities and give lectures on *nusach ha'tefillah*.

Who, in your estimation, are the best *chazzanim* of all time?

Rosenblatt, Hirschman, Koussevitzky – they're all great *chazzanim*, but that's not really what it's all about today. The synagogue service today is suffering from a lack of knowledge in terms of how to *daven*, so I'm trying to get away from that whole concept of "Who's the greatest *chazzan*?" If we don't know how to *daven*, what's the difference who the greatest *chazzan* is?

What do you mean by "don't know how to *daven*"?

Ninety-nine percent of the people don't know the melodies. They don't know how to set the text together.

Who decides what's correct?

There is a proper *nusach* for every occasion. If an individual leads a *Mussaf* service on Rosh Hashanah and sings something other than the traditional *Kaddish* tune before *Shemoneh Esrei*, it's not correct. And even if people are not knowledgeable, they know when it sounds right. They know when it's authentic.

In a lecture in 1977, the Rav – Rabbi [Joseph B.] Soloveitchik – said there's a tendency of *baalei tefillah* to use contemporary melodies for "*O'chilah laKeil achaleh fanav*" and it's very wrong. You're not allowed to do that, he said, because *nusach* interprets the text and it has *kedushah* because it has been handed down to us.

But aren't new tunes added to the *davening* over time?

There are certain parts of *davening* that are not set to any particular *nusach*. For instance, "*Lecha Dodi*" on Friday night. You can use many melodies for it. But when you're talking about *tefillos* like "*HaMelech*" on Rosh Hashanah or "*Tal*" and "*Geshem*" on *Pesach* and *Sukkos* – you can't change that. That has been handed down to us, generation to generation. It's our musical *mesorah*.

Are these what *chazzanim* like to call "*miSinai* tunes"?

Yes. There's also another term for it, "*skarbove,*" which comes from the Polish "*skarb,*" which means treasure. These are tunes that are held in such reverence that it is as if they came from Sinai. Take the tune for *Kol Nidrei,* for example. Can you imagine changing *Kol Nidrei* to a Carlebach tune? I'm not knocking Carlebach – his tunes are beautiful – but you can't change it.

And that's another aspect of the importance of *nusach. Nusach* unites people. No matter where you are, wherever you go, you're not going to hear a different melody for *Kol Nidrei.* The melody unites us as one.

Does the term "*miSinai* tunes" refer only to Ashkenazic melodies or Sephardic ones as well?

Ashkenazic only. Sephardic is a completely different world. And as a matter of fact, the Sephardic tradition is probably more authentic, especially the Yemenite one, since the *Teimanim* never left their *daled amos* and retained all their melodies from way, way back. Sephardic tunes are probably the closest to the way they sang in the *Beis HaMikdash.*

In a recent interview you said, "In many instances I have found that synagogue *nusach* and its music have brought people closer to observance." Can you provide an example?

About 30 years ago, the Joint Distribution Committee sent us students from Russia, and one of them was the chief cantor of Moscow. He couldn't read too well, he didn't know the melodies, and he didn't know too much about *tallis* and *tefillin* either. But when he came here, he became observant. If you have a certain music sensitivity, synagogue music can really inspire you.

How would you react to someone who says he prefers listening to a good *baal tefillah* over a professional *chazzan* since *chazzanim* tend to use pretentious, affected voices?

He's not a good *chazzan* if that's what he does. A good *chazzan* doesn't use a crazy voice. You sing with a normal voice. Have you heard some of the good *chazzanim* today? Let's say Helfgot. I'm not a big *chassid* of Helfgot. I'm not a *chassid* of any of the living *chazzanim* because all they do is imitate the recordings. Anyone can do that if they have some talent.

But the voice of a good *chazzan* should not sound – what did you say? – affected. It should sound like a natural voice. The *chazzanim* these people are listening to are not good *chazzanim*. I'm sorry. They have crazy voices but they're not good *chazzanim*. I agree, I'd rather hear a good *baal tefillah* than hear that kind of *chazzan*. I agree 100 percent.

— originally published October 28, 2015

Postscript: *In a March 2017 e-mail, Cantor Beer told me he currently conducts outreach seminars on nusach ha'tefillah and is set to soon release further volumes of the "Nusach Legacy" project (featuring Shachris of Rosh Hashanah and portions of the Shalosh Regalim davening).*

Charles Krauthammer

A Political Pundit With a Musical Passion

Charles Krauthammer may be paralyzed from the neck down, but that hasn't stopped him from becoming one of the most influential political commentators in America today. A contributing editor to The Weekly Standard and The New Republic, Krauthammer is also a nightly commentator on Fox News' Special Report with Bret Baier and a weekly panelist on PBS's Inside Washington. Close to 250 newspapers carry his weekly column, which earned him a Pulitzer Prize in 1987.

In addition to his political prowess, Krauthammer maintains a love for Jewish music. Several years ago, he and his wife Robyn founded Pro Musica Hebraica, which is devoted to "bringing Jewish music to the concert hall."

On December 2, the organization will hold a concert of cantorial masterpieces at the Eldridge Street Synagogue. The Jewish Press recently spoke with Krauthammer about the concert, among other topics.

The Jewish Press: What led you to found Pro Musica Hebraica?

Krauthammer: About eight years ago, my wife and I decided there was an area of Jewish culture that had been fairly neglected – great Jewish music in a classical setting – and we wanted to do something to bring it out to the world.

Is the music Pro Musica Hebraica presents really *Jewish* music or just music that happens to have been composed by Jews?

The idea is to bring Jewish experience, feeling, and history – "Jewish soul," if you like – as expressed through classical music.

So it doesn't matter who the author is. One of our concerts a few years ago was baroque Jewish music from 17th- and 18th-century Italy and Holland. It included the famous Sephardic Jewish composer Salamone Rossi, but it also had a selection by a Jesuit priest who was a philo-Semite and who set Psalms to baroque music. He was so much of a Hebraist that he actually wrote the music from right to left when he was transcribing it.

So we don't care about the origin of the composer, although, of course, most of the music is by Jews self-consciously reflecting their own heritage, past, and memories.

Why has this music been neglected?

Well, I'll give you one example. One of the major schools of this music was called the St. Petersburg school. Founded in 1908, this school consisted of students of Rimsky Korsakov. They were in the Russian conservatories, and their teacher basically said to them, "Why are you trying to compose Russian music? You're Jews. Compose the music of your own people."

So they sent ethnographic expeditions into the shtetl, listened to the music, and transcribed it. That was their inspiration for composing classical music with Jewish themes – the same way that Bartok, for example, produced classical Hungarian music from Hungarian folk themes.

This school thrived for 10 years. They put on concerts all over Russia, but then the Russian revolution came in 1917 and they were scattered to all corners of the world. Their music was largely forgotten, but we brought it back with Itzhak Perlman on the 100th anniversary of this school's founding to an amazing critical review in the Washington Post and tremendous public response.

This upcoming concert on December 2, though, will feature, not classical music, but *chazzanus.*

Yes, it's our first venture away from classical music towards more traditional liturgical music. It's also our first time in New York; we're usually in the Kennedy Center in Washington. Cantor Netanel Hershtik of The Hampton Synagogue, who is just exquisite, is performing, and the venue will be the Eldridge Street Synagogue, which is celebrating its 125th anniversary.

One theme that runs through this concert is redemption. It's a theme that's so prevalent in the liturgy that you can't go three pages in the *siddur* without coming across it. I think it's very important, particularly for those who may not be religious or aren't even Jewish, to understand that the idea of return, restoration – the idea of Zion – is not a modern creation but a theme going back to "*Im eshkacheich Yerushalayim,*" which was written 2,500 years ago....

One of the reasons I wanted to do this was because when I was growing up we would spend our summers in Long Beach where, once a year, Moshe Koussevitzky would perform at one of the synagogues at the far end of Long Beach. My father would take my brother and me, and we would walk for about an hour to hear him. I have never forgotten that. It was the most moving music or religious presence.

That tradition, though, really isn't around that much anymore. I have always wanted to have other people experience what I did when I was eight, nine, and ten. So for me, this is a labor of love. It has nothing to do with my work as a political commentator. It's purely an expression of my own Jewish experience and the desire to see it shared by others.

Do you find that your Jewish background and upbringing affect your work as a political commentator?

Well, I'm very wary of people who draw lines from the Bible to political platforms, but clearly my worldview is shaped by my upbringing and awareness of Jewish culture, life, and history. You can see it, for example, when it comes to my writing about Israel. It's very heavily influenced by the fact that I know it rather well and studied the history. If you had a Jewish upbringing like I did, it will inevitably shape your life and perspective on the world.

The other impact it had is that I studied Talmud very intensively during my school years, and I think that kind of critical textual thinking, which is the essence of Talmudic study, has carried over into the way I look at and interpret events, documents, Supreme Court decisions – all the things I deal with as a commentator.

You once worked as a speechwriter for the liberal Walter Mondale. How did you go from that to becoming one of America's most prominent conservative columnists?

I was young once. You know Churchill's quote: If you're not a socialist when you're 20, you have no heart; if you're not a conservative when you're 50, you have no head.

Was there a particular event or series of events that caused you to change your political views?

Well, I've always been pretty hardheaded on foreign policy. So on foreign policy I didn't change much; I'd say the Democratic Party did.

On domestic policy, I was a Great Society believer until the empirical evidence of the damage it did began to come in during the 1980s. As a former physician and having done some science, I am very open to empirical evidence. I don't doubt the good intentions of Great Society liberalism, but I'm firmly convinced that the empirical evidence shows that this is the wrong way to go about helping people. That led to a transformation of my views.

Many conservatives have been wringing their hands since Governor Romney's defeat on November 6. What's your take? Why did he lose?

A lot of reasons, but the main one, I think, is that he decided to run purely on economic conditions. It was a very good strategy in 2011, but the economy improved enough, or at least the perception is that it had improved enough, that it proved to be a losing bet.

Romney didn't campaign very much on the difference in political philosophies. I think if you run on Obama's liberalism versus conservatism the way potential 2016 candidates Paul Ryan, Marco Rubio, or Bobby Jindal might have run, conservatives win. The proof is the 2010 midterm elections which were purely ideological [and in which Republicans performed well]. To the extent Republicans could have made 2012 like 2010, they would've won.

But Romney, for all his sincerity – and I think he's a very good man and would've made a very good president – was simply not the best to make the conservative case. He spoke it like a second language, and that, I think, was a major problem. And then, at the very end when he had a scandal – Benghazi – which he could've really hit Obama hard with in the third debate, he just walked away from it. The press ignored it, Obama ignored it, and then Romney's momentum was stopped by Hurricane Sandy, and that was it. He fell short.

So you don't agree, then, with some conservatives who fear they have lost the country.

Not at all. In exit polls they asked people if government was doing too much or too little – which is a fairly good way to separate Left and Right. The "too much" won by eight points. That's pretty significant.

Many Jews feared Obama's reelection because of his stance toward Israel and Iran's nuclear ambitions. What's your opinion? Is Iran America's problem or Israel's problem?

It's the world's problem. It's a more immediate problem for Israel, more longer term for America – which is why their timetables are in such conflict.

What do you envision happening?

Well, everybody hopes sanctions will work. I'm very skeptical. If they don't, I think there's a very high probability that Israel will act. Whether America will support the act, I don't know.

What do you think America should do?

I think the duty of an ally is to allow an ally to defend itself.

You've been paralyzed from the neck down ever since a diving accident in medical school. Considering your handicap, how do you manage to accomplish so much?

I don't want to talk about that. It's not relevant to what I do.

In a way, it's inspiring, though. So many people nowadays complain about their lot in life and blame societal and economic forces for their failures. You could easily join this crowd, as could someone like Stephen Hawking, a world-renowned physicist who can't even talk without the help of a machine. But you don't. You just forge ahead.

Look I appreciate that, but I'm not going to comment on it. I took a vow a long time ago not to.

— originally published November 21, 2012

Postscript: *In 2013, Krauthammer published "Things That Matter: Three Decades of Passions, Pastimes and Politics." The book appeared on The New York Times' bestseller list for 38 consecutive weeks – 10 of them at the number-one spot.*

In the White House

Jason Greenblatt

Donald Trump's Dealmaker

(this interview only conducted by Jewish Press columnist Sara Lehmann)

While Donald Trump's daughter and son-in-law may be the most public Jewish faces of his campaign, a softer spotlight shines on newcomer Jason Greenblatt. Named by Trump as one of his Israel advisers several months ago, Greenblatt serves as executive vice president and chief legal officer of the Trump Organization. Having worked for Trump for almost 20 years, the Orthodox father of six from Teaneck, NJ, is emerging as a positive and constructive force in his boss' campaign.

I recently met with Greenblatt in his Trump Tower office in the hope of better understanding the Republican candidate through the lens of his trusted employee, confidant, and Jewish friend. While Greenblatt feels "incredibly fortunate" in his role as Trump's liaison to Israel, he does not take his job lightly. "I *daven* to Hashem each day," he told me, "to give me the wisdom, skill, knowledge, and ability to be able to help Israel and the people of Israel and the United States in the best possible way."

In the course of our interview, Greenblatt pledged to "do the best job I possibly can in whatever role, large or small, Hashem may destine that I play in this historic election."

The Jewish Press: Trump has resonated with many who are

increasingly disenchanted with political correctness and the establishment, yet finds himself under unabated attack. What's the best way to respond to a Trump hater?

Greenblatt: What I find is that Trump haters are very surface-oriented people. They'll grab a sound bite or something they either heard or misheard in a debate or read in a newspaper that's already been transformed into multiple messages with a reporter's or editor's bias. My goal when I speak to people is not so much to convince them to vote for Donald, although of course I'd love to be able to do that, but to have an intelligent conversation about what he really means and, also, where Hillary stands on the issue.

I would like to see more unity on the Republican side. It doesn't compute for me when staunch Republicans are saying, "Well, I'm not going to back him and I'm not going to vote." That essentially means they're voting for Hillary. You might not agree with everything Donald says, but either you're going to back him or you're going to back the other side. Certainly Jewish people need to think long and hard about where Hillary is on the issues as opposed to where Donald is. Particularly when it comes to security, because unfortunately terrorism is now also within our borders and not just in Israel.

What do you think Trump represents to Jewish voters and what would his election mean to them?

Trump is incredibly strong and supportive of Israel. He recognizes the very precarious area that Israel exists in, even more so in the past period of time because of the terror on our own shores. He recognizes that the terror is in large part caused by the preaching of hate to Palestinian children and he recognizes that Israel is doing its absolute best to keep its citizens safe. He isn't someone who is going to undermine Israel's ability to secure its borders and its people.

In a perfect world, he would love to be able to achieve peace. He sees his skills, his knowledge, his ability to talk to people as the traits that are necessary for someone who will come into a room with both sides and see if some sort of peace deal can be worked out. But he would never impose that deal on Israel, or the Palestinians for that matter. No peace deal is worth anything if some other country or countries try to impose it on them.

Would Trump agree that Palestinian recognition of Israel as a Jewish state should be a pre-condition to any deal?

Yes. He was very clear in his AIPAC speech that Israel is a Jewish state and will always be a Jewish state. Whether you couch it as a pre-condition or some other creative way to do it, he absolutely agrees that it has to be a Jewish state forever. If the Palestinians come to the table and say, "We want all of Israel and want the Jews kicked out," there's no point in having a discussion. But if they come to the table with a reasonably acceptable standard – reasonable to the Israelis, not just to Mr. Trump – then maybe the conversation can continue. But it's a little hard to predict because there is no partner right now at the table.

Can you comment on the criticism leveled at Trump for what some see as his tepid denouncement of anti-Semitic supporters?

I know there's been a lot of discourse in the Jewish community about how he hasn't gone far enough to condemn some of his followers who are anti-Semitic. I think that's very unfair criticism. Having worked here for 20 years as a *frum* person, I can tell you that Donald has been enormously respectful of my being *shomer Shabbos*. He has bent over backward to help me succeed in the company despite my being *shomer Shabbos*. That's who he is. He respects all kinds of people for who they are because he realizes that everyone brings something to the table.

He condemned David Duke. Did he condemn him the second everyone wanted him to condemn him? Our community has this sort of focus that we want something done a certain way; we want it done right away. We're not the only people in the country. He spoke to The New York Times, condemned Duke's remarks, said very clearly anti-Semitism has no place in society. I think his broad condemnation of anti-Semitism is even stronger than had he merely condemned irrelevant Twitter trolls. People need to look at the whole campaign story and not a particular story, biased or unbiased, in a particular newspaper on a particular day.

As someone who has worked with Trump for so long, how do you react to people who attack his temperament?

In my 20 years working for him, Donald has been nothing but extraordinarily respectful – not just to me, but also to my wife and kids. He is warm, caring, and compassionate. I don't think he's impulsive; he's energetic. He is excited to bring forth new ideas. That doesn't mean he's going to implement them without a lot of study and understanding.

He is a tough negotiator, absolutely, but that also doesn't mean he isn't capable of speaking thoroughly appropriately all the time. People see him on TV say something about a particular kind of person without understanding the context. Almost all those times he was attacked and was defending himself. He rarely goes on the attack, but he's definitely a counter-puncher. So if someone's going to attack him, he's going to attack back and attack strongly. But he's going to do it within the bounds of what makes sense.

How do you respond to those who accuse Trump of having a vague platform or flip-flopping on issues?

Donald has tremendous intellectual capacity. There are some people who perceive his big-picture ideas as vague, but you have to start with the big-picture idea. At least he's coming to the table with a lot of change, meaning he's saying the system doesn't work. Take security. Clearly the system isn't working. Yes, he has some big-picture ideas and he will have teams of really smart people to help him develop them. But you have plenty of politicians who are extremely specific – and where does that get us?

Regarding his position on issues: Look, he's been a businessman all his life. He's not been a politician. I personally don't think there's a problem if he learns more information and decides that his initial position on something maybe needs to be more nuanced or needs to change somewhat.

I think of that as a strength, not a detriment. If somebody is going to dig in their heels and say, "This is the way it's going to be," and they don't want to change their mind after a lot of facts are given to them, that doesn't make me feel comfortable. I think a leader needs to learn and maneuver as things come to light.

What would distinguish Trump as president?

I think what he brings to the table in a big way is looking at things the way I would want my president looking at things, not the way things have been done because they've always been done that way. That doesn't serve our country well. Things are constantly changing. The world I've been raising my kids in during the last few years is significantly less safe than even when September 11 happened. Therefore, it does me no good to have a leader who has all this so-called experience in terms of being an insider in Washington. I'm not going to feel any safer for myself and my family just because someone has been in Washington for a long time. If anything, I'm a big believer in someone who thinks outside the box, somebody who looks at things with a fresh pair of eyes. And I think Donald brings that to the table.

I'm always amazed when I come to him with an issue on a deal – just how quickly he gets it and how quickly he proposes, not just one but often several possible solutions. Some of them are super creative. He is always willing to explore ideas to figure out the right approach as opposed to saying, "This is the way it's done, this is the way it's always been done, this is the way we're going to do it."

Do you see Trump as a reaction to Obama?

Absolutely. Obama started out his presidency by apologizing left and right about who we are and what we stand for. We're an amazing nation. I say that as a Jew able to live and work here and keep Shabbos. This is an incredible country for Jews and other minorities. So what is there to apologize for? We are a nation filled with incredible people.

Obama definitely put our country on the defensive very early on, and we've lost respect around the world. I think there are other issues that he created for us, in particular regarding terrorism and security. Obama's legacy has left a huge portion of our population dissatisfied, and I think the antidote to that is someone like Mr. Trump.

— originally published July 6, 2016

Postscript: *Jason Greenblatt now serves as President Trump's special representative for international negotiations.*

Elliott Abrams

A Bush Administration Insider

The world of politics is divided between insiders and outsiders – those who know and those who don't, those who make policy and those who react to it, those who observe directly and those who peer from behind a curtain.

From December 2002 to January 2009, Elliott Abrams was an insider. As deputy assistant to the president and later deputy national security adviser – with the Middle East as his focus – Abrams interacted daily with such figures as President George W. Bush, Secretary of State Condoleezza Rice, and Israeli Prime Ministers Ariel Sharon and Ehud Olmert.

In his new book, *Tested by Zion: The Bush Administration and the Israeli-Palestinian Conflict,* Abrams shares his insider vantage point. Educated at Harvard University and the London School of Economics, Abrams also served as assistant secretary of state in the Reagan administration and today is a senior fellow for Middle Eastern studies at the Council on Foreign Relations.

The Jewish Press: You begin *Tested by Zion* with Bill Clinton warning Bush about Yasser Arafat. Can you elaborate?

Abrams: Every new presidential administration starts off with the old president and new president meeting in the Oval Office for a kind of handshake before everybody goes up to Capitol Hill for the inauguration. It's just a formality. But on January 20, 2001, when Clinton handed over to Bush, it was not a formality. Clinton had a message he wanted to deliver, which was basically, "Don't trust Arafat" – and he said it repeatedly. "He lied to me, he'll lie to you. Don't trust him."

The Bush administration, as you write, eventually adopted this position, but then decided to invest its efforts in Mahmoud Abbas – a man who spent 40 years in Arafat's PLO and argued in his PhD thesis that the number of Jews killed in the Holocaust was inflated by Zionists for their own ends. Why would the Bush administration trust someone like that?

In June 2003, Abbas did exactly what we hoped he would do. He met with Ariel Sharon in Aqaba, Jordan and said the armed Intifada is over. He said there's no justification for using violence against Israelis anywhere. That made a big impression on Bush. We saw no evidence – ever – in eight years that Abbas was involved in terrorism.

But even today you read occasional media reports of Abbas attending ceremonies at which Palestinian schools or streets are named after notorious terrorists.

This is a terrible problem. There is a culture of violence there, and one of Abbas' weaknesses is that he's not a violent person. He's never held a gun, and he's never been to an Israeli prison. The guys who are viewed as heroes by the Palestinians are people who have committed acts of violence.

Now, what do you do about that? What you ought to do is try to change the culture. Instead, what Fatah and Abbas have done is feed it – by glorifying the mothers of terrorists, glorifying terrorists themselves, and naming schools, streets, or squares after them.

We in the U.S. have never taken this seriously enough and, frankly, neither have the Israelis. We all say, "Oh, you should stop doing this," but we never insist on it. No one has ever said, for example, "U.S. support for the PA is going to stop on the first of the month unless that kind of stuff is eliminated."

And yet, the Bush administration – particularly Condoleezza Rice, as your book makes clear – pushed Israel to sign some sort of peace deal with Abbas. Why?

Condi thought a comprehensive peace agreement was possible. She and Olmert thought that if offered a sufficiently generous package by Israel, Abbas would sign.

I thought it was impossible – first, because the problems between the Israelis and the Palestinians are very deep (just think of Jerusalem, for example) and second, because I never thought Abbas had the courage to sign an agreement since he would be immediately accused of treason.

Did Condoleezza Rice and President Bush know your views on the matter?

They both knew. In fact, whenever I would go to Israel – which was very frequently – I would come back and the president would say, "What's up? Olmert is very optimistic," and I would say to the president, "Well, I know Olmert tells you he's optimistic, but I'm telling you there's never going to be a deal here."

So the president knew, and he would say to people, "Condi's optimistic, Olmert's optimistic, but Elliott's not optimistic."

How often would you speak with the president about the Middle East?

If we were both in Washington, probably on average twice a week.

Were these five-minute conversations? Half-hour conversations?

It would vary. I mean sometimes it was because a foreign leader was visiting the president, so if you count the time I spent briefing the president, the actual meeting, and then the discussion afterwards – that would be a couple of hours.

Sometimes it would be for a phone call. Let's say he was calling Sharon or Mubarak. So that would be more like 45 minutes. And sometimes it would just be a question. That would be 15 minutes.

Why would you be present during a phone call between Bush and a foreign leader?

The way business was done was, let's say we scheduled a call at 7:00 in the morning with the president of Egypt. I would go in about 10 minutes before and we would talk about why we were doing the call. I would also tell the president anything new that had happened in the last, let's say, 12 hours that might be important for the call.

For instance, if it was Mubarak's birthday, I would say, "You should wish him a happy birthday." It was kind of an update briefing. Then we would do the call – I would be in the room listening – and then at the end of the call we would chat about it and discuss the follow-up. [The president might say something like,] "That was interesting, but I need to talk to the Saudis now" or "I need to talk to Sharon now."

Many of Bush's critics portray him as something of a bumbling Texas idiot. You make it clear in your book that you disagree.

He was very smart. I mean, all you had to do was be in a meeting with him to see how smart he was – both about the issues and about the people.

He paid very close attention to his personal relations with foreign leaders. In this he was very much like Clinton and not at all like Obama, who seems to dislike spending time with foreign leaders. Bush liked it and thought it was important. He thought that if a relationship of confidence was established you could get more from these guys.

You write that Bush's Texas English threw foreign leaders off sometimes. Please explain.

Bush talked in one way to everybody – to his wife, to you and me, to the American people, and to foreign leaders. He had one way of speaking, which I would call "Texan." And it was funny because very often there were foreigners who didn't really follow completely. Ariel Sharon was one of them. Sometimes he would get lost in a meeting, and he would turn to his chief of staff, Dubi Weissglass, and say, "*Mah*?"

The president would use lots of colloquial expressions. For example, if he was asking someone whether he was going to join the United States in some action, he might say, "You know, the question is whether you're going to saddle up with us." Now, if you haven't watched a lot of Westerns and you're not an American, you don't know what that means.

Talking about Sharon, you quote Condoleezza Rice as saying: "[H]e's one of the very few people I know who spoke English better than he understood it."

She was right. Sharon seemed to have better English than he did because on most subjects you might want to talk to him about – Egypt, Syria, settlements, the IDF, Iran – he kind of had talking points in his head. He had the words ready. He used them a thousand times. But that didn't mean his comprehension was great. So often he would lose track of what was being said to him.

Of all the major figures in the White House during your tenure, who would you say was the most sympathetic to Israel?

I would say the president, first of all, and Cheney. They had a really deep appreciation for Israel, which I think was a great surprise for a lot of Israelis, particularly about Cheney, because he had worked in the Arab world for so long. I would say Rumsfeld was also a very strong supporter of Israel. Bob Gates, his successor, was not.

I think Condi was very sympathetic in the first term. After the Lebanon War in the summer of 2006, though, she was less sympathetic. I think she felt the Israelis had lost their way – that they had made a mistake in that war and had prosecuted it poorly – and that she was now going to have to take a much stronger hand in pushing them into an agreement with the Palestinians. She lost faith in Olmert, but also in the IDF.

How about Powell?

I think Powell was not sympathetic right from the start. Powell adopted, what I would call, the State Department view of Israel, which is basically that Israel is making trouble for us in the Middle East with our

Arab friends and that it ought to be pressured harder. This is the traditional State Department view, and I think Powell had that view right from the beginning.

In the book you refer to "the apparent American obsession with the Israeli-Palestinian conflict." Why is the U.S. government generally so obsessed? Why doesn't it take a more hands-off policy (as it arguably is doing now)?

I think it's partly because there is a mistaken view – and this has been held at the State Department for a very long time – that the central issue in the Middle East is the Israeli-Palestinian conflict, and if you were able to solve that conflict, all of our other problems would go away or be much easier to resolve. If you believe that, you're going to spend a lot of time on this issue.

I think it's ridiculous, though. Do you think that if you resolved the Israeli-Palestinian conflict, Iran would stop trying to get a nuclear weapon? Do you think the Syrians would stop killing each other? Do you think Egypt or Libya would become stable all of a sudden?

Did you ever get a sense while working in the White House that you were suspected of taking a more pro-Israel stance because you're Jewish?

Not from the president or the vice president or anybody else in the administration. Not from most of the Arabs either. I would say the exception was the Saudis, where I did have the feeling that they believed I was a kind of Israeli agent – that I was not working for the interests of the United States but for the interests of Israel.

— originally published April 24, 2013

Postscript: *Elliott Abrams' next book, "Realism and Democracy: American Foreign Policy After the Arab Spring," is scheduled to be published in September 2017.*

Dennis Ross

Advising Presidents Clinton and Obama

Few people have been more intimately involved in U.S. Middle East peacemaking efforts over the past 25 years than Dennis Ross. During the course of his career, he has served as director of policy planning in the State Department under George W. H. Bush, Middle East peace envoy for Bill Clinton, and special assistant to Barack Obama.

Ross is currently a fellow at the Washington Institute for Near East Policy and a professor at Georgetown University. The Jewish Press recently spoke with him about his new book, *Doomed to Succeed: The U.S.-Israel Relationship from Truman to Obama.*

The Jewish Press: In *Doomed to Succeed,* you describe the enormous amount of effort the U.S. has spent trying to resolve the Israeli-Palestinian conflict over the last several decades. Why does the U.S. care so much?

Ross: I think historically there's been a view that this conflict is a game changer in the region – that if you resolve it, it will improve our position in the Middle East and ease our relations with the Arabs. It's a view that's been embodied in almost every administration since Truman's time. I personally, however, have never believed this to be true.

Why not?

Well, it's pretty simple to explain today. If tomorrow you solved the

Israeli-Palestinian problem, it wouldn't stop one barrel bomb in Syria, it wouldn't push ISIS back one centimeter, it wouldn't change Iran's ambitions, it wouldn't stop the proxy war in Yemen, and it wouldn't change the struggle in Egypt between President Sisi and the radical Islamists.

Would it be good to resolve the Israeli-Palestinian problem? Absolutely. But it's not going to be a game changer, and it's not the source of the conflict in the broader region.

You write in the book that U.S. peace proposals are sometimes driven by European pressure. Why does Europe care about Israel-Arab relations?

Early on I think they cared because they were concerned about their access to oil. Later I think they have tended to see the Palestinians as victims and Israeli settlements as a form of colonialism, and they want to separate themselves from that because of their own history of colonialism.

Jimmy Carter is widely regarded in the pro-Israel community as the U.S. president most hostile to Israel. Do you agree?

No, I think Eisenhower was probably the toughest. Eisenhower saw Israel as an impediment to all of our strategic designs in the region. During the '56 Suez War, he even contemplated sending U.S. forces to expel the Israelis from the Sinai, and he had his undersecretary of state threaten the Israelis with expulsion from the UN.

I think Carter was tough toward Israel, but Carter is also the one who produced the Egyptian-Israeli peace treaty, which established three billion dollars a year in U.S. assistance to Israel. That's not a small thing.

How do you regard Obama? Is he Carter II?

I think you have to look at Obama as more similar to George H. W. Bush than Carter. On the one hand, Obama takes a very strong view of America's commitment to Israel on security. On the other hand, he sees Israel as being the strong party and the Palestinians as weak and, therefore, he puts the onus entirely on the Israelis to make peace.

So he has no problem distancing from Israel, and the first Bush also had no problem distancing from Israel even as he felt it was very important to be responsive to Israel's security needs.

Whom do you regard as the most pro-Israel president?

Bill Clinton.

It's interesting you say that because most right-wing Jews are not terribly fond of him.

Right, but Clinton had an emotional attachment to Israel, and he was the one president who emotionally believed it was a mistake to create any distance between the United States and Israel.

George W. Bush came to that point, but that's not where he started in his administration. In his first call to Israel after 9/11, George W. Bush pressed Ariel Sharon to have Shimon Peres meet Yasser Arafat, the man responsible for many of the terror attacks going on in Israel.

Bush changed, but Clinton throughout his administration thought it was a mistake to distance from Israel because Clinton believed we're Israel's only true friend and, therefore, although we may have disagreements, they need to be managed privately because if we create a public wedge between ourselves and Israel we will encourage Israel's enemies. Clinton was the one president who completely believed that.

In policy debates within the Obama administration, you often advocated the more pro-Israel position. Did White House officials ever intimate to you – directly or indirectly – that your Jewishness was influencing your views?

I think in earlier administrations – Truman, Eisenhower, Kennedy – there was an anti-Semitic undertone. Nixon said he wanted to keep Kissinger out of his policymaking the first couple of years because of his Jewishness; he thought it would make it difficult to reestablish ties with the Arabs. He actually said this.

But I think the turning point was really Reagan. Since that time, I don't think you find this anti-Semitic undertone.

In an interview with The Jewish Press two years ago, Bush official Elliott Abrams said he, too, never felt his Jewishness was an issue in the White House but said he sometimes felt the Saudis regarded him as an Israeli agent.

There was sometimes a sense in the Arab world: "Well, you know why Ross is so tough on us..." But I think that was convenient for them because they wanted to find reasons to explain why we were pursuing policies they didn't like or why they were doing something that might be hard for them. They could say, "Well, the Americans didn't give us a choice and look where the Americans come from."

Some people claim that the U.S.-Israel relationship is a one-way street. What's your take?

I argue quite the opposite. If you look in the military area alone, there are so many things we gain from Israel. Active armor on our armored personnel carriers and tanks has come largely from things the Israelis have developed. So much of our drone technology has come from the Israelis. So much in the doctrinal area about how you deal with asymmetrical warfare we get from the Israelis. The level of cooperation with the Israelis on intelligence is also something we gain very significantly from.

If you go outside of the military security arena, you can look at the Israeli companies that are in California now to help with the drought. You have Israeli universities producing drought-resistant agriculture that is a contribution to civilization, not just to the United States. There are so many different things we get from Israel.

In the book you write that the biblical Book of Joshua was a source of inspiration for Bill Clinton the night before the Oslo Accords were signed on September 13, 1993. How did the Book of Joshua, of all things, inspire Clinton, considering that it is all about the Jewish people conquering the land of Israel and annihilating most of its inhabitants?

You'd have to ask Clinton because I was quoting what he wrote. He says he couldn't sleep the night before the ceremony, so he got up and read the Book of Joshua. He describes this. And afterward he gave me and Warren Christopher a tie with trumpets on it [recalling the trumpets that toppled the walls of Jericho].

Some right-wing Jews believe it's a miracle Israel has the West Bank today considering the number of peace proposals America has pushed over the years; that if not for the Palestinians being so stubborn, they would have had 90 percent of the West Bank ages ago. What's your take?

It's true. Look, you had the Clinton parameters, and Arafat said no. You had what Olmert offered Abbas, and he said nothing. And you had what President Obama offered in March of 2014 to Abbas, and again he gave no comment.

There's an old saying of Abba Eban's: "The Palestinians never miss an opportunity to miss an opportunity." Since the year 2000 there have been three proposals to resolve the conflict that would have produced a Palestinian state, and the Palestinians have either said no or given no response.

— originally published November 11, 2015

Tevi Troy

Mitt Romney's *Frum* Adviser

Had Mitt Romney won the presidential election on November 6, Tevi Troy would be busy right now working as director of domestic policy on Romney's transition team.

Troy, who served as special policy adviser to Romney's presidential campaign, is a senior fellow at the Hudson Institute think tank. An Orthodox Jew who grew up in Queens, Troy has served in a number of government positions over the past 15 years, including deputy secretary of the U.S. Department of Health and Human Services in George W. Bush's administration. At one point he was also the White House's lead adviser on healthcare, labor, education, transportation, immigration, crime, veterans affairs, and welfare.

Troy is also the author of two books, *Intellectuals and the American Presidency: Philosophers, Jesters, or Technicians?* (2002) and *What Washington Read, Eisenhower Watched, and Obama Tweeted: 200 Years of Popular Culture in the White House* (forthcoming, 2013).

The Jewish Press recently spoke with him.

The Jewish Press: What exactly did you do for Romney?

Troy: I advised on a host of issues, including health policy, domestic policy, and also Jewish issues. I made TV and radio appearances, spoke to the media on Governor Romney's behalf, and even debated Jack Lew, White House Chief of Staff, at a Cleveland shul a few days before the campaign ended.

What was Romney like as a person?

Well, it's hard to say what he's like on a trip to Disney World or something like that. In terms of policy, he's very bright and knowledgeable and picks up stuff very quickly. I was in a series of policy meetings he had in Washington where he met with experts on various issues; I headed the healthcare briefing. He walked into that room with no notes, spoke off the cuff very knowledgably about healthcare, and then took questions from experts and responded knowledgably and skillfully with facts and figures.

How many times did you meet him?

Not that many. Three, four, or five.

Why do you think he lost?

It's very hard to beat an incumbent president. A president has four years to prepare for an election campaign. Only one incumbent Democrat has lost over the last century, and that was Jimmy Carter.

I also think the torrent of negative ads that hit Governor Romney over the summer at a time when he did not have the funding to respond was very damaging. Finally, the American people tend to want to give first-term presidents a second chance.

Some people think his toned-down performance in the second and third debates may have hurt him as well.

I don't think he toned it down at all. I think he was equally good in the second debate, and in the third debate I thought Romney had the right strategy, which is you don't want to get in an ugly brawl over foreign policy when you're trying to show the American people that you're ready to lead.

But it seems to me that we're in a more knuckle-baring era, and maybe the American people *do* want to see that kind of fighting in a foreign policy debate.

How would you compare Romney to George W. Bush?

It's hard to say because I spent more time with Bush. Bush was very good at getting to the heart of an issue very quickly. He asked very tough questions in policy meetings. He also seemed to have more of an easygoing manner than Romney. He was very good with people – the backslapping "Hey, I'm your buddy" kind of thing. That's a real skill in politics.

In other words, Romney is, as some people argue, a bit stiff.

I didn't say that at all. I didn't say anything against Romney. I'm just praising Bush for being a very good retail politician.

One of the reasons many Orthodox Jews voted for Romney was Obama's alleged anti-Israel bias. Yet, some people argue that Obama's position vis-à-vis Israel is identical to Bush's; that Bush, too, supported a two-state solution.

I don't buy that at all. First of all, President Bush worked much better with the Israelis. Second of all, President Bush supported a two-state solution, but with the Palestinians having corresponding obligations. And third of all, President Bush did not want to have pre-conditions before getting to the negotiating table, whereas President Obama presumed to draw what the final lines were in his speech before Netanyahu's visit a couple of years ago.

I think those are real and significant differences. I also think there were clearly rough and cold relations between the two countries for at least the first three years of the Obama administration, and I don't think any fair observer can claim otherwise.

To what do you attribute the administration's colder attitude toward Israel?

I don't know. [Political pundit] Peter Beinart argues that Obama didn't really know a lot about Israel growing up in Indonesia and Hawaii, and that his first real education on Israel came from some very liberal Jews in Chicago. That's one theory.

Another theory is that he came to the White House and thought he was going to reset relations with the whole world. He thought if he was colder toward Israel, the Arab world would be warmer towards us.

In your upcoming book, *What Washington Read, Eisenhower Watched, and Obama Tweeted,* you write that Obama is unusually well-versed in pop culture. Can you elaborate?

He watched a lot of television growing up and continues to watch television to an extent that I think is unusual for a president. "ESPN SportsCenter" is one of his favorite shows. He also likes "The Wire"; "Modern Family," which he watches with Michelle; "Homeland"; "Boardwalk Empire"; and "Mad Men."

I'm not a prude about pop culture. But I also think there are great ideas that have created our civilization that our founders were immersed in – great ideas about what leads to good government and the proper role of government in society. I think we as a nation benefited from the founders' immersion in those ideas, and I think presidents should at least take some time to focus on these issues as well.

Your first book, *Intellectuals and the American Presidency,* was published in 2002 and hence obviously did not include anything on Obama. If you had to add an Obama chapter to that book, what would be in it?

Well, I effectively did add an Obama chapter. I wrote a long article for National Affairs about Bush and Obama. I argued that Bush tried really hard – he read a great deal – to reach out to intellectuals, but, no matter what he did, he couldn't quite get their approval. Obama, on the other hand, doesn't even seem to try that hard. As I said, he watches a lot of TV and there are some indications that he doesn't read as much as his fans suggest he does. He was once asked what he was reading and he said he barely has time to floss and watch SportsCenter. Nevertheless, the intellectuals seem to fall all over him and praise him at every opportunity.

You worked in government for 12 years, Jack Lew is currently

Obama's chief of staff, Joseph Lieberman has been a U.S. senator for 24 years – are we seeing more Orthodox Jews in government than ever before?

It's hard to [know for sure], but I think there are more doors open for Orthodox Jews in politics than ever before and you see them appearing in senior positions.

Is that good, bad, significant, insignificant...?

I think it's a good thing. I think it's good for the Orthodox community to have its perspectives heard and that people don't just see Jews as a secular community. I also think it's good for America. Folding in different voices and perspectives is one of our strengths, so I want to see that continue.

Was your Orthodox observance ever an issue during your years in government?

There were times I couldn't work because of *Shabbat* or holidays, but for the most part I found people very accommodating....

When I worked in the White House, I had to be at work at such an early time that I couldn't *daven* at home, so I had to *daven* in the White House with my *tefillin*. A couple of times people walked in on me, but that's fine.

So, yeah, when you're an observant Jew, it's always an issue to some extent in that it's a daily part of your life, but it was never a deterrent or an obstacle.

Fifty years ago, Orthodox Jews generally did not wear yarmulkes at work. Today, most do. What was your practice while working for Bush and Romney?

It's an interesting question. I didn't wear a *kippah* at the time, but now I do full-time. A lot of it has to do with my kids. I just couldn't really explain why I don't wear it in the office. When I was growing up – I went to Ramaz – it seemed that people didn't wear a *kippah* at the office. Now I think we're just in a different phase.

So you wore a yarmulke while working for Romney?

Yes, including when I met with him, when I went on TV, etc.

When did you make the switch?

I actually started towards the end of the Bush administration. I brought everyone in for a family photo with President Bush and the kids were wearing *kippot,* so I wore a *kippah* too. And then I would bring my kids to work occasionally and in some ways it was more awkward to take it off with my kids there.

You know, at what point do you put it on and at what point do you take it off? It just didn't seem to make sense to me anymore. Do you do it when you get into the car? Do you do it when you get on the subway? Do you do it when you get off the subway? I just couldn't figure out the rationale for it.

And, you know, fortunately we live in a great country where there's relatively little anti-Semitism. I've had no repercussions from it. Very few gentiles even mentioned it.

Your brother is a presidential historian at McGill University who, like you, writes books on American history. Is there any sibling rivalry between the two of you?

No, he's written 10 books, so I'll never catch up to him. He's a great prolific historian and I'm honored to have him as a brother.

How did an Orthodox Jewish family from Queens manage to produce two distinguished American history buffs?

My father taught American history at a public school in Queens, and we both had a love for it.

— originally published December 5, 2012

Postscript: *In 2014, Tevi Troy founded a new think tank, the American Health Policy Institute, and, in 2016, he published his third book, "Shall We Wake the President?: Two Centuries of Disaster Management from the Oval Office."*

Rabbi Menachem Genack

Torah Emissary to President Clinton

When most Americans think of Bill Clinton, the Bible is probably not the first thing that comes to mind. And yet, as Rabbi Menachem Genack – CEO of the Orthodox Union's Kosher Division – discovered two decades ago, the former president is quite familiar with the Book of Books and has often sought solace and guidance in it.

Rabbi Genack first met Clinton at a fundraiser in New Jersey in 1992. "At the time," Rabbi Genack recalls, "there was a lot of discussion about President Bush's lack of vision, so when I introduced Governor Clinton I said, quoting a *pasuk* from *Mishlei*, 'Where there is no vision, the people perish.' Clinton liked the quote and said, 'You know what? I might use that in my acceptance speech at the convention.'" He did, and ever since, Rabbi Genack and Clinton have been friends.

Rabbi Genack is more than Clinton's friend, however. To some degree, he has also served as his rabbi, sending him numerous *"divrei Torah"* over the last two decades that he believed Clinton might find enlightening. After Clinton won a second term in 1996, Rabbi Genack began asking other people to pen short essays for Clinton's benefit as well – including such personalities as Rabbi Ahron Soloveichik, Rabbi Immanuel Jakobovits, Rabbi Israel Meir Lau, Dr. Bernard Lander, Senator Joseph Lieberman, and Cynthia Ozick.

These *divrei Torah* may originally have been intended for Clinton's eyes only, but several years ago Rabbi Genack thought that "just as they were useful to Clinton, maybe they'll be useful to the public." The result of that thought is *Letters to President Clinton: Biblical Lessons on Faith and Leadership,* containing over 100 miniature essays on such themes as leadership, faith, dreams and vision, and sin and repentance. Released last month, the book includes a foreword by Clinton and a preface by Rabbi Lord Jonathan Sacks.

The Jewish Press: What inspired you to start writing letters to Clinton and what gave you the confidence that he would actually read them? After all, many Americans probably think of writing to the president but don't bother, figuring their letters will just wind up in a secretary's wastebasket.

Rabbi Genack: Well, he would often invite me to the White House and we became pretty good friends. Also, I didn't mail the first letter I gave him; I handed it to him. I'd say the first 20 or so were handed to him. The Secret Service, though, thought that was unseemly, so President Clinton [arranged for me to send the letters through] different contacts in the White House.

How often did you send these letters to Clinton?

Usually every other week.

How do you know Clinton read them?

First of all, if you look at the book, you'll see that he responds to many of them in writing. Also, in her blurb to the book, Ann Lewis, who was the director of communications to the White House at the time, writes that I was once late in sending a letter, and President Clinton said to her, "It's been a long time since I've gotten a letter from Rabbi Genack; what's happening?"

By the way, in his memoir, *My Life*, Clinton mentions that among the things that gave him support during the period of the impeachment were the Bible and these mini sermons that he got from me.

Many readers may be surprised to learn this. After all, people don't

usually think of Clinton as a religious man.

Well, the word religious means different things for different people. What I indicate in the book is just that he's very familiar with the Bible. I'll tell you two stories. There was once a meeting in the White House with representatives from different Christian denominations and one of them said to Clinton, "Mr. President, I've been praying for you." The president said, "What have you been praying?" So he quoted a verse and said, "It's from Chronicles I." Clinton corrected him and said, "That's in Chronicles II."

There's another story concerning Ron Brown, who was the secretary of commerce under Clinton and was tragically killed in a plane crash. President Clinton went over to the Commerce Department to make some remarks in memory of Brown and asked his staff to find out what his favorite biblical verse was. They came up with something but they didn't know the source and it was sort of paraphrased. Clinton looked at it and said, "Oh, this is from Isaiah, I prefer the King James translation," which he cited by heart, unprepared, in his remarks.

Where did Clinton attain his biblical knowledge?

First of all, he's extremely smart. It's hard to quote a book to him that he hasn't read. He's constantly reading. And I guess maybe it's part of the Southern Baptist tradition.

Is it true that he asked you for advice when the Monica Lewinsky scandal broke?

I don't want to presume that I'm the only one he spoke to – obviously he spoke to a lot of people – but he did ask me what I thought he should say when he addressed the nation. I told him he should express profound remorse but I also said that presidents have a right to privacy.

The *Midrash* asks, "Why is it that animals can't speak?" and answers that if they could speak, they would tell our foibles and failings – since they are all over the place – and no one could survive. So the point I wanted to derive from the *Midrash* is not just that privacy is a right, but also that it's an existential need.

In his preface to *Letters to President Clinton*, Rabbi Lord Jonathan Sacks writes that Jews should be more active in sharing the truths of the Torah with the wider world. Do you agree?

I agree that the Torah has something to say about how we live our lives and that it has a universal message that is meaningful beyond our own *daled amos*. Adam HaRishon and Chava are buried together with Avraham and Sarah, and Rav Soloveitchik said this indicates that we're interested in mankind. We're part of *Knesses Yisrael* but we're also part of humanity, and we do have a message.

In fact, the basic documents of the United States [are based on] Jewish ideas – the dignity of man, "*tzelem Elokim*." These ideas were absent in the pagan world. So we can be proud that it was Jews who gave this to the world.

The letters in this volume are basically theological or ideological in nature. Why didn't you take advantage of your friendship with Clinton to write to him about specific issues of concern to the Jewish community, such as the imprisonment of Jonathan Pollard?

There were such letters. In terms of Jonathan Pollard, I was actually the one who spoke to him initially about reviewing the Pollard case. I spoke to him about Pollard several times, and I think he was sympathetic in thinking about it.

In terms of why that's not in the book: It didn't belong in the book. The book isn't about politics. It's about biblical themes. But I can tell you, having traveled with President Clinton several times and having spoken to him and seen him up close: He has a tremendous affinity and love for Israel.

It's interesting you say that because many supporters of Israel dislike Clinton. While the Oslo Accords may have originally been Israel's idea, many in the 1990s believed that Clinton pressured Israel into making concessions to the Palestinian Authority.

I disagree with that perception. I don't think Clinton ever pressured Israel.

How about when Benjamin Netanyahu was prime minister in the late 1990s? He clearly seemed ambivalent about Oslo at the time and many thought Clinton prodded him into making more concessions to Yasser Arafat than he otherwise would have.

I'm not a foreign policy expert. It doesn't make sense for me to debate Oslo with you. But I can tell you this – and this is true of both Bill Clinton and Hillary Clinton: They have a deep affinity for Israel.

— originally published November 14, 2013

Postscript: *Rabbi Genack was a vocal supporter of Hillary Clinton during the 2016 presidential election season. In a March 2017 e-mail to me, Rabbi Genack said he remains in touch with the former president.*

Jack Abramoff

Trying to Reform a System He Abused

In 2005 and 2006, Jack Abramoff was all over the news – for the wrong reasons. A high-powered Capitol Hill lobbyist, and an Orthodox Jew to boot, Abramoff found himself at the center of a federal corruption investigation that ultimately landed him in jail. Among other things, Abramoff was accused of conspiracy, bribery, tax evasion, and attempting to defraud his clients of tens of millions of dollars.

Today, Abramoff is a free man. Out of prison since 2010, Abramoff is now committed to reforming the lobbying industry he helped tarnish. In 2011, he wrote *Capitol Punishment: The Hard Truth About Corruption from America's Most Notorious Lobbyist.* The Jewish Press recently caught up with him.

The Jewish Press: What are you doing today?

Abramoff: I have my own radio show Sundays evenings on XM radio, and I travel the country speaking about politics, what goes on in Washington, and my past.

I'm working on a book on gridlock in Washington. I'm also working on television programming on the lobbying business and trying to move forward some motion picture projects – I used to be a movie producer. One film is sort of like "Lord of the Rings" and another one is an animated feature similar to "Shrek." Both of them have biblical backgrounds and undertones.

Finally, I'm working on efforts to reform the political system and helping other good causes as well.

What's wrong with the system as it's currently constituted?

The system is basically set up in a way that people who come in with money can buy outcomes. I'm working with reform groups – groups I used to oppose – to come up with some solutions to solve this problem.

How do people "buy outcomes"?

By giving politicians campaign contributions, taking them out to dinner, taking them to a ballgame, etc. If I'm asking you to do something for me for money, that's bribery – even if it's legal. Ninety-nine percent of what I did as a lobbyist was legal. It was only one percent, or even less, where I went over any legal line.

Your lobbying firm reportedly spent a million dollars a year buying congressmen tickets to various sporting events. Is this common practice in Washington?

No, I did things bigger than most people. But whether you're giving away six tickets or 60 tickets, the essence is the same.

You have publicly stated that you were morally blind as a lobbyist. How do you account for that blindness?

I didn't take the time to sit down and analyze the system. I just jumped in. I was into winning the fights I was in, and I felt the ends justified the means, so I went off track.

Incidentally, most people in the system today don't consider it immoral. Most congressmen who take these contributions don't feel they're being bribed.

What goes through a congressman's head, though, when a lobbyist buys him a ticket to a sports game? Doesn't he know the ticket comes with strings attached?

They think I'm their friend, and I thought I was their friend too. In other words, I was just taking my friend out. So, my friend happens to be a congressman and I happen to be asking my friend to help me out with something. Their attitude would be, "Well, if [the favor] is not something I would normally object to, what's the problem?"

There are all sorts of excuses you come up with to convince yourself it's not a bad thing. In fact, you tell yourself it's a good thing because you're going after worthy goals that would otherwise not happen if it weren't for your relationship with this congressman.

What worthy goals are you referring to?

I thought the clients I represented had worthy causes. I only took clients if I agreed with their cause.

How many lobbyists are there on Capitol Hill?

It varies. You get a count anywhere from 15,000 to 30,000. The top tier is under 100.

In your book, you offer a number of proposals to reform the lobbying industry. Can you detail some of them?

Well, as I mentioned earlier, removing the ability of lobbyists and special interests to use money in the political system is one of them.

Another one is to close the door between public servants and the lobbying industry. The people lobbying firms hire usually come from Capitol Hill [e.g., staffers to congressmen]. I used to hire people prospectively, offering them a job whenever they could take it up – in a year or so. I noticed that what would happen was that these people would start acting like they were working for me [immediately even though they were still employed by congressmen].

The only way to resolve this is to prevent staffers from actually getting the job for a few years. I have other proposals, but I think these are the kinds of reforms that are likely to obtain support on both the Left and the Right, and until something is supported by both the Left and the Right, it's not going to pass.

Under your proposed reforms, someone who donated a million

dollars to a congressman's reelection campaign would not be able to discuss politics with the congressman at a private dinner. His table talk would have to be restricted to family, friends, and the weather. Isn't it un-American to restrict free speech?

It's completely fair and completely American to say that if you want to have the right to do some things, you have to give up the right to do other things. For example, if you want security clearance in America, you have to give up the right to free speech.

Nobody's forcing you to lobby the federal government. If you make that choice, it's 100 percent fantastic. You just can't do everything else you wanted to do. It's not only not un-American, it's *very* American, and it's very necessary because right now Americans feel strongly that the system is rigged against them. And one of the ways in which it's rigged – and I know this firsthand having been on that side of it – is that people with unlimited resources, such as I had, can in essence get anything they want out of Congress.

You told "60 Minutes" in 2011 that you believed, as a lobbyist, that you were smarter than Congress – that no matter what reform bill Congress might pass, you would find a way around it. You are currently a reformer yourself. What makes you think lobbyists won't find a way around your reforms?

Every human law will contain a loophole that someone will find eventually. So it's not the kind of thing that's going to get solved with one set of laws. It's a constant process. But the changes that we propose were born from me contemplating, "What are the kinds of things that I would really have a tough time getting around if I were still a lobbyist?"

So while I don't for a minute presume that these rules are going to last forever, they'll do a lot of good and will change a lot of things for a while.

An acquaintance of yours claims you can "sweet talk a dog off a meat truck." What would you say to someone who doubted your sincerity and claimed all your reform talk is disingenuous? Someone who argued that Jack Abramoff is all about Jack Abramoff and is promoting reform

today because that's the only way he can get back in the spotlight and the center of things?

That kind of comment frankly almost doesn't merit a response. It's so ridiculous. I think, first of all, people need to judge me by what I do, not by what they think is in my heart. Unless they're *Hakadosh Baruch Hu*, they don't know what's in my heart.

And I'm not asking people to believe me. I'm not asking for anything out of this. I'm just saying what needs to be done. If they doubt my story in my book – which is told against my own interest – or if they doubt these things are going on, then they're either naïve or part of the system.

If they think I'm trying to get in the spotlight, what good is it for me being in the spotlight? I don't earn any money really off of anything like this.

Israel's foes sometimes portray the Israel lobby as an all-powerful force that controls Washington. As a former insider, what's your impression?

America's support of Israel is, in part, because pro-Israel forces are organized. But it generally flows, not from the so-called Jewish lobby – frankly, I fear there are more Jews lobbying against Israel than for Israel – but rather from the over 150 million Christians who believe strongly in the state of Israel. Otherwise there's no way in the world this country would be supportive of Israel.

You reportedly became *frum* at age 12 after watching "Fiddler on the Roof." Is that true?

It helped me. In those days, the early 1970s, there was no perceptible *baal teshuvah* movement. Where I lived in Beverly Hills, there were Jews, but the Orthodox were far away from us. I had no exposure to them. One of the first exposures I had was seeing "Fiddler on the Roof." It was literally one of the only times in my life I had seen traditional Jews. It wasn't the only thing that impacted me, but it certainly had an impact.

It didn't have the impact the author of "Fiddler on the Roof" intended, by the way. Shalom Aleichem was *anti-frum*. He's probably rolling around in his grave somewhere.

How did matters proceed after watching "Fiddler on the Roof"? Did you go to yeshiva?

No, I wanted to, but I wasn't allowed. It wasn't until I went to college that I was among *frum* people. I went to Brandeis. There actually weren't too many *frum* people there either, but that's where I could be more openly Orthodox.

As an Orthodox Jew, were you concerned about the *chillul Hashem* your arrest in 2005 caused?

Of course, I was absolutely concerned. I was mortified, but, unfortunately, I wasn't in control of it at that point.

When did you do *teshuvah*? At what point did you cease being a ruthless lobbyist and start becoming a reformer?

It wasn't until after my career ended and I started to sit down and analyze what I was involved in. I started to look at it honestly without having any skin in the game any longer. It was a process. It took months. They weren't quickly-reached conclusions and they weren't conclusions I didn't fight against, but I came to them anyway.

— originally published January 4, 2013

Postscript: *In two e-mails to me in early 2017, Jack Abramoff wrote that the TV programs and movies he discusses at the beginning of the interview are still in development and that he continues to speak out against corruption in Washington.*

Asked for his opinion on President Trump's vow to "drain the swamp," Abramoff wrote that Trump "should be commended for taking real steps to shutter the revolving door, where public servants become lobbyists. Unlike Obama, who focused on inhibiting lobbyists from entering his administration – which is not really the issue regarding corruption – Trump is stopping public servants from cashing in. The media have not given him credit – as usual – but he sure deserves it."

Rabbinic Wisdom

Rav Haim Sabato

The *Rosh Yeshiva* Who Writes Award-Winning Novels

Rashei yeshiva are not generally known for writing novels. Rav Haim Sabato, however, is not your average *rosh yeshiva*. Not only does he write novels, he won Israel's most prestigious literature award – the Sapir Prize – in 2000.

Critics have compared Rav Sabato to Nobel Prize winner S. Y. Agnon as both incorporate language from *Tanach* and other classical Jewish texts in their works. Indeed, gracing Rav Sabato's novels is almost an other-worldly aura or – as Haaretz described his writing – "music that slowly filters through to the soul of the reader."

Born in Cairo in 1952, Rav Sabato descends from a long line of Syrian rabbis. He currently lives in Maale Adumim where he serves as *rosh yeshiva* in Yeshivat Birkat Moshe. Among his works are *Adjusting Sights, Aleppo Tales,* and *The Dawning of the Day.* In September, Maggid Books will publish a collection of his essays on the *parshah, Rest for the Dove.*

The Jewish Press recently interviewed Rav Sabato via e-mail. His answers appear here in translation.

The Jewish Press: What would you say to people who might express surprise that a *rosh yeshiva* is also an award-winning novelist?

Rav Sabato: Anyone who studies Torah is constantly involved with sources, language, and the precise meaning of words. He is also exposed to various strata of Jewish culture – many of which are replete with beautiful literature, such as *tefillah, Midrash,* and *piyutim.* Finally, a yeshiva educator must be highly sensitive, which is a characteristic trait of artists and writers. So I don't see an inherent contradiction between [being an author and a *rosh yeshiva*].

It's true that there's been a rupture between the world of Torah and Hebrew literature ever since the Enlightenment due to the many people who were attracted to the latter and left the former in the process. But I believe that just as literature can have an effect in one direction, it can have an effect in the opposite direction as well – and express purity, beauty, truth, deep faith, and closeness to God.

And if those who feel these values deeply in their heart have the ability to write about them but don't, who will? Must we only read about heresy and lust in literature? Are faith, prayer, innocence, and repentance not sublime topics? Shouldn't *they* be expressed in literature?

Your writing style has been likened to S.Y. Agnon's. Do you embrace or reject this comparison?

Certainly I agree with it, although a simple writer like me is very far from a giant like Agnon. But I did not imitate Agnon; imitation is intolerable. I followed in his footsteps. In other words, I used the same [traditional Torah] sources he used because I'm at home with them.

I did not, however, follow Agnon in his habit of cynically injecting an element of "bitter fate" in his works, which pained me very much in my youth. I replaced it with an element of faith that casts an optimistic light even when very deep pain is being described.

Some people believe that authors and artists must have free range to express themselves – that expressing oneself is an end unto itself. Others strenuously disagree. What's your opinion?

I am among those who maintain that artistic expression that comes from inspiration is very valuable. Naturally, though, the more elevated the inner world of the writer, the more elevated the worlds he expresses in his writing will be.

How has the secular Israeli public reacted to your novels?

Amazingly. I've had responses from tens of thousands of readers. I'm very pleased that I received warm reactions from both members of HaShomer HaTzair *kibbutzim* and *mashgichim* of charedi *yeshivos* in Bnei Brak.

You come from an illustrious line of Syrian rabbis. Can you talk a bit about them?

My grandfather's grandfather was HaRav Aharon Choueka, who was the chief rabbi of Aleppo in Syria. He was a tremendous *gaon,* and the greatest *poskim* of his generation corresponded with him. His son was Chacham Menachem Choueka, a pious man, a *mekubal,* and an incredible *gaon* who learned the entire Talmud by heart by the age 18. He moved to Egypt.

His son, my grandfather, was HaRav Aharon Choueka who left Egypt and moved to Israel. He was a *gaon* in Torah but was mainly known as an excellent *darshan* who had an effect on thousands of Jews. He was among the most elite Torah scholars in Egypt and studied under Rav Ezra Attia whom he loved and greatly admired.

In an interview in 2006 you were quoted as saying, "Publishing? For me it's punishment.... due to the ensuing publicity. In the yeshiva we educate the students to find value in what is hidden." It's interesting you say that because in our society, promoting and selling oneself is highly valued and thought to be the only road to success.

Publicity and marketing have become such an intrinsic part of contemporary life that if someone does something without publicizing it, it's as if he didn't do it, and if he publicizes something without doing it, it's as if he did it. In Jewish thought, however, it's precisely the hidden *tzaddik* who is valued, and publicity, even if essential, is often regarded as a fate, or even a punishment, to be borne.

Publicity heightens external aspects and obscures deep inner worlds. Generally speaking, it is superficial. These drawbacks are in addition to the self-destruction that publicity causes famous people who start regarding themselves in accordance with the public's perception of them and who begin shaping their writings and public utterances based on how they will be accepted by others rather than their true worth.

What would you tell young Orthodox Jews interested in writing novels?

I would suggest that anyone who has an inner truth burning within and has the artistic tools to express it must do so with joy, and not because he wishes to be famous. Of course, it goes without saying that he must adhere to all relevant halachic restrictions. Literature does not give one license to break the rules of modesty or the boundaries surroundings male-female matters.

It's possible to write profound, beautiful, and meaningful works – on both the world within and without – amidst the all-encompassing perspective of the Torah.

— originally published August 5, 2015

Postscript: *A translation of Rabbi Sabato's latest work of fiction, "In the Beauty of Concealment," is set to be published soon. Rabbi Sabato is also nearly finished writing a book on Rav Saadya Gaon.*

Rabbi Berel Wein

A Jewish Historian, of the People, for the People

"I have always considered autobiographical works somewhat presumptuous. Why should anyone be interested in the details of someone else's life? Naturally, that observation applies to others' autobiographies. But sharing *my* life experiences with complete strangers is different, for they'll surely value my story."

Thus begins *Teach Them Diligently: The Personal Story of a Community Rabbi* by Berel Wein, recently published by Maggid Books. Born in 1934, Rabbi Wein fills his autobiography with stories and observations from his upbringing in Chicago; his rabbinic career in Miami Beach; his tenure as executive vice president of the Orthodox Union in Manhattan; his time as *rosh yeshiva* of Yeshiva Shaarei Torah in Suffern, NY; and his experiences in Israel since making *aliyah* in 1997.

Rabbi Wein, who is best known for his lectures and films on Jewish history, currently heads the Destiny Foundation. In November, the foundation hopes to premiere episode five of "Faith and Fate – The Story of the Jews in the 20th Century," a 13-part documentary series based on Rabbi Wein's book of the same name.

The Jewish Press: You begin your autobiography with a story about

Israeli Chief Rabbi Isaac Herzog, which, you write, has "continually inspired and challenged" you. What is that story?

Rabbi Wein: Rav Herzog came to Chicago after the Second World War and spoke in the Chicago yeshiva. He said he had just come from the pope in Rome and gave him a list with 10,000 names of Jewish children who had been sequestered in Catholic institutions during the war. He asked the pope to give him back the children, but the pope said he could not do so because all the children were baptized and once they were baptized they could not be raised in a different faith.

When Rav Herzog said that, he put his head down on the lectern and wept. And then he looked at all of us and said, "I can't do anything more for those 10,000 children, but what are you going to do to help rebuild the Jewish people?" Later on, when we all went to shake his hand and receive a blessing from him, he said, "Don't forget what I said, what are you going to do?" And that has reverberated within me all my life.

When most people hear your name, they think, "Ah, yes, the Jewish historian," and yet, as your book makes clear, history wasn't a career you chose. It essentially was the result of a fluke.

It wasn't a fluke, it was accidental. I was writing *sefarim* on the Talmud. Then one day in Jerusalem, a man came up to me – whom I never saw before or since – and said, "We've got plenty of people writing on the Talmud, but we don't have anybody writing on Jewish history. You should write on Jewish history." That man – the prophet Elijah, I don't know who it was – had an effect on me, and I began writing on Jewish history. I had always lectured on Jewish history, but I didn't start writing until later.

But recording and distributing your lectures on Jewish history wasn't exactly planned either.

No, it was not. I was giving a Jewish history class to women, and their husbands came and said they would also like a class. Many of them were physicians and did not have regular hours, so they asked me if they could send their tape recorders. I said certainly – especially since they had paid the registration fee – and after a while they came back and said, "You know, we circulate these tapes in the hospital to other doctors and everybody loves them. You should do something with them." I was head of the Shaarei Torah yeshiva at the time, so we started producing tapes and distributing them.

And the rest is history.

King Solomon said it long ago: "Cast your bread upon the waters" – because you don't know when you'll hit something. Our job is to do. We don't know how it affects people. I had no intention that thousands of people would listen to me, but I tried to do something and the Lord helped that it happened. Everybody should try to do that.

In your book you recount many interesting encounters you had with rabbinic greats of yesteryear. For example, you write that Rav Yaakov Kamenetsky once taught you proper etiquette toward tollbooth collectors.

I drove him once into the city and we came to the George Washington Bridge. It was a very long line, it was a very hot day, and by the time we got to the tollbooth I was completely exasperated. I gave the toll collector a 20-dollar bill, he gave me change, and I just zoomed off. Rav Yaakov bent over to me and said, "You forgot to say thank you to the toll collector." That's the kind of person he was.

You also relate several stories about Rav Yosef Shlomo Kahaneman, *rosh yeshiva* of Ponovitch, which surprisingly have a "Zionist" tinge to them. Can you share?

On *Yom HaAtzma'ut* Rav Kahaneman would fly the Israeli flag over his yeshiva. He told me that when certain fellows in town complained, he said to them, "On Lithuanian Independence Day in Ponovitch, I flew the Lithuanian flag. Here [in Israel] it's not worse."

The Ponovitch Yeshiva continues this *Yom HaAtzma'ut* practice to this very day, correct?

Yes. Rav Kahaneman was his own man.... I remember a speech he gave in the Chicago yeshiva in 1947. At the time there were seven members of the Irgun, or the Stern Gang, whom the British wanted to hang. Rav Kahaneman said, "If I had people who were as dedicated to building a Torah state as these people are dedicated to driving England out of the Land of Israel, we would have a Torah state."

This lack of vision or dedication to grander goals is still a problem today, is it not? Many Orthodox Jews in Israel focus on their individual communities and *yeshivos* but very few, it seems, are concerned with building a *national* Torah society.

That's always the problem. The trees or the forest – what are you looking at? We concentrate on the trees.

In a Jewish Action article several years ago you criticized *yeshivos* for teaching too much Gemara and too little *Tanach*. Can you elaborate?

I didn't say there's too much Gemara. I said the curriculum is skewed so that there is nothing, so to speak, *but* Gemara, and not everybody can deal with Gemara. Also, how can you be a Jew if you don't know *Tanach*, if you don't know *Navi*, if you don't know Hebrew? We're illiterate in our own language.

In that article you wrote that the "study of *Tanach* is almost an oxymoron statement regarding our schools."

It's true. It doesn't exist. If it does exist, it's very peripheral, usually very boring, and not challenging. But if you know *Tanach*, if you know *Trei Assar*, for instance, you know what's going on today. All of today's problems are reflected in *Trei Assar* – everything: assimilation, ignorance, *machlokes*, education, domestic problems, family. The *nevi'im* speak about it all.

Some people also bemoan the absence of *dikduk* in Jewish education.

You cannot know Rashi if you don't know *dikduk*. It's a lost art, a lost subject.

In one of your Jewish history lectures you attribute the loss of *dikduk* to a backlash against secular Zionists and other modern Jewish groups.

Rav Yaakov Kamenetsky said that. He said secular Jews stole the Hebrew language, stole the Land of Israel, and stole history and knowledge from us. And we let them have it. It'll come back, don't worry.

What will?

Everything.

Why do you think so?

Because all of these problems are cumulative and there comes a tipping point. There comes a time when it cannot go on any longer. It's true in all of history. There comes a moment – that's when revolutions come, that's when the Soviet Union collapsed. And now pretty much, the Jewish people are going through a few moments.

What makes you say that?

Because you can't have a system that's broke and expect it to go on forever.

You recently wrote an article criticizing Israel's charedi community for its stance on serving in the army. Can you elaborate?

Army service is a symptom of the problem. The problem is how to deal with the Jewish state. How do you deal with Jews who are not just like you? How do you deal with Jews who are not observant? Those are the issues. Until we come face to face and deal with them, you're only going to have arguments about symptoms, not about the cause.

For a long period of time we were able to deny that the state existed. We pretended that we were still in the exile except that it's a Hebrew-speaking exile. But that's part of the system that's broke.

We didn't really believe it was going to happen. But God fooled us. It happened – 66 years ago. And now that there's a Jewish state, we don't know how to deal with it.

You seem to straddle two worlds. Your education was black hat, but many of your views can be characterized as Modern Orthodox.

I'm not Modern Orthodox. I'm trying to be a *shomer Shabbos* Jew. I see myself as a continuity of my grandfather and my father and my teachers in the yeshiva. That's how I see myself.

It seems, though, that the two camps – black hat and Modern Orthodox – are drifting further and further apart. When you were growing up…

...When I was growing up, you knew every *shomer Shabbos* Jew in Chicago. That's how few there were, and no one could afford to say, "I don't go there," "I don't belong to that." We're a victim of our own success. Everybody's big enough so they don't need the other guy. It's a different world.

You write in your book that you completed a doctoral thesis…

I have a D.H.L. – Doctor of Hebrew Letters.

If so, why don't you call yourself Rabbi Dr. Berel Wein? It might lend your works greater prestige or acceptance.

I'm not looking for greater prestige or acceptance. Whatever I do has to stand and fall on its own merits – not on whether I'm a doctor or not.

In one of your lectures years ago you made an interesting observation on human nature based on your years in the rabbinate. You said a rabbi is forced by his position to pretend to care about other people. After pretending for enough years, though, a rabbi, you said, surprisingly begins to *actually* care. Can you elaborate?

A rabbi gets paid for doing *mitzvos* – visiting the sick, comforting the bereaved, listening to people. So you get paid for doing what you really should be doing anyway. The only thing is now it becomes your job. And after a while, it becomes part of you. That's why I think the rabbinate is a great profession even though it's a very, very difficult and wearying one.

— originally published July 23, 2014

Postscript: *In 2015, Rabbi Wein published "Who Knows Twelve?: Themes and Values in Trei Asar" (Maggid Books).*

Rabbi Dr. Warren Goldstein

Chief Rabbi of South Africa

Older Jews sometimes complain that *frum* Jews today value *chumros* over character and external posturing over inner piety. These Jews would likely enjoy *The Legacy: Teachings for Life from the Great Lithuanian Rabbis,* a new work by historian Rabbi Berel Wein and South Africa's chief rabbi, Rabbi Warren Goldstein. They might particularly enjoy Rabbi Wein's comment in the book's introduction that the "common response of Lithuanian Jews regarding the *frumkeit* of a person was, '*Frum iz a galach.*'"

Naturally, Lithuanian rabbis cared a great deal about halachic intricacies, and some of the most famous *chumros* practiced today come from the Litvish Briskers. But the real emphasis of Lithuania's rabbinical elite, Rabbis Wein and Goldstein argue, lay elsewhere.

Rabbi Goldstein, who has served as chief rabbi of South Africa since 2005, recently spoke with The Jewish Press.

The Jewish Press: What are some of the central Litvish values that you and Rabbi Wein identify in *The Legacy*?

Rabbi Goldstein: One is *mentchlichkeit,* another is *limud haTorah,* and a third is responsibility for *Klal Yisrael* – finding a sense of mission in servicing the *klal.*

Aren't these values part of basic Judaism? In what sense are they "Litvish values"?

I think the beauty of being part of *Klal Yisrael* is that different *hashkafos* emphasize different parts of our *avodas Hashem.* Rabbi Wein and I emphasized the values we received from our *rebbeim;* we believe they can be of great benefit to *Klal Yisrael.*

In *The Legacy* you write that Lithuanian Jews often quipped that "a Jew is not *frum;* a Jew is *ehrlich.*" What does that mean?

It's essentially talking about a refinement of character and a deep integrity and humility. Rav Shlomo Wolbe, who was one of the great *mussar* thinkers of the 20th century, explains that sometimes the drive to be *frum* can have harmful effects if it's guided by being self-centered and not by the right *middos* and values. So *ehrlichkeit* needs to channel any kind of religious passion.

In your discussion of humility in *The Legacy,* you quote a *teshuvah* of Rav Moshe Feinstein in which he writes that he avoids drinking blended whiskey in private (as some halachic authorities indicate the beverage is not *kosher*) but *does* drink it in public so as not to appear better than other Jews. What lesson do you derive from this *teshuvah*?

One has to be constantly aware of consequences. Rav Moshe was saying that the consequence of him not drinking blended whiskey in public would be to set himself apart from those around him. He would come across as superior, and that might affect his own arrogance internally.

One would never have the *chutzpah* to say this about Rav Moshe, but he writes it about himself. He's teaching us that we have to take a broad view of everything we do. Character, *middos,* and *bein adam lachaveiro* are all Torah values. It's all part of the same system.

In *The Legacy* you also quote two *teshuvos* from Rav Yitzchak Elchanan Spektor and Rav Mordechai Gifter addressing Jews who wanted to import or *shecht* their own meat because they were unhappy with their community's *kashrus* standards. Interestingly, both Rav Spektor and Rav

Gifter strongly discouraged these Jews, arguing that maintaining communal unity was more important. Can you comment?

What these *rabbanim* were saying is: Let's make a *chumrah* of, what they called, the "*tzuras hakehillah*" – the unified communal structure. Torah is a comprehensive system and every part of it affects the other parts. That's why it's important to identify key essential Torah values because if these values are given more importance than others, they will be "trumping values" as well.

Another interesting or unusual statement in *The Legacy* is the comment of Rav Yerucham Levovitz that inner serenity is "the sum and crown of all positive traits and accomplishments." What precisely did Rav Yerucham mean by this? Why should inner serenity be so important for a Torah Jew?

Serenity comes from one's *neshamah* being at peace with who we are and what we're doing in this world. And that comes from doing the right thing – for two reasons. First, we were designed to serve Hashem, so when we're doing that we're living in accordance with our life's purpose. And second, Hashem created the Torah perfectly in such a way that it is the blueprint for ideal living and balances all the different parts of who we are.

You're the chief rabbi of South Africa. For those who don't know much about South African Jewry, what can you say as a quick primer on the subject?

The South African Jewish community is, *baruch Hashem,* a very vibrant, active Jewish community. Numbers in international terms are relatively small – about 70,000-75,000 Jews – but 90 percent of them are actually of Litvishe origin; hence my connection to the subject.

It's also a community that has some of the lowest rates of assimilation in the Jewish world, and which, in the last 20-30 years, has experienced a *baal teshuvah* movement that's unprecedented. There's hardly a family in the country that hasn't been touched by the movement, particularly in Johannesburg. So it's very Jewishly aware and Jewishly proud. Even those who are not *shomer mitzvos* have a tremendous amount of Jewish pride and great respect for *rabbanim* and Torah as well.

Finally, it's a community that has a very strong *tzuras hakehillah.* We have one *beis din* that deals with all *kashrus,* all *gittin,* all *kiddushin,* all *geirus* – everything is under one structure.

What's the denominational breakdown of South African Jewry?

Orthodoxy is dominant in South Africa. Even though there are obviously many Jews who don't keep *mitzvos,* the *kehillah* is 90 percent-plus Orthodox-affiliated. So even if you have Jews who are not *shomer mitzvos,* they belong to Orthodox shuls. All of the schools are also within an Orthodox framework, which means the schools only have Orthodox *rabbanim* teaching.

I think that's been a key in the success of the *baal teshuvah* movement – because even though Jews have drifted from practice, they were within an Orthodox framework and so there was always a way to reach them.

— originally published March 27, 2013

Postscript: *Several months after this interview was published, Rabbi Goldstein launched the "Shabbat Project," now an international program which, in 2016, drew more than a million participants from 95 different countries around the world.*

Rabbi Paysach Krohn

A Modern-Day *Maggid*

Few writers and speakers inspire like Rabbi Paysach Krohn. The author of 12 books – including his famous Maggid series of short stories – Rabbi Krohn travels the world regaling audiences with tales that stimulate the heart and soul.

Rabbi Krohn is a fifth-generation *mohel* and, at 21, was the youngest person ever to be certified by the Brith Milah Board of New York. His latest book, *The Maggid at the Podium,* was published by ArtScroll this past November.

The Jewish Press: How did your career as an author begin?

Rabbi Krohn: Ever since I was a little boy, I loved writing. My mother was a great writer, and she taught me. We would underline expressions in newspapers and pick up great alliterations. In school, in secular subjects, the writing and literature teachers were always my favorite.

Then, in 1976, ArtScroll came out with its first book – *Megillas Esther* – and it was written in such a beautiful way. Very quickly almost 100,000 *Megillas Esther*s were sold and everybody was overwhelmed. So I went to Rabbi Meir Zlotowitz and said to him, "I would love to be part of your team. Would you mind if I write *Koheles*?" He said, "We're doing the five *megillos,* but if you want to do anything else, just write it and we'll edit and print it."

So I asked if I could do *Mishlei*. I soon realized, though, that it was going to take over my life. It was just an impossible task because every *pasuk* is a book by itself. So, after a while, I stopped. But I loved writing and wanted to do something, so it occurred to me: Maybe I can write on *bris milah*, [and that was the genesis of] my first book: *Bris Milah: Circumcision – The Covenant of Abraham*.

How about your popular Maggid books? How did those come about?

Right before my father passed away in 1966, the Maggid of Yerushalayim, Rav Shalom Schwadron, came to America and stayed in our home for six months. I had never seen a *maggid* before, but my father had always taught us about the Dubno Maggid, and the thing I loved about the Dubno Maggid was that he took parables or examples from real life and used them as lessons. Rav Shalom Schwadron was fabulous at that. In the same speech, he could make an audience laugh and cry. He was able to talk to people and change them.

Now, I must admit, I had never thought of writing Rabbi Schwadron's stories, but when my friend Hanoch Teller started writing books with stories, I said to myself, "Wow, that's a great idea." So, as I was finishing the *bris milah* book, I called Rabbi Schwadron...

...and the rest is history.

Well, ArtScroll had never published a book of Jewish short stories. But within a month of *The Maggid Speaks* coming out, they sold 5,000 copies, which was absolutely amazing for them because they had only printed 5,000.

Then, one day, I came to ArtScroll's offices and met Rav Nosson Scherman. He said to me, "I just got back from South Africa where I was invited to speak and when I walked into one of the *yeshivos* there, I saw your book on the desk of one of the *rebbeim*." I said, "In South Africa?" He said, "Not only in South Africa.... And this teaches us that you must write another book."

I said, "What do you mean? What should I write about? Where am I going to get stories? I already used Rabbi Schwadron's best stories." He said, "Somehow you have to find stories because if the rebbes are teaching children your stories – which contain *mussar, yiras shamayim, ahavas Hashem,* and *ahavas haTorah* – then you have an obligation."

Twenty-five years later, you've now published eight Maggid books containing hundreds of stories. Where do you get so many stories?

For the second book in the series, I went to Rabbi Schwadron and asked him if he had more stories. But then I started getting stories from different *rabbanim* and *askanim.* And then many [ordinary] people started telling me stories because, if you tell a story, people want to tell you one in return.

And it just grew. Wherever I was invited around the world, I always met with people and let them know that I wanted to hear great stories. That's how these books are written. People stop me in the middle of the street or on an airplane to tell me a story.

How do you decide which ones to put in your books?

Ninety-eight out of 100 stories I can't use because they don't contain universal lessons. A story in a book has to be something that somebody's going to read it and say, "Oh my, if that person could do that, I can too. I can change."

In your books and speeches you seem to have a special ability to motivate and inspire. What's the secret of your success?

There are two things that are very important. One, never ever write or tell a story you don't believe in. You have to believe there's a great lesson in it. It can't be half-hearted. It has to be total. And I think when you tell stuff you really believe in, or that has inspired you, you tell it with such power and fervor that that comes across.

People ask me, "Do I get nervous when I speak?" and the answer is, "No, I get nervous when I prepare." When I'm preparing, I could be sweating like I just went through the most diligent workout because I'm trying to figure out which story to use, how to present it, etc.

So the first thing is you have to only tell something you believe in very, very strongly. The second thing is: Don't get caught in the details. That makes it boring. Get to the point. If you're talking about a trip you made to Israel, it's not important what airline you went on, and it doesn't make a difference that the plane came five hours late. That's not the point. If you went to Israel and you met a certain *tzaddik*, you should be at the *tzaddik*'s home by the second sentence of the story.

Many times people will say to me after a speech, "You put five speeches into that one speech," and that's true because many speakers will say the same story and repeat it and review it and tell it another time in another way. The same is true of a Torah thought. Say a thought, finished. The audience has to be at the edge of their seats. They can't fall asleep – and they won't fall asleep if they know they're going to miss something.

You once described yourself as a "*mohel* who has a mission." What did you mean by that?

When I do a *bris*, especially for a family that's not religious, I feel I have a responsibility to make it such a meaningful event that they will never forget it. A family that's not religious doesn't have too many religious occasions. We have Shabbos and *Yom Tov* and all the *mitzvos* – we have ways of being inspired – but how are these people going to get inspired?

So you have to do something at the *bris* to make them feel a connection to the previous generations, to Hashem, and to Torah. One of the ways I do that is I have one of the parents speak about the person the baby is named for. When you do that, all of a sudden the *bris* takes on a totally different approach because they realize they're not only talking about the future of this child, but the legacy of his past.

I always tell people that the Rebbe Reb Elimelech writes that when you name a child after someone, you make a connection between the *neshamah* of that child and the *neshamah* of the person he's being named for. When I was writing that for the *bris milah* book, I took the page out of the typewriter to write the word *neshamah* [in Hebrew]. Now, write for yourself the Hebrew word *neshamah*. What do the middle two letters spell? *Shem*. Isn't that incredible? When I saw that, I thought I would faint. The word *shem* is right in there – the two *neshamos* are connected through the name!

So that's what I tell people, and that's what I mean by a mission. The *bris* is not just the technical aspect. It's being *mekadesh shem shamayim* in such a way that the people leave elevated.

What would you say is the most interesting *bris* you did for a non-*frum* family?

One of them was for a Russian family. The father called me up and said he wanted the *bris* in the afternoon after he came home from work. So I came to the house on Tuesday – eight days after the child was born – but there was nobody there except the mother, the grandmother, and the baby. The mother looks at me, and says, "What are you doing here?" I said, "What do you mean? I told your husband, Ivan, that the *bris* is today." She said, "He thinks it's tomorrow, everybody's coming tomorrow."

So I called her husband. He was in the gym, working out, and I said, "Ivan, listen, I apologize, maybe I didn't make myself clear, but today is the eighth day. We have to do the *bris* today."

I thought for sure he was going to say, "Listen rabbi, we're not doing it, come back tomorrow." But instead, he said, "Rabbi, how much time do we have left?" I said, "Half-hour." He said, "Okay, you get everything set and I'll be there."

I couldn't believe it. So I'm setting everything up and he walks in about 15 minutes later, sweating. I told him to wash up [because he had to be the *sandek*], I gave him a yarmulke, and we did the *bris*. We finished five minutes before sunset.

Then I said, "Listen to me, Ivan. I have to come visit the baby, so I'll be here at the exact same time tomorrow. Don't say anything to anyone and tomorrow we're going to make a beautiful ceremony."

So the next day, I come. Many people are there and everybody thinks we're making a *bris*. We bring out the baby, I say *"Baruch haba,"* and then I put my arm around Ivan and said to everybody: "You don't realize what kind of *tzaddik* you have as a friend. You see, Ivan never went to yeshiva and he couldn't possibly know how important it is to have a *bris* on the eighth day, but his *neshamah* told him that if God says it's supposed to be on the eighth day, you do it no matter what, even if nobody's here."

So I said, "*Rabbotai,* I'm going to go through a ceremony and I'll explain the whole ceremony, but I want you to know that your friend did the *bris* yesterday and you can be so proud of him."

It was so moving.

— originally published April 24, 2014

Postscript: *In November 2016, Rabbi Krohn published yet another book in his Maggid series, titled "Illuminations of the Maggid." As for his other activities, Rabbi Krohn wrote to me in March 2017: "This past year I led trips to Italy and another to Southern Spain and Gibraltar. I've led these types of tours since 2003 and by now perhaps close to 1,000 people have been on these tours, which include Greece, Lithuania, Poland, Prague, the Austrian Alps, Frankfurt, Hungary, Morocco, and Vienna.*

"I am blessed that I love everything I do – the brissin, the speaking, the writing, the touring – but more than anything else, what means most to me is my family, and they know it as well, which is so important."

Rabbi Zevulun Charlop

A Rabbi With Innumerous Tales From Yesteryear

Rabbi Zevulun Charlop is a mind rich with fascinating stories and historical anecdotes. The son and grandson of distinguished rabbis, Rabbi Charlop was head of Yeshiva University's Rabbi Isaac Elchanan Theological Seminary (RIETS) from 1971-2008. Today he is special adviser to YU President Richard Joel on yeshiva affairs and *rav* of Young Israel of Mosholu Parkway. The financially-strapped Bronx congregation – which once boasted hundreds of members – has not *davened* together since July due to extensive water damage to its synagogue, but Rabbi Charlop has not entirely given up hope of it meeting again.

The Jewish Press recently met with him in his Washington Heights office.

The Jewish Press: What's your background?

Rabbi Charlop: I was born in the Bronx, and I think the Yankees and I are the only ones who never left.

My father, Rav Yechiel Michel Charlop, was one of the most famous rabbis in the country. He was born in Yerushalayim and studied in some of the finest *yeshivos* there. He also had a special *chavrusa* with both Rav Kook and Rav Yosef Chaim Sonnenfeld and was the conduit between them. Each one used to ask about the other and would send his regards through my father.

Rav Isser Zalman Meltzer wrote a *kuntrus* for my father. I met Rav Shneur Kotler – Rav Meltzer's grandson – and he said, "It's impossible! My grandfather never wrote a *kuntrus* for anybody." But I found it and showed it to him. When my father left *Eretz Yisrael,* my grandfather said he never knew anyone who left to America knowing all of *Bavli* and *Yerushalmi baal peh....* My father wrote three *sefarim* on one *amud* of *Shas.*

When did your father come to America?

In 1920. In America he studied in [RIETS]. In fact, he received the first Rokeach Award. Rokeach, the famous company, was founded by a very religious man who came from Kovno. He's famous for making kosher soap [since soap is usually made with tallow]. Many *rabbanim* gave *heterim* because soap is *eino ra'ui l'achilas kelev,* but Rav Yitzchak Elchanan, the *rav* of Kovno, felt soap needed to be kosher. So he sent a call out to all the chemists, and Yisrael Rokeach made this soap. The bars were blue and red – for *milchig* and *fleishig.*

It was such a successful business that the Russian government was going to put Rokeach in jail in order to take it over. Rav Yitzchak Elchanan found out about it and told him to run to America. So he came here and many years later he offered a $5,000 prize for getting the highest *yoreh yoreh, yadin yadin.* My father won the first one.

Later, my father served as a rabbi in Canton, Ohio, and Omaha, Nebraska, and, in 1925, he became the rabbi of the Bronx Jewish Center, which was the largest synagogue in the Bronx. The Bronx had close to 700,000 Jews at the time – more than the entire Jewish population of Israel in 1948.

What schools did you attend growing up?

Yeshivas Salanter, which was the only yeshiva in the Bronx, TA [Talmudical Academy], Yeshiva College, Columbia University, and RIETS. From there I became the rabbi of the Young Israel of Mosholu Parkway. This year would have been my 60th in that shul.

Is it true that the teachers in Yeshivas Salanter taught in *ivris b'ivris*?

Yes, not *ivrit b'ivrit,* but *ivris b'ivris.*

I found a remarkable letter signed by all the *rebbeim* of RIETS which was sent to Yeshivas Salanter – I think it was instigated by Rav Moshe Soloveitchik – and it stated that the only way to learn Gemara is in Yiddish. [They stated their opinion] as a *halacha.* They said Yiddish has been used for centuries, the thinking is in Yiddish, and that Yeshivas Salanter therefore has to teach Gemara in Yiddish, not *ivris.*

The only one who didn't sign the letter was [YU founder] Dr. [Bernard] Revel, and I think it's probably because he didn't approve.

What was the logic behind teaching in *ivris* and not *ivrit*?

The great Hebraists throughout the world spoke in *ivris* because it was *lashon ashkenazis.* That's the way people read Chumash and *davened.* Many Hebraists felt that was the real Hebrew.

Can you speak a bit about your grandfather, Rav Yaakov Moshe Charlop? He was a close student of Rav Kook, correct?

My grandfather was a great *tzaddik* and *gaon*.... When the state was established, *gedolim* went to Ben-Gurion and asked him not to draft women and, later, yeshiva *bachurim.* If you read history books, they'll name all the *gedolim* who [supposedly convinced Ben-Gurion not to draft women and yeshiva *bachurim*]. But the truth of the matter is that he rejected them. It was only because of my grandfather who came to him and cried.

Wasn't it the Chazon Ish who convinced Ben-Gurion?

According to a new biography about my grandfather that just came out, the Chazon Ish asked my grandfather to go to Ben-Gurion. It's in the [official record] of the Knesset. When Ben-Gurion said he's making these exemptions, his own party asked, "What's going on here?" Ben-Gurion said in the Knesset: "I did it only for Rav Yaakov Moshe Charlop."

Why would he do it for your grandfather?

Because my grandfather loved all Jews and was a lover of *Eretz Yisrael.*

How close was your grandfather to Rav Kook?

He was a *talmid chaver.* He was the only one in the room when Rav Kook died, and he gave an initial *hesped* when they were *metaher* Rav Kook's body....

They wrote amazing letters to each other. Someone once publicly called my *zeidy* a *talmid chaver* of Rav Kook, so my *zeidy* wrote to Rav Kook, saying, "I apologize, I never said to anybody that I'm, *chas v'chalilah,* your *talmid chaver.* How could I even dream of being your *talmid* – let alone your *talmid chaver?*" And Rav Kook wrote back, "How could I say that you're my *talmid?* You're my *chaver.*"

How did your grandfather become Rav Kook's *talmid*?

He was charedi, completely charedi, like all the other *Yerushalmim.* He was considered a *tzaddik* when he was 20, 25 years old.

His father came to *Eretz Yisrael* in 1842 or 1843 as part of one of the last waves of [*aliyah* by] the Vilna Gaon's students. My great-grandfather was one of the *dayanim* of Reb Yehoshua Leib Diskin, who was the greatest *rav* of his time. They say that whenever Rav Chaim Soloveitchik and the Beis HaLevi saw a piece of Torah of Reb Yehoshua Leib, they would begin to shake. We can't even imagine that today. When my grandfather was a *bachur,* from the age of 12 and on, he worked with Reb Yehoshua Leib, helping him *mesader* his writings because Reb Yehoshua Leib was already nearly blind.

My grandfather was known as one of the great *iluyim* of Yerushalayim, maybe the greatest. He got *semicha* from the Ridvaz, and the Ridvaz said he could be the rabbi in the greatest Jewish cities in the world. This was when my *zeidy* was in his early 20s.

If he was so charedi, how did he become close to Rav Kook?

When he was very young, he used to learn so hard that he wasn't well and the doctor told him to go to Yaffo. So he went. It was the year, or the year after, Rav Kook came from Europe, and they had big signs on the walls of Yaffo that Rav Kook was speaking between *Minchah* and *Maariv*. My *zeidy* debated with himself whether he should go because everybody said Rav Kook was too modern.

But he knew that Rav Kook was a great *gadol*, so he decided to go. He walked into the shul, which was packed, and stood in the back. He listened and was transfixed. He began to stare at Rav Kook, and Rav Kook saw this tall young man fixated on him, and he became fixated on my *zeidy*.

When it was over, Rav Kook looked for him but couldn't find him. So he went over to the great *posek*, Rav Tzvi Pesach Frank, who was also there, and asked him, "Do you know that tall young man who came in?" Rav Tzvi Pesach Frank said, "Yes, that's Rav Yaakov Moshe Charlop, one of the *iluyim* of Yerushalayim." He said, "I want you to find him and tell him to see me." The rest is history.

What about Rav Kook so impressed your grandfather?

His greatness. He saw that Rav Kook was a *gaon olam*, even as he was a *gaon b'machshavah*. My *zeidy* was very big in *machshavah* himself.

As dean of YU's rabbinical school for 37 years, you obviously interacted with many interesting *rabbanim*, such as Rav Yoshe Ber Soloveitchik, Rav Dovid Lifshitz, and Rav Mendel Zaks, the Chofetz Chaim's son-in-law. Can you talk a bit about Rav Zaks?

Rav Mendel Zaks was the *bochen* of the yeshiva. He was a *gadol* and the *rosh yeshiva* of Radun while the Chofetz Chaim was still alive. I remember at his *levayah*, Dr. Belkin [YU's president], who received *semicha* from the Chofetz Chaim when he was 17, said he knows for a fact that Reb Mendel edited [portions of] the *Mishnah Berurah* and that the Chofetz Chaim accepted all his emendations.

Reb Mendel Zaks had a son, Reb Gershon Zaks, who was a *gadol olam*. He began the Chofetz Chaim *yeshivos* in Monsey. Reb Gershon gave *shiurim* and some of the biggest *rebbeim* here at YU went faithfully every week to hear him.

What was your relationship with Rav Soloveitchik [popularly called "the Rav"] like?

I saw the Rav every week. At the beginning [when I first became dean of RIETS], the Rav would walk into my office several times a year to show that I was like his boss, *chas v'chalilah*. I was very upset, and later on he didn't do it.

He was a great supporter of mine. At the time, the relationship between the Rav and Dr. Belkin was very difficult – which was very well known – but they both, for reasons unbeknownst to me, liked me very much and trusted me, and I helped bring them together.

You must have had many interesting encounters with Rav Soloveitchik. Can you share just one?

The story that is most interesting and unbelievable is one I told at his tenth *yahrzeit*.

There was a man, a judge in New Jersey, who was married to a cousin of the Lubavitcher Rebbe. The couple was married for 11 or 12 years but didn't have any children, so they decided to adopt. She went to the Lubavitcher Rebbe, her cousin, but the Rebbe was very much opposed to adoption because of the problem of *yichud*. There are *heterim*, but the Rebbe was against it. He said, though, that she should go to Rabbi Soloveitchik, and he'll allow you to do it. Something like that.

So the husband came to me and said he wanted to see the Rav. I told the Rav the story, but he got very upset. He said, "The Rebbe sends him to me [implying that the Rav was a *meikil*]? It's his cousin and I should *pasken*?" He was very much opposed. So I told him, "They're going to get divorced. Also, the Rebbe didn't say no to them. The Rebbe wanted to save his cousin, but he just couldn't do it because he publicly came out against adoption."

The Rav was finally assuaged, and because the Rav was the Rav, I couldn't imagine he wouldn't give them a *heter*. After meeting the Rav [and not getting a conclusive answer], they wanted to meet him again. But the

Rav backtracked and said he didn't want to see them. Later he agreed, but when they knocked on his door, he didn't answer. I called him up and said, "They're knocking on your door..." He said, "I don't want..." He was backtracking again.

Finally, he opened the door and took them in. Now, I had told the husband that the Rav understands the situation and I'm almost sure he'll say it's alright. After the meeting, I spoke to him and he said the Rav was going in that direction but then stopped and said, "Come back in a year. If you don't have a child in a year, ask me again."

It was a crazy answer. I called the Rav and said, "What happened?" He said, "I was going to do it. But then," he said, "I told the *Eibershter*: If You don't give this woman a child within a year, I'm going to give her the *heter*!"

About four or five months later, the man called me up and said his wife became pregnant for the first time. She gave birth several weeks before the year was up. They wanted the Rav to be the *sandek*, so I went and spoke to the Rav. He started to laugh. "I'm not a *rebbe, chas v'chalilah*. I didn't do it. What did I do?"

— originally published April 14, 2014

Postscript: *Young Israel of Mosholu Parkway was finally forced to close permanently. Rabbi Charlop now lives in Teaneck, New Jersey.*

Rabbi Marvin Tokayer

The Young Man Who Went (Far) East

Ministering to Jews in Japan is not exactly what Rabbi Marvin Tokayer had in mind when he studied rabbinics at Yeshiva University and the Jewish Theological Seminary. But ultimately that is what he did, spending over a decade in the Far East and writing no fewer than 20 books in Japanese, including a book on the Talmud that became a bestseller in South Korea.

Rabbi Tokayer, who currently lives in Great Neck, NY, is also the author of *The Fugu Plan: The Untold Story of the Japanese and the Jews During World War II* and *Pepper, Silk & Ivory: Amazing Stories of Jews and the Far East*. He currently is writing volume two of the latter work as well as eight books on the Jews of India and a commentary on *Meseches Avodah Zarah* from an Oriental perspective.

The Jewish Press: How did a Jewish boy from New York wind up becoming a rabbi in Japan?

Rabbi Tokayer: I was a chaplain in the Far East with the U.S. Air Force in the early 1960s, but I had nothing to do with the local Jewish communities. I wound up serving as a rabbi in Japan because of a meeting with the Lubavitcher Rebbe. I'm not a Lubavitcher, but when I was a student [at the Jewish Theological Seminary] there was a young man teaching Lubavitch philosophy as a volunteer and I went to his class.

I didn't understand what was being taught, so I asked many questions and the constant reply to my questions was, "The Rebbe knows." I said, "I don't know what you're talking about." He said, "If there's a problem, the Rebbe has studied it and resolved it. If it's okay with him, it's okay with me."

Well, that wasn't okay with me, so this young Lubavitcher said to me, "Why don't you write to the Rebbe?" So I wrote a letter and got a response that the Rebbe would like to meet me. I was given two minutes and was there for about two hours.

How did that meeting lead you to Japan?

Well, many years later, when I was finished with the military, I was engaged to be married and the *mashgiach* for the caterer of my synagogue happened to be Lubavitch. He said to me, "You know, the Rebbe has total recall. Why don't you invite him to your wedding?" I said, "I have enough people coming to the wedding." He said, "The Rebbe isn't going to come, don't worry. But maybe he'll invite you for a *beracha* and it'll be a chance for your fiancé to meet the Rebbe."

So I sent the Rebbe an invitation and shortly thereafter I get a call that the Rebbe would like to see me and my fiancé. So we went to see him. We walk in, and the Rebbe smiles and says, "I haven't seen you for a long time, you disappeared on me." And then he says to me, "Stop working with the dead, start working with the living." I didn't understand. So I said, "Excuse me, but I don't understand." He repeats it: "Stop working with the dead, start working with the living." I still didn't understand. So he said, "I read somewhere that when you were in the military, you discovered a Jewish cemetery in Nagasaki. Why are you wasting your time looking for cemeteries? There are living Jews in Japan and you should go there and be their rabbi."

That was out of nowhere. We came to say hello, and he says we should go to Japan. I looked at my fiancé, who did not understand Yiddish, and said, "The Rebbe suggests that we go to Japan." Her reaction was that it may be closer to go to the moon.

But no matter what I said, the Rebbe boxed me into a corner and wouldn't let me out. There's a Peace Corps mentality, he said. We help the whole world, we also have to help ourselves. Go to Japan, represent the Jewish community to the government. Make sure they have a good school. Make sure the synagogue is functioning. Give some years to the Jewish people. Japan is a changing country. Go there and be their rabbi. It'll be great for you, and it will be wonderful for the community.

Ultimately we said, "Thanks, but no thanks. We're not interested." And he gave us a nice *beracha*. Bottom line: Within a year we decided to go to Japan.

What changed?

Well, a couple of months after this meeting, I got a telephone call from somebody at Kennedy Airport. He said, "I'm in between planes and, sorry to impose, but I would appreciate if you could meet me at the airport. I want to talk to you about something." I had never heard of this guy, but I was curious, so I went.

His name was Shaul Eisenberg, president of the Jewish community of Japan, and he said, "I'd like to offer you the position of rabbi of the Jewish community of Japan." It came as a shock. I said, "You know, I heard this once before, and we're really not interested." He said, "I'm going to be back in New York in a couple of months, can I speak to you again?" I said yes, and we met again.

And then my wife and I gave it some thought. We were a newly married couple, and maybe the Rebbe knew something we didn't. Maybe for a young couple to go so far away to be by ourselves and to open up to the world of China, Japan, Burma, and India would be an interesting honeymoon.

I was at a synagogue at the time, so I went and asked for a two-year leave of absence, knowing they wouldn't give it to me. Nobody gets a two-year leave of absence. But, surprisingly, they did. So we went – and forgot to come home.

What year was this?

It was 1968. We spent 10 years there. I was the only English-speaking university-trained rabbi from India to Japan. If anybody was interested in Jews, anti-Semitism, the Holocaust, the Bible, Judaism, I was the only number to contact. So it opened up many opportunities for me.

And it was fascinating to learn about the Jewish experience in the Far East. Jews have been in China, for example, for 1,800 years and in India for 2,200 years – from before the story of Chanukah.

What kind of Jews attended your shul in Japan?

They were third-generation, primarily Russian Jews who before or during the Russian Revolution went south from Siberia into China. They lived in northern China, which was called Manchuria at the time, and from there they went to Shanghai and Japan. In addition, there were some Sephardic Jews who came to Japan from Iraq via India and China. These weren't tourists or businessmen from America or Israel. That's who's there now, but not in my time.

In your book *Pepper, Silk & Ivory*, you mention a number of interesting *minhagim* you came across during your time in the Far East. Can you describe one or two?

Well, in India, the mezuzah on the door is not some piece of plastic or metal that you buy in the Judaica store. It's a palm print. You dip the palm of your hand in blood on *erev Pesach* and put it on the doorpost. Another interesting *minhag* is the Chinese Jewish tradition of the Torah reader wearing a veil just like Moshe did after he came down from Mount Sinai.

In the book you also note, amazingly, that a Jew wrote the orchestration for the music of the Chinese national anthem.

Yes, his name was Aaron Avshalomov. He was born in northern Siberia to a Russian Jewish family and spent most of his career in China. He lived in America for a while, but his best music was produced in China, and he encouraged the Chinese to use their own music rather than imitate European classical music. When he wrote an opera, it was half Chinese, half Western music.

What was Avshalomov doing in China?

His family lived there. There were 50,000 Jews in China. The parents of the former prime minister of Israel, Ehud Olmert, spoke Chinese at home. His grandparents are buried in China. The city of Harbin in northern China was a booming Russian Jewish city, maybe one of the finest Jewish communities ever produced in the diaspora. There were two Jewish banks, two Jewish schools, many shuls, Jewish soup kitchens, a Jewish hotel, and a Jewish high school that the actor Yul Brynner attended.

Are there other Jews who made a significant historical mark in the Far East?

The first prime minister of Singapore, David Marshall, was the president of Singapore's Jewish community. The first person to introduce psychiatry to China was a Jewish woman from Vienna, Fanny Halpern. And the closest friend, adviser, and bodyguard of the first president of China, Sun Yat-sen, was Morris Abraham Cohen. He was an unbelievable person. He saved Sun Yat-sen's life several times and was instrumental in getting China not to vote "no" on the partition of Palestine to produce a Jewish homeland.

The New Yorker recently published an article on the popularity of the Talmud in South Korea which credits you in large part for this phenomenon. Apparently your book of Talmudic stories and proverbs in Japanese was translated into Korean and became a bestseller in South Korea. How do you explain Koreans' fascination with the Talmud?

The Koreans think: If we are studying very hard – which they are – and working very hard – which they are – how come we don't have a Nobel Prize? And how come the percentage of Jews with Nobel Prizes is off the charts? What do the Jews have that we don't? They think studying the Talmud is our secret.

You've written some 20 books in Japanese. What are they about?

At first I wrote about Jewish proverbs, ideas from the *Chumash*, the Jewish home, the Jewish school, Jewish holidays. Then I started to compare and contrast – our history with Japanese history, the Jewish school with the Japanese school, the Jewish mother with the Japanese mother, etc.

What was your purpose in writing these books?

To put the Jews on the map. Let them know who the Jews are because you also have anti-Semitic books floating around. The Japanese have no history with Jews. What do they know about the Talmud? What do they know about Shabbos? What do they know about the Bible? They never heard of any of this. So I wanted them to have a correct image of the Jew.

You wrote these books in Japanese?

It was spoken in Japanese.

You speak Japanese?

Yes. When we came there, nobody spoke English, so you had to learn the language. If you spoke to the dog in English, it did nothing. If you spoke to it in Japanese, it understood and did what you wanted. So we figured: If the dog could learn Japanese, we could learn it too.

— *originally published October 1, 2015*

Postscript: *In November 2016, Rabbi Tokayer received the highest-ranking Japanese civilian award – the Order of the Rising Sun – for his contributions to Japan and creating friendly relations between the Jewish and Japanese peoples.*

In early 2017, Rabbi Tokayer told me he has completed the sequel to "Silk & Ivory" (under the title "Sugar in the Tea"), which will be published later this year. His volumes on the Jews of India and Maeseches Avodah Zarah are works in progress, he said. He also mentioned that he has been approached by PBS to do a three-hour documentary on the Jews of China, Japan, and India.

Rabbi Avraham Peretz Friedman

FBI Consultant, Batman Aficionado, *Kiruv* Rabbi

The resume of Rabbi Avraham Peretz Friedman (also known as Cary A. Friedman) almost reads like a bucket list. Study Torah with Jonathan Pollard? Check. Consult for the FBI? Check. Graduate from Columbia University with a Master's in electrical engineering? Check. Teach Gemara to the dean of Duke University's law school? Check. Translate the *divrei Torah* of a 17th-century rabbi? Check. Write a book on Batman? Check. Get a black belt in Shaolin gung fu? Check.

Rabbi Friedman, who currently serves as associate director of the Center for Tactical Resilience and Ethical Policing, published his seventh book over the summer, *Beautiful Days, Holy Days: The Majesty and Profundity of the Jewish Holidays*. His previous works include *Table for Two: Making a Good Marriage Better, Chanukas HaTorah: Mystical Insights of Rav Avraham Yehoshua Heschel on Chumash, Spiritual Survival for Law Enforcement,* and *Wisdom from the Batcave: How to Live a Super, Heroic Life*.

He and his wife live in Passaic, New Jersey, and are the parents of six children.

The Jewish Press: How does an Orthodox rabbi come to write a book on Batman?

Rabbi Friedman: Well, I grew up kind of obsessed with Batman. And what happened was: I had been learning and teaching in *Eretz Yisrael* for a number of years, and I came to back to the United States as part of a Torah Umesorah program to do *kiruv* at Duke University. One of my *rebbeim* said to me, "They're going to melt in the face of your Torah." But I showed up and the students weren't particularly interested.

So I decided to incorporate Batman into my classes since it was really the only anchor I had in popular culture. I would bring in a page from a Batman comic book with some ethical dilemma and then ask the students how they would resolve it. The kids would start arguing and after five minutes I would hand out, *l'havdil,* a photocopy of a page of Gemara and say, "Matt, the point you're advocating is the view of the Baalei Tosfos. And Jessica, your view is what the Ritva says. And Jeff, your position is what the Ramban says."

So Jeff, who wouldn't know the Ramban if he tripped over his turban, would suddenly be battling away to defend the Ramban's view. It was devastatingly effective. I did that for four years, and the class became very popular.

Would you recommend your Batman book to Orthodox Jews or is it just meant as a *kiruv* tool?

I think there's a value in *frum* people reading it too. To live a Torah life means to be heroic. It calls upon us to transcend our instincts and reach amazingly high levels that we wouldn't have thought possible, and one of the defining lessons of the Batman persona is the idea of overcoming adversity – of responding to a tough life by rising above it and doing something great.

So if people within a Torah society have good parents and teachers and are excited with this sense of being heroic, I wouldn't necessarily say, "Go and find out about Batman." But if someone doesn't have any other source that would impress upon him the importance of being heroic, I think it's a great idea.

Turning to your police work, what exactly do you do at the Center for Tactical Resilience and Ethical Policing?

I'm a police trainer. I started the company together with two other nationally-known trainers, one of whom is the chief psychologist for the Navy SEALs. We assist police agencies in helping their officers deal with the physical, psychological, emotional, and spiritual stresses of the job. We work all over the country. This month, for example, we'll be in Chicago addressing 3,000 police chiefs.

In your book *Spiritual Survival for Law Enforcement*, you write that people don't realize how mentally tough being a police officer is – to the point that the police suicide rate is apparently three times higher than that of the general population.

Many police officers considered entering the clergy before law enforcement, so they [clearly] have an instinct to do good in the world. They believe in some transcendent value or truth, they care for human beings, and they have self-confidence in themselves. Think of these as spiritual "bank accounts." The lives of police officers, however, contain all kinds of experiences that drain these accounts. They see suffering, randomness, and evil every day, and they begin to think there's little they can do in the face of so much horror.

So what happens is these three accounts get drained very quickly and police officers go into spiritual overdraft and become embittered. What I do is sensitize them to the fact that there is this drama playing out, and then I help them create exercises and tools to replenish these accounts. Basically, I distill a lot of *mussar* literature so that police officers can stay healthy.

Is that also what you do as a consultant for the FBI?

Yes. For the last 15 years I've been a consultant to the FBI's Behavioral Science Unit, and I designed a course for them on spiritual survival for law enforcement. For about seven years I taught at Quantico a few times a year.

What is your sense of the mood of police officers right now with the increase in anti-police sentiment in the United States?

They're bewildered. It's kind of a sad thing that society dismisses the extraordinary work they do. I mean, they put their lives on the line every day to protect strangers. It's one thing if a person risks himself to protect his family, but police officers protect people they've never met before.

So the fact that there is this kind of wide-scale negative portrayal of the police in the liberal media is sad to them, but I really believe that most decent people in this country are very strongly supportive of the police – as they should be.

When you lived in North Carolina in the 1990s, you studied Torah with Jonathan Pollard in prison every week for four years. What were your impressions of him?

I thought he was an extraordinary human being. He has a brilliant mind, and I enjoyed learning with him very much. It was very difficult for me to see him in that kind of environment, but amid all the harshness of the place, he retained his dignity throughout, and his *middos* were, I thought, exemplary.

What did you study with him? Was there a *sefer* he particularly enjoyed?

We studied *Chumash* and Gemara, and we spent a lot of time on hashkafic topics as well. Pollard and I also went through every word of the first two volumes of *Hegyonei Halacha* by Rabbi Yitzchak Mirsky. Finally, Pollard had a copy of *Gateway to Happiness* by Rabbi Zelig Pliskin, which he loved more than anything else around him.

As the author of *Table for Two: Making a Good Marriage Better,* what would you say is the key to a good marriage?

There's nothing magical about making a marriage good. Marriage is composed of two people, and both have to refine their personal character and work on their *middos*. If a person uses marriage properly, it becomes the vehicle by which he or she can reach very high levels of *shleimus* and *tikkun hamiddos*.

In fact, it doesn't even require two people. Even one person working hard on him or herself can make amazing differences and use that as a springboard for improving his or her marriage.

You write several times in the book that there's "no *mitzvah* to be natural" in a marriage. What do you mean by that?

I think a lot of people within marriage say, "I just want to be myself," "I'm going to let it all hang out," "I want to just relax and be the person that I am." And that's never a formula for success. Success comes when a person transcends him or herself.

There was a movie when I was a boy called "Love Story" and its tagline was, "Love means never having to say you're sorry." That's *sheker v'chazav*, it's *rishus* – because love means *always* saying sorry, *always* working on oneself, *always* demanding more of oneself and trying to raise oneself up to a higher level in terms of sensitivity and kindness and consideration for one's spouse.

Why do you – a rabbi – have a black belt in Shaolin gung fu?

I think it's important for everybody – for every Jew especially – to defend him or herself. In addition, for me, Shaolin gung fu is an adjunct to my *mussar* training. It teaches a person to confront his fears and sense of limitations and then to just smash through them. I'm involved now in teaching Shaolin gung fu to some of my own children.

On the front cover of some of your books you are "Rabbi Avraham Peretz Friedman" and on the cover of others you are "Cary A. Friedman." Why?

I want to make people comfortable. When I submitted *A Table for Two*, the people at Targum Press said, "We're not sure people will be comfortable reading a book written by Rabbi Cary Friedman. They might think it's a woman. We want people to have a sense that this book is appropriate for them."

In the outside world, though, "Cary" is a little less scary. If the cover of my police book said "Rabbi Avraham Peretz Friedman," I don't think there's a police officer in the country who would read it – and I don't blame them. I mean, would we pick up a book if it was very clearly written by a priest?

So both names are fair expressions of who I am. I am Cary A. Friedman, and I am Avraham Peretz Friedman. I don't see any *setirah,* but on the covers of my books I put the name that won't turn the audience off because the most important thing for me is that they open the book and experience the Torah that's inside.

In your latest work, *Beautiful Days, Holy Days,* you write interestingly that *Megillas Esther* is almost an anti-Cinderella story. Can you elaborate?

The outline of the Cinderella story is that a heroine with humble origins is elevated to some high position due to the intervention of an otherworldly being, and her success is a function of her beauty.

In *Megillas Esther* we see a rejection of all this. Esther doesn't want to become queen and she gets the job not because of her beauty – in fact, *Chazal* say she had unappealing features – but because of her *middos,* her intellect, and the greatness of her *neshamah.* She even refuses to wear cosmetics when they're offered to her. And when Esther becomes queen, the only value she sees in it is the potential to save *Klal Yisrael.* So *Megillas Esther* is a rejection of the values of the Cinderella story right down the line.

— originally published September 9, 2015

Postscript: *Rabbi Friedman and his two business partners continue teaching the police community. In late 2016, Rabbi Friedman wrote to me: "I see – daily – the power of Torah as the insights I provide save officers' lives, careers, marriages, and integrity."*

He is currently writing several more books, including a commentary on Pirkei Avos, a practical training manual for police officers, and a second volume of essays on the yamim tovim.

Mohammed's Sword

Katie Hopkins

Fighting English Liberalism With Gusto

(original interview, published here for the first time)

In the West, common sense is not so common anymore, and individuals willing to speak freely – even if it means earning the scorn of liberalism's politically-correct elite – are even rarer. Katie Hopkins is one such person.

A popular columnist for the Daily Mail, Hopkins is fiercely critical of the West's approach to battling Islamic terrorism and was perhaps Donald Trump's most vocal supporter in the United Kingdom in the lead-up to the 2016 presidential elections.

Like other provocative conservatives, Hopkins has been harassed for her views, even once being questioned by the police for language she employed in a 2015 column titled, "Rescue Boats? I'd Use Gunships to Stop Migrants." She vows, however, to continue speaking her mind, even if it lands her in jail one day, she told this writer.

Resnick: Many people believe that the proper response to terrorism is carrying on as if nothing happened. If you act scared or even differently, you're "letting the terrorists win," people say. During a recent TV appearance, you mocked this belief. Why?

Hopkins: I feel that the West's response to terror attacks is completely unacceptable. We almost have a process for dealing with them now. The leader of the attacked country says, "We strongly condemn this attack," other world leaders say they stand shoulder to shoulder with the country, somebody turns off the lights of the Eifel Tower, we light up a public building in the colors of the country's flag, and then people come out with their tea lights and hashtags.

Why do you disapprove of this reaction?

Because it's not a *response* to terror, and what it means is the same thing will happen again. It's all very well for Theresa May to say after the Westminster Bridge attack, "We stand united" or "We are not cowed" – or any of those other phrases that people think makes everyone feel better – but in reality we are just ants scurrying about, defenseless, waiting for the next footstep to fall.

And the fact is that we *are* afraid and we *are* cowed. People now accept terror as normal and think they're brave for just walking across Westminster Bridge. To this we've been reduced – to thinking that walking across a bridge is brave.

When I'm in London now, my mum texts me to make sure I'm okay. That's madness. I'm 42 years old. When I cross a city road with my children, I tell them, "Stand next to this lamppost; keep it between you and the traffic in case anyone mounts the curb." That's a mad conversation to have with children in the 21st century in Europe – equipping them for a truck attack if they're walking down a [sidewalk]. But that's where we are.

Much of the West seems strangely resigned to living with terrorism as opposed to defeating it. Why is that? Why does London's mayor claim that terrorism is part of living in a big city when there are many big cities – such as Tokyo and Warsaw – that experience zero terrorism?

You're right. It's a narrative they want us to buy into that this is just part and parcel of being in a city, that we should accept it as "the new normal" – part of the great multiculturalist project.

Of course, all this is the opposite of how I think and it's the sort of thing that drives me mad. We need to stand up for Britain and our national sovereignty. We need to say to people, "If you wish us harm, you have no place in this country."

What practically can be done to prevent future terrorist attacks?

Let's take one example. The Westminster terror attacker, who grew up with the name Adrian, converted to Islam and became an extremist after a spell in prison [where he changed his name to Khalid]. Then he visited Saudi Arabia on a number of occasions; then he moved to Luton in the same area as an extremist Islamic network; and then he was flagged by MI5.

So we knew he was going to be a problem, but failed to stop him when he changed his name, failed to stop him when he came out of prison, failed to stop him when he returned from Saudi Arabia, failed to stop him when he moved into the very community we know is a threat to us, and failed to stop him again when MI5 realized he was part of the problem.

We need to look at our prisons and perhaps create special wings for Islamic extremists where they can be kept in isolation so they can't radicalize others. We need to stop individuals from coming back to the UK if they were radicalized abroad. I don't know why we always judge in favor of personal freedom, or human rights. I would prefer for us to focus on the human rights of the innocent individuals who end up being killed by terrorists.

In the 1980s, Rabbi Meir Kahane advocating kicking the Arabs out of Israel, in part because of the terror threat they posed. Should countries like England consider such a solution for their own hostile populations? Or is this solution too radical?

I think it is a radical solution. But I do think we have to accept that multiculturalism has failed in all but the richest areas of England. Until we do that, we can't move forward.

I would also place everyone on the terror watch list behind bars if they're British nationals or deport them to the countries they came from if they're not. I don't see why the UK should continue to host them.

I would also stop the boats crossing the Mediterranean because that's where the next population of terrorists is going to come from. Eighty-five percent of those crossing the Med are not refugees or asylum seekers, and I would make strong borders so that we stop allowing individuals into this country we can't police.

We all know that discriminating against good populations is wrong. But many liberals seem to believe that it's wrong to discriminate against *any* group, even if it is the source of much evil. How do you explain such thinking?

It's perverse. And I can't help explain it because it makes no sense to me at all. I completely agree with you....

People always say, "Well, if you stop people coming, maybe one or two of those people will be asylum seekers who need our help" – and all of me says, "You know what? Tough." If it means my country stays safe and more British nationals stay safe – tough. And I don't care if I hurt or offend a few people by saying that.

You write a lot about terrorism, but you also address cultural issues in your columns, and the language you employ is not always prim and proper. How would you respond to more traditionally-minded readers who may be uncomfortable with your language?

When I think something, I say it or write it. And I don't mind if people find those opinions offensive or brilliant. All I do is say my stuff. And it so happens that the reason I have such a big following is because many people feel silenced. I'm kind of a conduit for people who think the way I think but can no longer say it because the list of things you can no longer say is longer than the list of things you can.

Dr. Phyllis Chesler

A Feminist Who Dares Criticize Islam

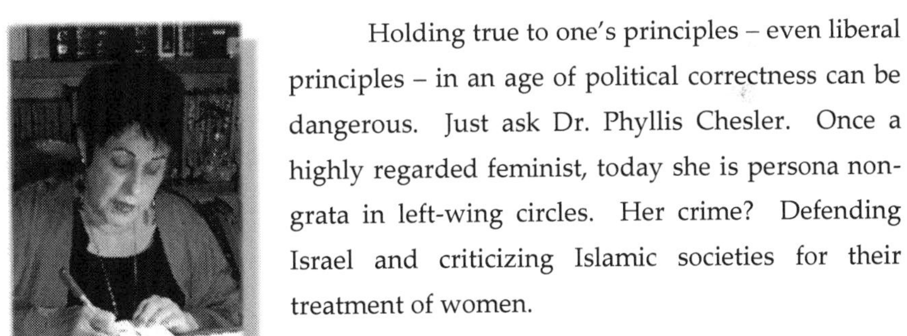

Holding true to one's principles – even liberal principles – in an age of political correctness can be dangerous. Just ask Dr. Phyllis Chesler. Once a highly regarded feminist, today she is persona non-grata in left-wing circles. Her crime? Defending Israel and criticizing Islamic societies for their treatment of women.

Dr. Chesler is the author of 16 works, including *The Death of Feminism* (2003), *An American Bride in Kabul* (2013), and, most recently, *Living History* (2015).

The Jewish Press: Do you still regard yourself as a feminist?

Dr. Chesler: I do, but the vision of universal human rights has died in the feminist movement, and what has taken its place is this multicultural relativism in which anybody formerly colonized, not white, preferably Arab, and – most importantly – "Palestinian," is the victim *de jure*, the victim *uber alles*.

You write in your latest book, *Living History*, that at a certain point in your career you "lost most of [your] intellectual and feminist friends." When did that occur?

The New Anti-Semitism, which I first published in 2003, was the first time in my career that a book I had written was not reviewed. It was ignored by the mainstream media – the very media where I was once very prominent. And any number of my feminist friends were angry, shocked, or, at best, silent.

Then I began to publish in conservative venues – because they applauded the book – for which I was severely castigated by my friends. They said, "You're making alliances with right-wing Christians and Jewish conservatives." I replied, "But you're making a perfect storm of an alliance with misogynist, Islamist barbarians."

How can America defeat Islamists, considering that they are so dispersed geographically? Should we go to war against states like Saudi Arabia and Iran that fund radical Islam to the tune of billions of dollars? Should we stop all immigration from the Middle East? What should be done?

Let me say a number of things. I work with Muslims who are dissidents and Muslim feminists who are anti-Islamist. Having said that, the majority of Muslims are just like the majority of Germans under Hitler. Yes, they themselves may not act on their beliefs that infidels should be killed, but they're guilty because they're bystanders.

So what do we do? The first thing is we have to tell the truth and it has to be repeated as often as necessary. The second thing is we have to influence legislators about immigration. I'm happy to have America give asylum to the victims of Islamic persecution – Christians and females. But I'm not happy to allow in fanatics who are about to bring this country down. We therefore need to have immigration people who are trained to tell the difference and to make very hard, firm decisions. And they have to be legally empowered to do so. Otherwise we will become like Europe.

What is your take on Europe and radical Islam in light of the recent attacks in France?

Sometimes I think Europe has reaped a karmic destiny. It was complicit in the murder of six million friendly, non-violent Jews, and for that crime it has now reaped a whirlwind of many, many millions of very hostile

Semites who wish to take Western civilization down.

Some conservative pundits like Mark Steyn believe Europe is lost – that hostile Muslim immigrants will take over the continent within the next century by virtue of their high birthrate. Do you agree?

Well, the demographics are against Europe because as women become more educated and men become progressive about women's rights, the birthrate goes down. If you're not under siege, this is fine – you have two children instead of eight. But if you [accept within your midst] a culture that believes in polygamy and believes that a woman should have eight children, your country will be flooded.

Now, that doesn't mean we want to force white Caucasian women to breed, breed, breed, but it does raise questions about immigration, deportation of radicals, restriction of access to radical mosques, etc. It also raises questions about using European laws to punish very seriously honor and shame crimes committed on European soil.

You write in *Living History* – in reference to standing up to radical Islam – that people would "rather live on their knees than risk dying on their feet." Can you elaborate?

Jews are an anxious group – understandably so, given the millennia of persecution – and want to have no trouble. They don't want to bear the burden – or glory – of having to support a Jewish state that has been demonized into pariah status. They don't want to spend their lives fighting. They don't want their salaries risked. They don't want to receive hate mail. They want to have opportunities and take vacations.

Anyone who takes up Israel's cause is demonized as a "Zionist," a "conservative," and a "Republican." These are all curse words. And once you defend Israel – even if you are a staunch civil libertarian, as I am, or a committed feminist, as I am, it doesn't matter – you have crossed the line of what is permissible and nothing you say thereafter will be deemed credible. The litmus test for political correctness is where you stand on Israel.

Why, in your opinion, do many liberals focus on the occasional

Muslim killed in self-defense by Israel when Muslims are killed in far greater numbers in so many other places, such as Syria where more than 200,000 people have died as a result of the ongoing civil war there?

It's a good question, and I think part of the answer – the darker part of the answer – is that nobody really cares about Muslims. The world doesn't care about barbarians vs. barbarians, or Muslims vs. Muslims or persons of color vs. persons of color – just as in Ferguson and Baltimore nobody really cares about the black-on-black crime. They care only if a white policeman is killing a young black man.

In addition, it's a psychological defense mechanism. Rather than focusing on real genocide committed by Islam in terms of religion and gender – which is a bigger and harder problem to solve – you focus on the tiny, not totally perfect, state of Israel. That way, people don't have to feel helpless in the face of terrorism or barbarism but rather can feel: "If only Israel were abolished, everything would be okay."

In your 2013 book, *An American Bride in Kabul*, you reminisce about your marriage to an Afghani Muslim 50 years ago. How did a nice Jewish girl from Brooklyn wind up eloping with a Muslim to Afghanistan?

I was a born rebel. In 1948 in Boro Park, where I grew up, I joined a left-wing Zionist group, Hashomer Hatzair, which envisioned a mystical, political, and harmonious union between Yishmael and Yitzchak. Perhaps that concept reverberated with me over time so that my guard was not up as it should have been.

But I was not openly rebelling by the time I got involved with this man. I was a child and I knew no danger and it was a great adventure. I had no intention of staying in Afghanistan, nor did I wish to get married, but he said, "I can't introduce you to my family and we can't travel the world unless we are married," so I said, "Well, all right." It was a civil ceremony that meant little to me.

However, once we landed in Afghanistan, they took my American passport away and I became a citizen of no country and the property of a very large, wealthy polygamous Afghan family. And this is a man whom I met in college – very urbane, very sophisticated, very well-spoken. We never once discussed religion. He had no problem with the fact that I was Jewish. It's something that no one talked about in 1960 in America. Islam was not taught anywhere in colleges, and I did not understand how wild [that part of the world] really was.

I was not prepared and was held captive for five months. I came back and literally kissed the ground when I arrived [in New York], something I've only done once since – on my first visit to Israel.

How did you manage to get back to America?

I nearly died in Afghanistan. I was very ill with hepatitis. I had made many escape plans, all of which failed, but at the last minute, my then-father-in-law gave me an Afghan passport. He probably didn't want a dead American kid on his hands and clearly his son, my husband, was not letting me go, so he let me go.

I'd say I got back because I was blessed by God. And maybe it was all *bashert* because otherwise how could I understand the Jew-hatred that's endemic in the Islamic world? How could I teach it at this moment in history?

And how could I know what I know about the burqa and women in the Islamic world had I not been there, had I not witnessed it and endured some of it myself? So maybe this was all part of some divine plan.

— originally published May 13, 2015

Postscript: *Dr. Chesler is currently completing three books: "Memoir of a Politically Incorrect Feminist" and two volumes of her collected writings on honor killings and "Islamic gender apartheid." She remains a fellow at the Middle East Forum and, as she wrote in a recent e-mail to me, "continues to monitor the dangerous rise of anti-Semitism, anti-Zionism, and politically-correct poisoned propaganda."*

Mitchell Bard

Taking an Honest Look at Radical Islam

Mitchell Bard has written and edited 23 books, including *The Complete Idiot's Guide to Middle East* and *The Arab Lobby: The Invisible Alliance That Undermines America's Interests in the Middle East*. Bard, who has a PhD in political science from UCLA, is also the executive director of both the American-Israeli Cooperative Enterprise (AICE) and Jewish Virtual Library, an online encyclopedia of Jewish history and culture.

He has appeared on CBS, NBC, and Fox News, and numerous other television and radio programs. He recently spoke to The Jewish Press about his latest work, *Death to the Infidels: Radical Islam's War Against the Jews*.

The Jewish Press: *Death to the Infidels* argues that the Arab-Israeli conflict is about religion. Many people, however, think it's about land. Why do you think they're wrong?

Bard: If it were about land, you wouldn't have Islamic groups saying it's inconceivable that Jews should rule over Muslims. It's also telling that only Muslims have turned to violence. Palestinian Christians are in the same situation as the rest of the Palestinians in the territories and yet they have not chosen violence or martyrdom. If anything, they feel just as persecuted as Jews.

If you're right that the conflict is rooted in religion, what are the ramifications?

The ramifications are that there is no solution – that there never will be peace between radical Islam and Israel. That doesn't mean you can't reach an agreement – Israel was able to make agreements with Jordan and Egypt – but those agreements didn't bring peace to the region. Radical Muslims continue to wage war against Israel.

The problem is that too many people think in terms of some sort of perfect peace like the Garden of Eden – or at least like the United States has with Canada and Mexico. And that just is unrealistic.

You write in the book that Arabs possess a very different sense of time than Westerners. Can you elaborate?

When Americans think of the good old days, they think of the 1950s or 1960s. When Muslims think of the good old days, they think of the 1240s or the 1540s – or the 840s – when there was this glorious Islamic empire that dominated most of the world.

They think it's just a matter of time before they overwhelm the Jews and acquire nuclear weapons. So this idea of getting Iran to agree to [put its nuclear program on hold for] 10 years... for them, 10 years is nothing. They're willing to wait 50 years to have the capability to destroy Israel. And this is something most Westerners don't appreciate. You have people in the Middle East say things like, "It took us 200 years to drive out the Crusaders, but we did. And it may take us 200 years to drive out the Jews, but we will."

You have an interesting line in your book: "The media and diplomats often divide the Muslim world into moderates and radicals, but those involved in the conflict with the Jews would be more accurately described as radical and more radical."

I think if you look at the current leadership of the Palestinians, for example, that's really what the choice is. Mahmoud Abbas and the rest of them are not moderates by any means. They talk about liberating Jerusalem and the Jews trying to blow up the al Aqsa mosque. That's really not very moderate.

A moderate would be someone who says he's prepared to live in peace with the Jewish state and is against terrorism and doing everything possible to stop terrorism and incitement.

You write about the U.S.-Saudi Arabia relationship and note that the Saudis get a pass from the U.S. on, for example, human rights violations and the funding of terrorism and radical Islamic education around the globe. Why do they get a pass?

Well, they've gotten a pass for the entire history of the relationship – going back to the late 1930s when oil was discovered. The Arabists in the State Department, in particular, have been able to convince successive administrations that the Saudis literally have us over a barrel. They believe we can't afford to pressure Saudi Arabia because the oil will be cut off.

Isn't that true?

No, because they can't live without selling oil. They can't drink it. They need to sell it somewhere, and we can use a lot more leverage to change their behavior.

As someone who has written extensively on the Arab-Israeli conflict, what do you find are the biggest misconceptions people have about Israel?

One big misconception is that Israel is not interested in peace. And the other big misconception is that settlements are the obstacle to peace when they empirically are not. From 1948 to 1967, there were no settlements, and yet there was no peace. And from 1967 to 1977, there were very few settlements, yet there was no peace.

How is someone with a Master's degree from Berkley and a doctorate from UCLA so conservative?

I don't think I'm particularly conservative. On most social issues I'm very liberal, and if you look at some of the things I've written on the Middle East, they're much more on the liberal side than the conservative side. For example, my longstanding position on the Middle East peace process is that Israel should unilaterally withdraw from the territories because if Israel controls or annexes the territories, it faces the dilemma of "How do you remain a Jewish democratic state?"

Withdrawing from the West Bank would entail the expulsion of settlers from their homes. If we're already talking about expulsion, why should we, as Jews, advocate the expulsion of our own rather than the expulsion of Arabs? Why is expelling Jews moral but expelling Arabs not?

I don't believe in the expulsion of Jews. My view has always been that Jews who live in the territories should have the choice. If they really believe that what's most important is the Land of Israel rather than the State of Israel, let them stay. But then they are going to be in Palestine and subject to the laws and security of the Palestinians – and that's probably not a good idea. But as far as I'm concerned, they should be able to have a choice.

— originally published April 15, 2015

Raheel Raza

A Muslim Who Won't Be Silent

Criticizing Islam or Islamic society is often risky business. Say an unkind word about it and one is liable to be vilified as an intolerant, ignorant bigot.

Documentary producer Raphael Shore knows this firsthand. His films "Obsession: Radical Islam's War Against the West" (2005) and "The Third Jihad: Radical Islam's Vision for America" (2008), were branded Islamophobic and attacked by liberal watchdog groups.

Undaunted, Shore recently produced yet another controversial documentary, "Honor Diaries," which highlights the pervasiveness of underage marriage, honor violence, and female circumcision in Muslim societies. Although intended to help women, the film has been harshly criticized by the Council on American-Islamic Relations (CAIR), which successfully lobbied to have screenings of the film at the University of Illinois and University of Michigan canceled.

The Jewish Press recently spoke to Raheel Raza, president of the Council for Muslims Facing Tomorrow and one of nine activists prominently featured in "Honor Diaries."

The Jewish Press: This film bills itself as "more than a movie, it is a movement to save women and girls from human rights abuses – around

the world and here in America." Interestingly, though, it seems that conservatives are the ones championing this film while liberals, who claim to fight for human rights, are generally standing on the sidelines. Why is that?

Raza: It's always been this way. I've been an activist for over 25 years, and I have always found that there's a deep silence when it comes to issues relating to women – especially Muslim women. Western feminist groups and liberals don't want to touch the topic; they drop it like a hot coal.

One reason is political correctness. A second one is fear. They're coerced into silence by Islamist organizations telling them they'll be called racist or that there's no need for them to speak about someone else's culture. But we [believe] that cultural relativism should not trump human rights. It's not about religion or culture or a specific group of people. It's about human rights. And those who are trying to shut down dialogue or are not supporting this cause obviously don't care about human rights.

But some people believe it's wrong to interfere in someone else's culture.

Why is it wrong to interfere? As a human being, if you see someone else being hurt, are you just going to look the other way and allow them to be hurt because it happens to be another culture or because it happens to be justified by part of their faith? Why? Why this exception only in terms of Islam or Muslim societies? They would speak out for anyone else.

There are people who champion animal rights. Are women not as important as animals? Are they not our sisters? Are they not our daughters? So to me it seems to be a double standard. It's looking the other way, and it's absolutely appalling and unacceptable because unless we create awareness we're not going to be able to solve the problem.

And these practices are not just happening in other countries. They're happening in the U.S. and in Canada too, and they're on the rise.

How do you respond to the claim that what you're fighting is, in effect, Islam since Islam condones some of the practices that "Honor

Diaries" finds deplorable? Take the issue of child brides, for example. Some Muslims argue that they are simply following the example of Mohammed, who married a six-year-old girl when he was 50 years old.

Well, that is their ignorance speaking. Those people have not read their history properly. And again, this is not about religion. It's about a human rights violation.

And let's say for a moment they believe this happened in the 7th century. That's no reason to validate it in the 21st century.

How do the majority of Muslims living in America regard Western values? Many Americans sometimes wonder if the Muslims among them aren't much more radical than the media and others portray them to be.

I can't speak for all Muslims, but if I were to make a generalization I would say they believe in different things, and the majority of them believe in leading a 9:00 to 5:00 life, earning a good living, and going to bed at night knowing their children are fed. They're the silent majority.

Unfortunately, after 9/11 we've been put into a position where unless all Muslims speak out, by default they're considered terrorists or prone to violence. Obviously that is not the situation, so there has to be better understanding by the masses who are not Muslim and there has to be more outreach by Muslims as well, [making it clear] that organizations like CAIR and ISNA – the Islamic Society of North America – do not speak for them.

There are many interpretations of the faith. Unfortunately, we are faced with the most violent interpretation today, and the battle for the soul of Islam at the moment is to take back that voice.

"Honor Diaries" has been translated into Arabic and Farsi. Is this film being shown in the Middle East? Is it allowed to be?

The Facebook Arabic page for "Honor Diaries" has more than 100,000 likes.

People are afraid to show the film publicly, especially in a country like Pakistan where the Taliban operate, but they're more than willing to show it in private homes. In Pakistan, the rate of honor killings is very high. In Egypt, female genital mutilation is very common. So they are showing the film, but it's not public screenings because they're afraid for their safety.

You're the president of the Council for Muslims Facing Tomorrow. What exactly does your organization do?

First of all, I specifically chose the name Muslims Facing Tomorrow because we have a huge problem of Muslim societies living in the past. For example, the Taliban and the extremists believe the only good Muslim is a 7th-century Muslim. We say no, we must look forward, we must look ahead.

So we hold seminars, we bring in speakers, and we also host events for youth because they're very confused. They don't know what is right and what is wrong and which path to follow. We embrace individual freedom, freedom of expression, freedom of choice, the value of living in a pluralistic society....

We also want to bring back the beauty that was part of Islam – music, art, and culture – all of which has been totally subsumed by extremism.

— originally published May 28, 2014

***Postscript:** Raheel Raza continues to fight for moderation in Islamic society. In late 2015, she narrated a short film, "By the Numbers" – viewed more than four million times on YouTube – in which she cites research revealing that hundreds of millions of Muslims worldwide believe that apostates should be executed, honor killings and suicide bombings are sometimes justifiable, and Sharia law should govern society. The West, she argues, must confront these facts if it wishes to remain free and safe.*

Leo Hohmann

Sounding the Alarm on a "Stealth Invasion"

(original interview, published here for the first time)

Many Muslims are peace-loving – but many are not. The precise breakdown is up for debate, but since no one can really tell what lies in another man's heart, why does the United States permit so many Muslims to immigrate to its shores? This question seems rather important, but few among America's political class appear interested in addressing it. And so, not only has America's Muslim population not stabilized in the 16 years since 9/11; it has actually nearly doubled in size.

In *Stealth Invasion: Muslim Conquest Through Immigration and Resettlement Jihad,* veteran journalist Leo Hohmann reveals the extent of America's radical Muslim problem, arguing that time is running out for this country. If it wishes to avoid the constant scourge of suicide bombings, shootings, and car rammings currently plaguing countries like France, England, and Belgium, it must get its Muslim immigration problem under control, he says.

Hohmann currently serves as news editor for WorldNetDaily.

Resnick: You write that America allows far too many Muslims into this country. How many, in fact, do we allow in?

Hohmann: The numbers have been steadily rising. If you include only those coming here on green cards, you're looking at about 130,000 per year. If you also include – and I think we should – people who come here on visas that allow them to stay for two years or more, it's about 260,000 per year.

Why should we include people who come here on temporary visas?

Because many of them end up renewing their visas for another two or three years, and by the time that's done, they're often in a position to get a green card.

The student visa program in particular is exploited by Muslims. Most of our major universities have large populations of students coming from Saudi Arabia and other hotbeds of Wahhabism and Salafi Islam, which is the most virulent strain of Islam. These students immediately start chapters of the Muslim Student Association, which is very radical and an offshoot of the Muslim Brotherhood.

Then you have entrepreneurial visas and religious visas. The latter is especially troubling because we're importing foreign imams from Saudi Arabia, Egypt, Iraq, and other hotbeds of Islamic radicalism to run our mosques. In many cases, mosques in the United States are actually more radical than those in the Middle East.

You write that the government settles many Muslim refugees in small towns across America, often disturbing the social fabric of these areas. Why would the government act in this manner?

When people think "refugees," they automatically think of big cities like New York, Chicago, Miami, and L.A. But that's the furthest from the truth. Stone Mountain, Georgia, has received more Syrian refugees than New York City. Places like Awatana, Minnesota, and Twin Falls, Idaho, are getting overrun with refugees. If you do your homework, you'll find out that there's often a meat-packing plant or maybe an aluminum manufacturer or fiber glass company in the area, and these companies want cheap foreign labor.

Some people claim we have nothing to fear from Muslims moving

to this country. They argue that just as Irish, Italian, German, and Jewish immigrants in earlier times embraced this country and its values, so will Muslims immigrants. How do you respond?

When my grandparents came here from Italy, they did not bring an allegiance to Italian law with them. They did not refuse to assimilate. They came here with the intention of becoming full Americans. In fact, they recoiled whenever anyone would refer to them as Italian-Americans. They just wanted to be Americans.

This is the complete opposite of today's immigrant from Saudi Arabia, Syria, Somalia, or Sudan. They're coming with an allegiance to a foreign legal system – Sharia law – and Sharia law is completely incompatible with freedom of religion, freedom of press, and freedom of speech.

Is the problem their refusal to accept Western values or their apparent desire to impose their values on the rest of America?

Well, I'm not even saying it's 100 percent the fault of the Muslim immigrants. Some of it is our own fault because we don't expect these immigrants to assimilate. And there's something about Islam that senses weakness. It senses openings in the spiritual gate, so to speak. When you have spiritual weakness, which ends up in political weakness, Islam swarms into that vacuum and exploits it. And that's what we see right now in Europe, and I'm afraid we're heading down that same path in America.

In your book, you quote President John Quincy Adams who argued that the "precept of the Koran is perpetual war against all who deny that [Mohammed] is the prophet of God." Many argue that this characterization is false – that Islam is a "religion of peace," as President George W. Bush famously proclaimed. What's your opinion?

There are a few peaceful sects of Islam, but they are not in the mainstream and they are in fact persecuted in almost every country by the mainstream Islamic culture.

There is no such thing as a radical Muslim. You have what I call "good Muslims" and "bad Muslims." The "good Muslims" are the ones who go to mosque regularly and believe what the Koran says. They believe Islam should be the supreme religion of the world and that anyone who doesn't submit to Islam – and that's what Islam means, submission – is somehow less of a human being and must ultimately face the sword.

Those are your *good* Muslims. They believe what their Scripture tells them. The *bad* Muslims – whom we see as the *good* Muslims – are the ones who are *not* devout, *not* observant, and *don't* believe all this nonsense.

President Trump has called for extreme vetting of all future immigrants to this country. You argue, however, that vetting Muslims for potential terrorists is impossible. Why is it impossible?

Because the perpetrator of every single one of the recent attacks on U.S. soil was either an immigrant who came here as a young boy or was born to an immigrant. How do you vet against that? The Chattanooga shooter, Muhammad Abdulazeez, came here at age six. You can't vet a six-year-old.

Abdulazeez attended public school, went to college, and got an engineering degree from the University of Tennessee at Chattanooga. But he suddenly became more devout after he graduated from college. He looked at himself and said, "Oh my goodness, I'm frittering away my life. I'm 24 years old and have been living a Western lifestyle. Allah would not be happy with me. I need to become more devout."

This is a pattern you find if you study Islamic terrorists. Many of them were born in the West to immigrant parents and led Western lifestyles. But after they got through their formative years and were in their mid-20s, it suddenly dawned on them, "Am I going to be good Muslim or a bad Muslim?" And one way to become a good Muslim if you've been a bad one is to commit jihad. You go straight to heaven and all is forgiven.

What, then, is the solution to prevent future terrorist attacks in the United States?

I think it's three-pronged. First, we need to drastically cut back Islamic immigration. Second, we must demand assimilation of those

Muslims whom we allow to immigrate here. And the third facet is maybe the most important: Declare the Muslim Brotherhood a foreign terrorist organization. This would shut down all the mosques that are currently under the spell of the global Islamic Salafi revivalist movement.

Why in your view should we not cut Muslim immigration entirely?

Well, the more we can cut it to the point of eliminating it, the better. But even more important than the number of Muslim immigrants is what happens once they get here. They shouldn't get any special accommodations that are not being given to other religious faith members. Because that's where it starts. If you feel like you're special and your government is cow-towing to you and is intimidated by you – that sets the stage for violent jihad.

We play footsy with our Muslims here. We won't even name Islamic terror as a threat in our FBI training manuals. All the language that was deemed offensive to Muslims was scrubbed in 2011. We are letting them set the rules of the game.

Israeli Mystique

Saul David

Revisiting the Miraculous Entebbe Mission

July 4 is always a joyous occasion in the United States, but in 1976 American Jews had an additional reason to celebrate: On that day, Israeli special forces flew 2,500 miles from home and rescued 102 hostages held by Palestinian and German terrorists at Uganda's Entebbe Airport.

In anticipation of the 40th anniversary of the mission, military historian Saul David this month published *Operation Thunderbolt: Flight 139 and the Raid on Entebbe Airport, the Most Audacious Hostage Rescue Mission in History*. To learn more about the book and the rescue mission – whose execution was far less seamless than is generally known – The Jewish Press spoke with David.

The Jewish Press: People tend to think of Yitzhak Rabin and Shimon Peres as cut from the same political cloth, but when it came to the Entebbe hostage crisis their views seem to have differed sharply.

David: That's correct. Rabin was the prime minister and Peres was the defense minister, but they had very different strategies when it came to dealing with terrorist threats. Rabin was of the opinion that you only use force if it has a possibility of succeeding. Peres, it seems, felt that force needed to be used as a matter of principle – that you shouldn't cut deals with terrorists because it encourages them to keep coming back for more concessions.

What were Rabin's hesitations in using force to rescue the Entebbe hostages?

As an ex-soldier, Rabin knew that special-forces operations conducted far away from Israel had a very low probability of success. So he wanted to make sure the intelligence was as thorough as possible: everything down to which way a door opens – does it open outward or inward? – because in a hostage rescue vital seconds are crucial.

Where, in fact, did Israeli intelligence get its information in preparing for the raid?

From a number of sources, including the released hostages. Probably the biggest mistake the terrorists made was to release some of the hostages, because when they got back to France they were debriefed by Mossad operatives. So they learned key things like the layout of the rooms, the habits of the hijackers, the sort of weaponry they had, and the likelihood of the building being wired with explosives. Actually, the Israeli in charge of intelligence told me that even when they launched the operation they still didn't know for sure that there weren't any explosives there.

They also found out that the Ugandans were cooperating with the terrorists. Now, this was crucial because up until that point they were thinking of various plans that were going to get them into Uganda where they would neutralize the terrorists and then hand themselves over to the Ugandans. When they realized that was no longer possible, they not only had to have a plan that would get them to Uganda, they had to get back as well, which meant they had to find a way to refuel the planes, which was a problem all of its own.

There's no question that by the time they launched the operation on Saturday morning, they did not have everything they needed. In fact, the intelligence officer I mentioned before said to me, "Our information was 70 percent; we had a 30 percent intelligence gap" – which is quite big.

You describe the rescue plan in the book, which entailed landing at Entebbe Airport at midnight and then driving a black Mercedes to the

terminal building where the hostages were being held. Since this model was the vehicle of choice of Ugandan generals, anyone seeing it would assume a Ugandan general was inside until it pulled up to the building. You write, though, that the Israelis completely botched this portion of the operation and lost the crucial element of surprise.

Exactly right. It was a very clever plan because the Israelis knew they had to get through the outer ring of Ugandan soldiers guarding the airport cleanly because if there was a firefight at the outer ring, the terrorists would be forewarned and have a chance to start killing the hostages. So one of the senior special-forces officers on the raid, Muki Betser, told his commander, Yoni Netanyahu, that whatever happens, even if they were challenged, "Don't stop and don't fire." He thought Yoni Netanyahu had agreed to this.

But what actually happens is that as they're driving toward the terminal at 40 miles an hour with the lights on – pretending to be a military convoy – they see three Ugandan sentries, one of whom raises his rifle to his shoulder as if he's going to fire. Now, Muki knows from his time in Uganda that this is just standard procedure, so he says to Yoni, "He won't fire, just keep going." But for some reason Yoni ignores him and says to the driver, "Swerve slightly to the right, I'm going to take him out with a silenced pistol."

So he and another officer draw their pistols and shoot at the sentry. He falls and they think they managed to kill him silently. But he's not dead and he gets up a second later and raises his rifle to shoot, so one of the Israeli soldiers in the truck behind the Mercedes opens fire with his Kalashnikov. And this starts a massive firefight because not only do the Israelis on all three trucks start firing now but so do the Ugandans from various vantage points. And as far as Muki Betser is concerned, this is a total disaster because it's given the terrorists a chance to start killing the hostages.

Why, in fact, didn't they kill the hostages?

This is the other amazing thing about the story, and it's hard to know. I was able to track down one of the terrorists' accomplices, Gerd Schnepel –

he was actually the boyfriend of the female hijacker – and he gave me what I think is a very credible reason. Two of terrorists inside the building were Revolutionary Cells terrorists from Germany, and they weren't killers, Schnepel told me. They were idealists. And when they realized the game was up, when they realized they weren't going to get their fellow terrorists in Germany released from prison – which is why they participated in the hijacking – they decided not to become murderers and kill defenseless men, women, and children.

Whether that's entirely true – whether they weren't entirely sure who was coming through the door – we will never know, but I think they must have had a pretty good idea that a rescue was underway given the firing that was going on outside.

No one knows for sure. Maybe it was confusion or worry that the Ugandans had gone loco. Maybe they were frozen with shock. I don't know. Maybe they just weren't as hardened and ruthless as the terrorists we're used to dealing with today.

Is it possible they were so taken in by Rabin's efforts to negotiate with them that they didn't even consider the possibility that the Israelis at that point would attempt a rescue mission? Rabin, after all, was genuinely prepared to give in to the hijackers' demands until virtually the last second.

Yes, I think that must have been a factor. Dan Shomron, the Israeli commander who led the whole rescue operation, said afterward that the reason it succeeded was because no one thought in a million years there was any possibility they would launch such a rescue operation, partly because logistically it was so hard to do.

Israel was also apparently lucky that the Ugandan reinforcements didn't rush to the airport to confront its rescue team. Why didn't they?

It seems the Ugandan military was paralyzed because ever since Idi Amin became president of Uganda, his chief fear was a military coup. So when he heard about the shooting at the airport, he thought elements of his armed forces had turned on him and he left the presidential palace and hid in the gardener's house. So he was completely out of the game.

And the senior commanders who were responsible for security at the airport also disappeared or went into hiding when they heard all this firing going on because they thought it was military forces turning on their officers. So there was no one really to coordinate a proper response.

You write interestingly that one of the outcomes of Israel's raid on Entebbe was a new policy among Western powers not to negotiate with terrorists.

Yes, as a broad policy, that is exactly what happened. The UK, the U.S., and a lot of other Western countries moved to a position where if there's a terrorist situation and hostages are being held, they first look for a military solution. And of course you have many examples of that – the German GSG-9 rescuing its hostages at Mogadishu Airport in 1977; the Americans attempting to do the same with its hostages in Tehran in 1980; and the British rescuing hostages at the Iranian embassy in London in 1980.

Hijackings also apparently stopped.

Yes, pretty much. I mean you get Mogadishu the following year, but given that this is a time when you were having scores of hijackings every year, it reduces to a trickle. So this scourge of the late '60s up until the mid-1970s is pretty much put to bed by Entebbe.

In the book you also make the interesting observation that if not for the raid on Entebbe, Benjamin Netanyahu might not be prime minister of Israel today.

That's correct. Benjamin Netanyahu was brought up in America and, given that he trained to be a management consultant, there was every likelihood that he was going to continue his career in the U.S. Overnight, though, his brother Yoni became a national hero since he was the only Israeli soldier to die at Entebbe and he was the leader of this famed special forces group, Sayeret Matkal.

So overnight the Netanyahu family went from being completely invisible in Israeli politics to being the most famous family. And it's pretty clear that Benjamin Netanyahu launched his political career off the back of his family's fame and has been using Entebbe ever since as a way of building up his strongman credentials.

Several films were made in the aftermath of the rescue mission. Which do you think is the most historically accurate?

Probably the Israeli film. Of course every feature film is going to take a few liberties, but the Israeli film is the closest to the truth – probably because they had the best access to the real version of events given that a lot of the hostages and the rescuers and politicians were all Israel-based.

— *originally published* December 2, 2015

Postscript: *Participant Media bought the film rights to "Operation Thunderbolt" in 2016. Its film is scheduled to premiere in the U.S. in the fall of 2017.*

Saul David is currently working on a historical novel set in the late 19th century, "Hart and the Prince's Folly," to be published later in 2017, and is also writing a proposal for a "Band of Brothers"-type book about a U.S. special forces unit in World War II.

Nancy Spielberg

Turning a Camera to Israel's Miracle in the Air

When Israel was established on May 14, 1948, it had no air force. Two weeks later, four Israeli fighter planes stopped Egypt's army from invading Israel. Where did these planes come from? Who flew them?

Although hard to believe, credit for Israel's success in the air in 1948 is largely due to foreigners – Jewish idealists in America who helped smuggle planes into Israel and World War II pilots who volunteered to fly them. The remarkable story of their heroism is told in "Above and Beyond," a new documentary produced by Nancy Spielberg, sister of the legendary filmmaker Steven Spielberg.

The Jewish Press: What led you to make this film?

Spielberg: I was inspired by an obituary somebody showed me in 2011 which was titled "Godfather of the Israeli Air Force Dies," but went on to talk about an *American* – Al Schwimmer. The details were so incredible and unknown to me. It felt like a Hollywood movie – the adventure, the clandestine operations, the FBI chasing these [American Jews] because they were breaking the law. These guys were war heroes, and they risked their lives for Israel even though they weren't Zionists. I said to myself, "This story has got to be told. We're losing this generation of World War II and if we don't listen to them now, we've lost it."

You say these Jews were not Zionists. What, then, motivated them to fight for Israel?

The guys I interviewed were all raised with a lot of anti-Semitism. They got bullied and beaten up coming from and going to school. They were not proud of their Judaism. It never helped them. When they came back from World War II, no commercial airlines would hire Jewish pilots.

But they were involved in liberating the camps, and they saw these survivors in Israel walking into another potential genocide. I think that's what spurred them, but in the process they actually discovered, or rediscovered, their Jewish identity.

It's amazing that Israel had to rely on volunteers from abroad to build its air force in 1948.

Israel had been under British control up to that point, and the Brits didn't really allow the Jews to arm themselves. So they had no air power, and when the war started, they were bombed on a regular basis by the Egyptians. That's what was so incredible. We have footage in "Above and Beyond" taken by somebody who went out and filmed an Egyptian Spitfire flying over Tel Aviv, bombing it. Nobody could stop it. All they could do was get a camera and film it.

And yet, just two weeks later, Israeli fighter planes – made in a former Nazi factory in Czechoslovakia – helped stop an invasion of Israel by Egypt's army.

The Egyptian army was less than 30 miles outside of Tel Aviv and moving in with all its forces. That would've been the end. And that's when these pilots took off and totally surprise attacked them.

They didn't cause a lot of physical damage, but they psychologically frightened the Egyptians because they suddenly realized that there was some competition in the sky. Also, the Egyptians thought this was just one piece of a much bigger air force. So psychologically, it literally crippled them, and they never went beyond that point.

Many Jews know that President Truman recognized Israel 14 minutes after its founding. Few, though, realize how hostile the U.S. was to Israel's fate immediately afterward. According to your documentary, not only did America impose an arms embargo on the Middle East, it also sought to prosecute American Jews trying to help Israel.

I was told by many historians that it was really Truman's cabinet that pushed for these embargoes. The British also put a lot of pressure on the Americans to stay out of it. Everybody thought the situation would be resolved in a couple of weeks because you had all these Arab armies attacking, and there really was no chance Israel was going to survive....

Al Schwimmer [the "godfather of the Israeli air force"] lost his American citizenship because of his efforts. And there were fines and jail times slapped on others.

Where did you find the veterans you interviewed for the film? They must be in their 90s.

I think the youngest person I spoke to was 88. The oldest guy now is 95. But there are really not a lot of them left.

Did your brother, Steven Spielberg, help you in making the film?

I didn't really want his help. I had a vision of what I wanted to say, and I wanted to stay true to that.

But my brother was helpful in the sense that he's my brother and was loving and supportive and wonderful. I got a big *beracha* from him – like he put the big Spielberg stamp on my forehead and said, "Great idea, Nancy! Go do it!"

Of course I did show him a rough cut, and I remember he came to me and said, "I love your film." I said, "I'm so glad. Can I have your notes [of criticism]?" He said, "I don't have any notes except that I'd like to recommend it to the Cannes Film Festival." And I was like, "Oh my God." I couldn't have asked for more.

What was the biggest surprise for you personally in making this film?

What surprised me was that I really identified with these guys. As I listened to them talk about growing up with anti-Semitism and being alienated from their Jewish roots, it really brought back to me my own childhood growing up in Phoenix where we moved in 1957 when I was under a year old. We were the only Jews on the block and many times we were called "dirty Jews" and made to feel like we didn't fit in. So I really identified with them.

At the same time, I think I saw my dad in them, and in many ways I made this film for my dad. He's 98 and he used to fly in the back of B-25s doing radio communications in World War II.

Your father is still alive?

Thank God. He's going to be 98 in February. He was very sick, and we almost lost him. But he's getting stronger now. He came to Jerusalem with me to screen the film, and he came to San Francisco for our premiere at the San Francisco Jewish Film Festival. He is *shepping nachas* galore!

— originally published January 28, 2015

Postscript: *Nancy Spielberg continues to screen "Above and Beyond" around the world. Since this interview, Spielberg has also executive produced "On the Map" – about Maccabi Tel Aviv's European Championship victory in 1977 – and is now working on several other films, including "Who Will Write Our History?" – about a secret effort to record daily life in the Warsaw Ghetto – and a feature film based on "Above And Beyond."*

Spielberg has also become a public lecturer (on her Jewish identity and why she started producing inspirational Jewish films) and hopes to soon create a film fund of $10-15 million, enabling the production of future films about Jewish culture, heritage, and history that will instill Jewish pride in viewers.

"Somewhere in there," she wrote to me, "I'm hugging my husband, two daughters, and dog!"

Zev Golan

Biographer of Lechi Founder Abraham Stern

The Irgun is famous; Lechi – the other underground Jewish group fighting the British in the 1940s – less so. With only 1,000 fighters, as opposed to the Irgun's 5,000, Lechi is sometimes thought of as the Irgun's "kid brother."

Yet, Lechi possesses a fascinating history of its own. Founded in 1940 by Abraham Stern, Lechi devoted itself to an uncompromising war against Great Britain. Unlike the Irgun, Lechi fought the British throughout World War II, and while the Irgun generally gave the British time to evacuate buildings before it blew them up, Lechi did not.

Lechi's goals were as radical as its deeds. In its 18 "Principles of Rebirth," Lechi called for conquering all the territory from the Nile to the Euphrates (the Irgun "only" called for conquering both banks of the Jordan), as well as rebuilding the *Beis HaMikdash*.

A new book by Zev Golan, *Stern: The Man and his Gang*, records the history and ideology of this unusual group while also profiling some of its more famous members. Golan has authored five previous books and, from 1992-2003, directed the Israel office of the Institute for Advanced Strategic and Political Studies.

The Jewish Press: For those unfamiliar with Lechi's activities, can

you recount some of the group's more famous exploits?

Golan: Perhaps its most famous exploit, if you can call it that, is the assassination of Lord Moyne in Egypt. Lord Moyne was the highest British politician in the Middle East, and it was his decision not to save the Jews of Hungary. He said to the messenger who came to him with plans to save them, "What would I do with a million Jews? Where would I put them?"

Lechi didn't know about that at the time – it was only revealed 15 years later – but Lechi did know that Lord Moyne was responsible for closing the gates of the homeland to Jews trying to get in during the Holocaust. So they assassinated him.

Another thing Lechi is famous for is its conduct in British courtrooms. Lechi's fighters were the first to turn these courtrooms into a battlefield. Starting in 1944, when they were put on trial, they refused to recognize the court's authority. Instead of claiming they were innocent, they said, "Yes, we carried arms, and we're going to fight you and throw you out of the country."

This changed the attitude of a lot of people in *Eretz Yisrael* in the 1940s from "We have to bow down to a foreign power" to "What are the British doing in our land? We're the descendants of King David; this was his country, and we have a right to be here – not them."

What about Lechi's assassination of Count Folke Bernadotte in September 1948?

That is perhaps Lechi's second most famous action. It was also its last. Bernadotte had been appointed by the UN to negotiate peace in *Eretz Yisrael,* and he decided to come with his own plan that he would force upon the parties. His plan called for taking, not only Yerushalayim, but also large portions of the country that the UN had originally designated part of Israel and giving them to the Arabs. He even wanted to ensure that no Jew of military age would enter the country and intended to station agents at airports and seaports around the world for that purpose.

Lechi held a rally at which they said, "Leave the country, you're not wanted here." Bernadotte didn't listen, so a group of Lechi members assassinated him. That ended the Bernadotte plan, but it also ended Lechi because Israeli Prime Minister David Ben-Gurion used the attack as an excuse to arrest most of its members.

In the book, you profile 13 leaders and members of Lechi, including a Chabad *chassid*, Moshe Segal. Can you talk about him?

I don't know if he was Chabad at the time, but he certainly was afterwards. He set up the women's seminary in Kfar Chabad and was its principal for several years in the 1950s. He also corresponded not only with the seventh Lubavitcher Rebbe but with the sixth one as well.

Rav Segal was the leader of a religious underground called Brit Chashmonaim. He was a member of the Irgun high command before he joined Lechi, and he was the first Jew to blow the shofar at the *Kotel* when the British made it illegal. He was arrested, and only when Rav Kook, the chief rabbi at the time, threatened a hunger strike did the British agree to release him.

Every year afterwards, young Jews went to the *Kotel* and blew the shofar, and Rav Segal often coordinated [this operation]. The shofars would be smuggled to the *Kotel* area without the British knowing, somebody would blow it, hand it off to somebody else – often a young woman, who was less likely to be searched by the British – and then try to escape. This went on until 1947, and it made the *Kotel* an area that symbolized Jewish pride.

Many years later, in 1967, Rav Segal became the first Jew to return to the Old City as a resident. He rebuilt the Chabad synagogue with his own hands and continued to blow the shofar at the *Kotel* until his death in 1985. He died on Yom Kippur at night.

In the memoirs of Lechi leader Israel Eldad, which you translated and published in 2008, Eldad writes: "Between [Lechi founder Abraham Stern] and even the best among his opponents there still lay this tremendous difference in approach: They admitted we must fight in order to be free, and he said we must fight because we are free." What did he mean by that?

Stern was, in his soul, a sovereign, free, proud Jew living in the Jewish state. If I can return to an earlier question, Rav Segal told me that when he put the *tallis* over his head and blew the shofar at the *Kotel*, he was living in a free Jewish state. There was a little area under that *tallis* where no non-Jew could tell him what to do in his homeland.

These people were free in their souls and that's why they fought. They said, "Nobody can oppress us, nobody can tell us when to blow the shofar, nobody can tell us that we can't bring our brothers and sisters who are being persecuted in Europe to live with us here." Other Jews, even the best of them, looked around and said, "We're oppressed, we want to be free. How can we best realize that goal?" When you start thinking like that, there's a lot of room for political negotiation and machinations, or being docile because "it's not the right time."

You argue in the book that Lechi's ideology, which you call Revolutionary Zionism, is still very much relevant today. How so?

Revolutionary Zionism means that nothing competes with the importance of liberating and establishing Jewish sovereignty in the land – and bringing redemption. So, as long as the land – from the Nile to the Euphrates – is not liberated, we have to liberate it. As long as the people are not living entirely in *Eretz Yisrael*, we have to bring them back to *Eretz Yisrael*. And as long as we don't have the Temple, we have to build the Temple.

What about Lechi's attitude toward dependence on others?

The Jewish people and the Jewish state shouldn't be dependent on other states. We need to be truly free and in charge of our own destiny. We shouldn't want foreign aid; we should want to stand on our own legs.

We also shouldn't be turning to other countries and saying, "Solve our problems for us, worry about Iran for us, worry about Hamas for us." Rather, we should take care of our own problems and decide what our destiny is by ourselves.

In the book you mention a group, the Zionist Freedom Alliance, which you write has adopted many of Abrahams Stern's ideas. This

group, among other things, opposes Israel's security wall, which many right-wingers support. Why would an organization following in Stern's tradition oppose this wall?

It's dividing the homeland. Dividing the land or living behind a wall for protection is returning us to the ghetto. It's not returning us to sovereignty in our land.

But many people argue that the wall saves Jewish lives.

Beating the enemy would also save Jewish lives.

Many of these ideas – inspired by Stern – sound "harsh" or "extreme" to many people, and, yet, you write in the book that Stern was a very calm and gentle person by nature.

It has been said that to see injustice and not scream or do anything is a crime. I met many Lechi members later in their lives. Rav Segal, for instance, was always calm. He never ever got angry. Stern is described by many as never raising his voice. He was a student of Latin and Greek literature in Hebrew University.

These people saw millions of Jews who were going to be killed or, later, actually being killed in Europe. They also saw their homeland being occupied by an enemy that was determined to let, or help, these Jews die. They also saw this enemy determined to imprison the Jewish people for years to come in the future. And so they were forced in their minds to become revolutionaries. The alternative, as they saw it, was death – death for themselves, death for their relatives, and death for their nation.

— originally published November 16, 2011

Postscript: *Zev Golan has since written a book, "Machtarot Bemaasar," on underground members incarcerated in the British Central Prison of Jerusalem; produced a DVD, "Zion, Will You Not Ask After Your Captive?" of underground songs performed by popular young Israeli singers; and composed a play, "The Ghosts of Mizrachi Bet Street," about the final morning of Abraham Stern.*

Shimon Mercer-Wood

An Israeli Spokesman With Roots in Ghana

Shimon Mercer-Wood is the spokesperson and consul for media affairs at the Consulate General of Israel in Manhattan. A product of the London School of Economics and Yeshivat Ma'aleh Gilboa, Mercer-Wood previously served as political officer at Israel's embassy in New Delhi and press officer at Israel's embassy in London.

The Jewish Press: What's your family background?

Mercer-Wood: My mother's family is from Transylvania, which is Hungarian-speaking Romania, and my father's family is from Ghana in West Africa. My father's uncle was the ambassador of Ghana to Israel in the 1960s, and he brought along my father with him.

Why did he bring your father?

They were very close. Also, in that part of Ghana it's actually a matrilineal society, which means the person you inherit is not your father, but your mother's brother. So as part of his being groomed to take over from his uncle, he went with him and was kind of like his protégé.

And then your father stayed in Israel?

In 1967, on the eve of the Six-Day war, Ghana's embassy was ordered to evacuate because everyone was sure Israel was going to be destroyed. In Israel they were preparing mass graves in the public parks because they thought there would be, *chas v'shalom,* many casualties, and in Holland they were preparing refugee camps for all the Jewish refugees they were certain would end up in Europe.

But my father had developed an interest in Judaism and felt it was disloyal to abandon the Jewish people in a time of danger, so he stayed in Israel. And then my father got swept up by the very obvious miracle of Israel going from the brink of peril to unprecedented victory in such a short time. So he stayed, converted to Judaism, joined the army, and has basically been in Israel ever since.

It's quite a story.

Apart from it being my personal family story, though, it also speaks to Israel's relationship with Africa in that time. Israel was a huge player in the African continent in the 1960s. This was part of Golda Meir's policy to find friends around the world and to fulfill the aspiration of being an *ohr la'goyim.* So Israel was very active in introducing modern agriculture to Africa. In fact, Israel at that time had more embassies in Africa than any other non-African country in the world. The relationship was so close that when my uncle was shifted from the Ghana Embassy in China to the Ghana Embassy in Israel, it was considered a major promotion.

What do you do at the Israeli consulate in Manhattan?

We try to introduce positive material about Israel into the media output, and I would divide that into three "battles." The first battle is to engage with those journalists who write primarily about the Israeli-Arab conflict and provide them with information that may help them be more sympathetic to the Israeli position.

The second battle is to provide stories to journalists who are interested in writing about Israel. So, for example, we met a producer at one of the news channels who said, "I want stories about Israeli startups. Please feed me with stories." Our job then is to seek out such stories – be in touch with relevant authorities and hubs in Israel – and build up story pitches.

The third battle, which is the most interesting, is to reach those journalists who don't even think about writing about Israel, and introduce Israel to them. Recently, for example, we sent a journalist to Israel to cover a conference on accessibility – especially how to make tourism more accessible for people with disabilities. This is a writer to whom it would never have occurred to write a story about Israel. But she came back from that conference very enthusiastic, and it was a huge success. It's very gratifying to find someone like that and put Israel on their radar in such a positive context.

I should add that we place a special emphasis on Jewish media, because the most important asset this building is charged with safeguarding is the relationship between Israel and American Jews. I very often meet people who adore Israel but their conception of Israel is kind of what Israel was like in the 1980s. Israel is a very dynamic place – it's constantly changing – and it's important for me to make sure people see Israel as it is today.

Why is that important?

Because we're one nation, we're one people. At the end of the day, on the face of the planet, we only have each other. And just like you keep in touch with your brother who lives in another city and you want him to know what's happening in your life and you don't want his perception of your life to be stuck like when you were in college, it's important for the different components of the Jewish nation to know what the others are going through. It's not because you want their "support." It's because that's what it means to be one people.

Those who dislike Israel sometimes call it racist. When you speak to such people, do you find your skin color helpful in combating this argument?

There's a spectrum of anti-Israel attitudes. On the light side you have ignorance, and in that case perhaps it helps. But further along the spectrum, there is entrenched hostility to Israel, and then nothing helps because they don't really care. It's not about knowledge or understanding. It's an emotional issue. It's a feeling of commitment to a struggle against Israel. And you can really see it physically when you speak to these people, how much their whole being is fired up with attacking Israel.

So I don't bother arguing with them, because a) they don't deserve it and b) it's completely pointless. We really should focus our efforts on those who don't have that level of hatred. I often hear people say, "Show them the facts!" They don't care about the facts. They operate in a cultural sphere in which facts are of no importance. It's part of a certain brand of post-modern mode of thought that says that everything is subjective and relative and facts are just not important.

What's Israel's opinion of Donald Trump?

It's important to understand that Israel has a relationship with the United States that exceeds the relationship with the president of the United States. So it sounds like a talking point but it's actually true: Whoever the American people elect, Israel will be happy to work with because they will have been elected by the American people.

What's very important, though, is that the political relationship between Israel and the United States remain bipartisan. There are people in America – on both sides of the political spectrum – who are trying to undermine the bipartisan nature of this relationship for their own political reasons. These people don't have Israel's best interests in mind.

Several media outlets have reported that Bernie Sanders' supporters hope to amend the Democratic Party's platform so that it is less pro-Israel or even anti-Israel. Is Israel concerned?

I'm not going to comment on anything a particular politician is doing, but, in general, the attempt to make Israel a divisive issue is exactly what I was talking about before. Israel shouldn't be a divisive issue. I also think that recognition of Jerusalem as Israel's capital is not an "Israel" thing. It's a Jewish thing. When someone wants to remove reference to Jerusalem as the capital of Israel, they are trying to erase one of the most fundamental features of the Jewish heritage. You want to criticize Israel, go ahead. But if you erase reference to Jerusalem as our capital, you're insulting every Jew who has ever lived.

Syria is currently a mess. What are Israel's hopes for the conclusion of that conflict?

Israel's policy on Syria is that we don't care who rules them, how they are ruled, what sort of government they have, etc. It's none of our business. We just want to be left alone.

But the prime minister has laid down three red lines. First, anyone who shoots at us, we shoot back. Second, we will not allow Syria to become a conduit for advanced weaponry reaching Hezbollah in Lebanon. And third, we're not going to allow anyone to build an infrastructure that can be used to threaten Israel in the future. So if we see someone building a terrorist network, the purpose of which is to threaten Israel, something may happen to that person. According to certain reports, these things have happened in the past and they will continue to happen so long as there are people who want to use Syria as a base for attacking Israel.

I have to add that on a human level it's very sad to see such unspeakable suffering, and we try to extend humanitarian aid wherever we can. There's an Israeli NGO called IsraAID which set up shop on the island of Lesvos in Greece giving medical care to refugees. Other Israeli NGOs are providing food and supplies in refugee camps in Jordan.

How is Israel dealing with Russia's interests in Syria?

It's a very complicated issue. Our interests in Syria do not correlate with Russia's. Russia wants to keep Assad in power. Keeping Assad in power means strengthening Iran's influence and presence – which is the main threat to us. And the Russians are also fighting shoulder to shoulder with Hezbollah, which is one of our main enemies. So our interests do not correlate. Having said that, Israel and Russia share enough interests elsewhere and on other levels that we both have the motivation to make sure the conflicting interests don't result in a direct conflict.

What "other interests" are you referring to?

I won't go into too many details, but there are other issues on which Israel and Russia cooperate so that both countries wish to maintain cordial relations.

It's also interesting to note that Russia sees Israel as a special case on account of its huge population of Russian Jews. I remember meeting the Russian ambassador in Israel, and he said, "Since I've come to Israel, my English has deteriorated because from the supermarket to the president, everyone speaks to me in Russian." So they feel there's an important link there, and I think that makes for a different attitude.

What's Israel's current policy toward Iran? Are we now beyond the point where destroying Iran's nuclear facilities is possible?

Israel's fundamental policy hasn't changed. We will take every means necessary to make sure Iran doesn't get nuclear weapons. What has happened is that because of the Iran deal, the crunch time – the point at which you have to make a decision – has been pushed off by a few years. But when we reach that crunch time again, I have no doubt that the prime minister of Israel will not hesitate to act.

— originally published June 22, 2016

Postscript: *In the summer of 2017, Mercer-Wood became spokesperson at the Israeli embassy in Paris, France.*

Knesset Outliers

Rabbi Dov Lipman

Fighting for Charedi Integration

The biggest surprise of Israel's elections in January was the phenomenal success of Yesh Atid – a new party headed by Yair Lapid that won 19 seats and is now part of Prime Minister Netanyahu's coalition government.

Yesh Atid is sometimes perceived as avidly secular, but two rabbis currently serve in the party as MKs. One is Rabbi Shai Piron, Israel's new education minister. The other is Rabbi Dov Lipman, the first American-born Knesset member since Rabbi Meir Kahane. A graduate of Yeshivas Ner Yisroel and the holder of a Master's degree in education from Johns Hopkins University, Rabbi Lipman made *aliyah* in 2004 and lives with his wife and four children in Beit Shemesh.

Last month, Rabbi Lipman was named a member of the Knesset's Committee for Immigration, Absorption and Diaspora Affairs.

The Jewish Press: What is an Orthodox rabbi doing in a party that's widely regarded as secular?

Rabbi Lipman: Before Yair Lapid even went into politics, he stood up before a charedi audience and said, "You won." At the beginning of the state, he said, there was a battle for what Israel was going to be. Was it going to be secular, without Torah – possibly even without God? Or was it going to be religious-based? He said that we on the religious side have shown that there is no basis for us being in Israel without God. And then he said, "Now let's work together."

So from my perspective as someone who is charedi, to hear that call from a secular person and *not* to respond would be the worst thing I could do. Therefore, I decided to see what Yair was all about, and I got to know him well. He's not anti-religious, he's not anti-Torah, he's not anti-anything. He wants to work together on the things that we all agree about and move the country forward. He wants to break down the walls between the secular and the religious.

And that means what, for example?

We have a plan for national service – a compromise plan that takes into account the sensitivities of the charedi community. We also have an education plan which says, on the one hand, that there should be general studies on the religious side, but also that there should be more Jewish studies on the secular side.

We also want to help charedim get to the workforce. Can you imagine that the charedi parties have never had a task force to help charedim enter the workforce? I started that task force because I'm not interested in trying to keep us secluded and creating more walls.

There has been much hysteria over the proposed draft of charedim into the IDF. What is Yesh Atid's precise position on this issue?

The starting point of Yesh Atid's plan is that everybody serves – either in the military or in national service – but there will be exemptions for those who are the real *iluyim.*

The same way you have *yeshivot hesder* for the religious Zionist community, we will have similar programs for the charedi community that combine Torah learning and service. It will take five years to build those plans. In the interim, the plan states that any charedi who wants to leave yeshiva or *kollel* and go to work can do so – legally, as opposed to now where it is illegal [to work during the years of draft eligibility]. It is estimated that as many as 30 percent of charedim might take up that offer and leave tomorrow to learn a trade or go to work because right now, economically, they're starving.

Some people argue that the charedim aren't bothering anyone. They just want to study Torah and be left alone. Why can't you respect their wishes?

Three answers. First, it's destroying us as a people. Having a separate camp that does its own thing and doesn't view itself as part of society is destructive. We were one people for 2,000 years, and if we were one people while we were persecuted, let's be one people here in Israel. That's number one.

Number two: Economically, it can't work. You can't have a society where this large of a population lives off the tax base but doesn't contribute to it.

Number three: From my perspective, [we charedim] have never been people who didn't join the workforce or didn't view ourselves as part of the nation. Charedim should be the leaders of the nation. They should be involved in the country instead of building walls. Building walls is destroying us as a people. Let's get back to the way it's always been where people were *bnei Torah* and also part of society.

Is that really the way it's always been?

Yes. Historically we've never had a population that said, "We don't work." The Smag says that it's a *mitzvat assei min haTorah* to work. The mishnah in *Pirkei Avot* says that Torah without work leads to sin. The Gemara says that a father must teach his son a trade.

Let's go further. The Rambam says anybody who chooses to learn Torah and forces others to sustain him disgraces Torah, disgraces God's name, and has no portion in the World to Come. Let's learn the *Shulchan Aruch*. Every morning, it says, a person *davens*, learns Torah, and then goes to work.

That's who we've been throughout our history. It's a new phenomenon [to not work]. Many people say it's because after the Holocaust we had to rebuild Torah because it had been destroyed. I get that. But we've rebuilt

Torah, we've done it. Now let's get back to the combination of the two.

Would you be happier if all charedim acted like some Satmar groups who don't serve in the army but who also don't take funding from the state?

I certainly think it's more consistent, although you have to ask yourself, "What does not taking from the state mean?" Do they take garbage collection from the state? Do they take streetlights from the state?

More importantly, though, to take that approach is to say we're going to have polarization and lack of *achdus* in *am Yisrael,* and I think that's wrong. I think the correct approach is to say, "Let's be part of *am Yisrael.*" If *bnei Torah* are part of Israeli society, I think you'll see an amazing response on the *chiloni* side. I'm not talking about their individual level of *shemiras hamitzvos,* but their perspective toward Judaism and Torah and their pride in being Jewish.

Some observers have pointed out that Israeli charedim are more extreme than their American counterparts. Is that true?

There's no Ner Yisroel in Israel. There's no Chaim Berlin where guys go to Brooklyn College at night. There's no Monroe, NY where Satmar provides a few hours of English and mathematics in high school. It doesn't exist. These are things which I very much want to try to change.

Among Yesh Atid's goals is converting Israel's non-Jewish Russian population to Judaism. Even some Orthodox Jews support this move, fearing Israel will have a huge intermarriage problem on its hands if it doesn't. However, before possibly converting these Jews, shouldn't charedi MKs like you push to amend Israel's Law of Return so that henceforward only halachic Jews can move to Israel and attain automatic citizenship? Otherwise, we might face this problem all over again in the future.

We don't have Russians coming en masse anymore. So let's first deal with the 300,000 who are here. Let them convert. Rabbi Chaim Amsalem wrote a *sefer* of a few hundred pages with all the sources allowing this. Let's begin with that.

You publicly identify as charedi, yet many of the positions you've outlined are hardly "black hat." How do you explain that?

If charedi means that I force other people religiously, that I'm not Zionistic, and that I only wear a white shirt – then I'm not charedi. If charedi, however, means that I'm a *chared b'dvar Hashem,* that I'm very careful in my life about Torah and *mitzvot,* that I'm concerned about the influence of the outside world on my children, and that my wife and I bring up our children where genders are more separate – then I am charedi.

[People identify charedi with "extremism,"] but I don't think that's what charedi has always meant. On a certain level, therefore, I'm fighting for the integrity of [the word]. There's a political party here in Israel called Tov that has 40,000 charedi members who believe charedim should work and have general studies. They're growing in terms of their political power and they take great offense when people talk about them as the "new charedim." They say, "No, we're the old charedim. The other guys have changed things."

My dream, by the way, is that one day no one will have to label himself anything. You'll just be a Jew.

There are 39 Orthodox MKs in this Knesset – more than any before in history. What's the significance of this?

I think the question isn't about significance but responsibility. With such numbers, I think we have a responsibility to do something. We can have a tremendous influence on the country.

You wrote an article last year bemoaning the absence of God in Israel's political culture. You compared Israel to America where almost every politician ends his speech with, "God bless America." Why is God so absent in Israel?

You know what's amazing? Yesh Atid has brought more Torah to the Knesset than there's been in decades. The number of people in our party who said *tefillot* and quoted from *Tanach* or the Gemara in their inaugural speeches in the Knesset is way beyond what Israel has seen before. I end every one of my speeches with, "May God bless Israel."

As far as why God is normally absent in Israel, it's because religion in Israel has become something people are afraid of. They're afraid it will be forced. So even secular people who believe in God and want some Judaism in their lives don't talk about it.

Yesh Atid is trying to bring about an environment where God is not a negative topic – that mentioning God or our classic sources doesn't mean that the next step is we're forcing religion on you. We're trying to create an environment where people can embrace Judaism and feel proud to be Jews.

When you became an MK, you were forced to renounce your American citizenship. You reportedly cried when you did so. Why?

Because America gave my family every opportunity to live as religious Jews. My father, *zichronah livracha,* was a federal judge and my father-in-law was a chaplain in the U.S. Army. I was able to pursue every dream I wanted. So when you have to stand up and raise your right hand and say, "I renounce my U.S. citizenship with free will," it felt like *kefiyat tova* – that I was being an ingrate a little bit. It was very hard to say those words.

— *originally published April 10, 2013*

Postscript: *Rabbi Lipman is now an independent consultant on Israel advocacy and Israel-diaspora relations. He also writes a column for the Jerusalem Post and Times of Israel and has written four books on Judaism and Israel since this interview.*

In a January 2017 e-mail to me, Rabbi Lipman wrote, "I am happy to report that thanks to our efforts, charedi male employment has risen to over 50%, there are more charedim in the IDF than ever before, and there are 10,000 charedim in higher education. Projects we helped start are helping tens of thousands of charedim get training and find jobs. Thousands of charedi families are seeking English education for their sons.... The process of charedim recognizing that they can be Talmudic scholars, fervently religious, and support their families with dignity is off and running."

Moshe Feiglin

Promoting a Destiny-Defined State

For over a decade, Moshe Feiglin has been working toward becoming prime minister of Israel with the aim of "turning the state of the Jews into the Jewish state." He still has ways to go, but on February 5, he advanced one step closer when he was sworn in as a Knesset member for the first time.

Ahead of a dinner celebrating his victory next week in the Chateau Steakhouse in Queens, NY, Feiglin spoke to The Jewish Press.

The Jewish Press: You've been trying to get into the Knesset for a long time. Now that you're in, what do you hope to accomplish?

Feiglin: I hope to advance the concept of Jewish leadership to the state of Israel – a state that is based on Jewish identity and not just survival.

What does that mean?

One example is the two-state solution. If you understand that we came back to Israel after 2,000 years of exile to achieve a goal and not just to survive, then you understand that we need the whole country. We long for Jerusalem, the Temple Mount, Shechem, Chevron – all these places that connect us to our identity.

When the goal is survival, Tel Aviv is enough. When the goal is to create a special society that carries a message to the entire universe, then questions like [surrendering land to the Arabs] are not even considered.

You often write that you want to create a Jewish state. For some people, that means a halachic state.

No, I'm talking about something much, much wider. I'm talking about making the Torah part of our culture.

But some argue that a Jewish state means one in which Torah law reigns supreme – with police enforcing the laws of *tzniyut*, for example, as they do in Iran.

No, nothing can be forced. The whole concept of force is against Judaism because Hashem tells us, *"U'vacharta ba'chaim"* – you should choose, and if you're being forced, you cannot choose.

Are you saying there was no force in the times of *Bayit Rishon* and *Bayit Sheni*?

I'm saying that this is what we need today.

A number of years ago, you wrote that Israel should make Sunday a day off like in America. You argued that many Israeli soccer fans, for example, might observe *Shabbat* if games were played – and televised – on Sunday rather than Saturday.

That is a good example of how to build a modern Jewish state that gives its citizens the capability to have a real *Shabbat* even though they're not religious right now. What we need to do is be more open and give Israelis the ability to be who they [truly] are. If you give them the opportunity to choose, most of them will choose the right thing.

Some people might say this claim is naïve since Israelis, by and large, are secular.

I think they're totally wrong. When you ask Israelis what they are first – Jewish or Israeli – more than 80 percent say first of all, and above all, they're Jewish. When you ask Israelis to describe themselves, only 19 percent say they're secular, 50 percent say they're traditional, and the rest say they're *dati* or charedi. So those who say Israelis are secular don't really understand where Israeli society is holding.

In your articles, you often write about the importance of building the *Beit HaMikdash,* calling it "the direct link between the Almighty and His world" – a place that allows us "to synthesize between the physical and spiritual...to create a life of harmony between the two." Your average Orthodox Jew, though, believes we must wait for Mashiach to build the *Beit HaMikdash.*

We just read in last week's *parshah,* "You should make a Sanctuary for Me." It doesn't say "Mashiach should make a Sanctuary for Me." So what can I tell you? It's written clear and simple right there.

Why do so many Jews believe otherwise?

You should ask them.

You descend from a Chabad family and went to religious Zionist schools growing up. How would you describe yourself today?

I'm Moshe Zalman Feiglin. There's no [label] that describes me specifically. Sometimes you can call me Chabad, sometimes you can call me *dati le'umi,* and sometimes you can even call me not religious at all since I don't identify with the concept of "religion." Religion, to my understanding, is not a Jewish concept. The first person who uses the word "religious" in the Bible is Haman HaRasha.

Judaism is not a religion; we should remember that. Religion is just part of the Judaism that served us in the diaspora, but now that we've come back to our land, we should open that to a full culture because otherwise Judaism cannot fulfill its message.

There's a reason why the punishment of not willing to go from the Sinai desert to *Eretz Yisrael* was much bigger than the punishment the Jews received for *cheit ha'eigel*. For *cheit ha'eigel* – which is, so to speak, a religious sin – we can do *teshuvah* and start from the beginning. But when you're not willing to go to *Eretz Yisrael,* you're basically saying, "I give up on the Jewish mission" – which can only be fulfilled from the land of Israel.

Rav Samson Raphael Hirsch also disliked the word "religion" to describe Judaism since it implies that Judaism concerns only one aspect of life when, in fact, Judaism encompasses and is supposed to permeate and inform *every* aspect of life. Is this your line of reasoning as well?

We took the concept of religion from Christianity, and we should understand that this is not what Judaism is all about. It's not just about religion. It's much wider than that. Of course I'm not talking about giving up *Torah u'mitzvot*. On the contrary. I'm talking about *Torah u'mitzvot* with a national purpose. Not just a private purpose or a family purpose – not even a community purpose – but a national purpose.

On that level it can be done only in the land of Israel with Jerusalem, the Temple Mount, and, *b'ezrat Hashem*, as soon as can be, the *Beit HaMikdash*.

Whom do you regard as your heroes?

David HaMelech.

Anyone else?

Herzl is also definitely a hero. Not that I agree with everything he said, but definitely a person with a vision who changed history. If you want to talk about non-Jews, we can talk about Churchill who saved his people from Germany.

Both your friends and enemies sometimes compare you to Meir Kahane. Do you embrace this comparison? Reject it?

You can find places where we say the same things. You can also find places where we are different. I was in the army when Meir, *Hashem yikom damo*, was most active, so I didn't get to know him so well. But I can definitely say that the slogan "*Kahane tzadak* – Kahane was right" has proven itself many times.

When you first started your campaign to become Israel's prime minister, terrorism was rampant and Israel's leaders were constantly

negotiating to surrender land to the Arabs. Matters seem to have improved somewhat since then. For people who only care about land and security – rather than the ideological vision you outlined earlier – why is it important that you become prime minister?

Well, I don't agree with the way you describe the situation. Just a few months ago, we had missiles being shot from Gaza at Tel Aviv. It reminds me of the joke of a person falling from the roof of a skyscraper and somebody in the middle of the building is looking from the window and asks him, "How is it going?" and he answers, "So far so good."

Israel is being targeted by terrorists and losing its credibility all over the world. We have the strongest economy, we have accomplished miracles, but we have also lost our roots and our ability to justify our existence. We definitely need Jewish leadership.

Do you genuinely believe you will become prime minister one day?

I have no doubt that sooner or later Israel will have Jewish leadership.

But not necessarily you?

Of course not necessarily me. I am not the message; the *message* is the message. I'm looking right and left and don't see anybody else, but it's not about me.

President Obama is visiting Israel in March. What would you advise Prime Minister Netanyahu to say to him during his visit?

Netanyahu should demand that Obama come with Jonathan Pollard before anything else. That should become the number one issue when it comes to the relationship with America. If, God forbid, Jonathan Pollard dies in jail, this black moral cloud above Israeli and American society will not be able to be erased.

Why is securing Pollard's release more important than anything else?

Because I see [the neglect of Pollard] as treason against our fellow brother who gave his life for us, and I believe that morality changes history.

The bottom line is that when something immoral happens for such a long time in such a terrible way, it has an impact on the moral foundation of the Jewish state.

— originally published February 20, 2013

Postscript: *In 2015, Moshe Feiglin quit Likud and founded his own party, Zehut, which aims to run in the next elections for Knesset.*

Religion vs. Science?

Rabbi Yosef Bitton

Finding Science Confirmed In *Bereishis*

The age of the universe. Fifteen billion or less than 6,000? The debate shows no signs of letting up in the Orthodox community.

One of the latest to toss his hat in the ring is Rabbi Yosef Bitton, formerly chief rabbi of Uruguay and today head of a Syrian community in Manhattan Beach, Brooklyn. In his recently-published book, *Awesome Creation: A Study of the First Three Verses of the Torah,* Rabbi Bitton scrutinizes the Torah's words and those of *Chazal,* analyzing them in light of contemporary science.

The Jewish Press: What kind of insights does your book offer on science and religion?

Rabbi Bitton: I examine, in depth, the first word of the Torah, "*Bereishit.*" As you know, the beginning of the universe was proven when scientists detected that the universe is expanding. So, in a sense, modern science is discovering what the first word of the Torah said thousands of years ago. I show that the prophets referred to the expansion of the universe when they said, "*noteh shamayim,*" that God stretches the heavens.

I also analyze every single word of the second verse of the Torah. I show that many translations reflect non-Jewish ideas. For example, "*tohu vavohu*" is usually translated as "chaos" even though this translation differs from how *Chazal* and most classic commentators understood these words. If you interpret *"tohu vavohu"* as chaos, you are, in a sense, following the Platonic view of creation. According to Plato, God was not the creator of the world but the one who put a chaotic universe into order.

Another example is *"ruach Elokim."* It should not be interpreted as "spirit of God." According to *Chazal, Targum* Onkelos, Maimonides, Radak, Ibn Ezra – practically all commentators – *"ruach Elokim"* means a physical wind. "Spirit of God" is a Christian concept that reflects the doctrine of the Trinity: the father, the son, and the Holy Spirit.

Now, when you remove all these mistranslations, the second verse gives us an inventory of sorts of how the world looked in the beginning, and it's very close to what modern science describes: a lifeless world, covered by water, with a dense and dark atmosphere.

How do you deal with the age of the universe in your book?

I show that time was a consequence of the act of creation. *Chazal* said, *"Kol ma'asei bereishit bekomotan nivra'u,"* which means that all creation was created in a mature state. That mature state creates the illusion that things are older than they really are. For example, *Chazal* said that Adam HaRishon was 20 years old when he was created. So five minutes after he was created Adam was, chronologically speaking, five minutes old. Nonetheless, he had the body of a 20-year-old man.

So if a scientist determines that the light of a certain star took several billion years to reach Earth, you would say that God created the world with that light already reaching Earth.

Yes, if I am a scientist and I try to track back creation – without considering the act of creation – then of course I will add billions of years to the equation. When scientists analyze and examine the world, they don't consider an act of creation, which is the big difference between what the Torah says and what science says.

It makes sense that God would create a star whose light is already visible at the moment of creation. Why, though, would He create dinosaur

bones underground that appear to be millions of years old. Why would He mislead us?

I don't want to refer to that right now. I'm planning to write another book on the appearance of life, evolution, and dinosaurs. In this book, I deal with the creation of the world as a structure, not with life.

In your book, you discuss the Big Bang, a theory which most people today regard as almost "obvious." Few seem to be aware how revolutionary this theory actually was in the history of science-religion debates.

Exactly. Popular knowledge has it that the Big Bang and creation are far apart, but that couldn't be further from the truth. After thousands of years of holding the Aristotelian view of the eternity of the universe, science [since the mid-1900s] now asserts that the universe had a beginning. That's a breakthrough, and it's the closest that science has gotten to the first word of the Torah: "*Bereishit.*"

You cite an interesting *mashal* by the Rambam about the limits of human knowledge in your book. Can you give a shortened version?

I adapted the Rambam's *mashal* for the modern reader. I said: Imagine if robot-like scientists from a different planet would come to Earth, kidnap a three-year-old boy, and study him for two months to learn about the human species. They would see him grow one inch and, working their way backwards, they would conclude that he was originally only one inch tall or less.

From studying this boy for two months, they would never be able to deduce the processes of pregnancy and birth. Why? Because they never saw a woman, and all the laws of pregnancy contradict what they know about biology. This boy, after all, has to eat and breathe, and so they would never be able to conceive – or even imagine – that this boy was in somebody else's body with no air, food, or water.

Similarly, we have to understand that information about creation might not only be beyond our knowledge, but also beyond our imagination.

You quote a British philosopher who compares human knowledge of electrons to that of monkeys and concludes that not only will monkeys "never be able to understand an electron the way we do," but they are "*cognitively closed* to it."

Yes, there are limits to our epistemological capabilities.

You often quote the Sephardic sage Menashe ben Yisrael in your book, the man who was largely responsible for the return of Jews to England in the mid-1600s. Why?

Many reasons. First of all, because I happen to love his style. Second, because I'm trying to do a kind of *techiyat hameisim* with him and other unknown writers. His book was translated into English in the 19th century, so I used it in the hope that this book and others like it will become better known to the general public.

On your website, you post mini-biographies of various Sephardic rabbis. Why?

Because I think Sephardic rabbis are unfortunately unknown to mainstream Judaism, and they have a lot to say. In my opinion, they represent a model of integration between erudition in Torah and general knowledge. They never saw a contradiction between the two, so I think they are a model that is very necessary today to inspire other Jews to follow Torah 100 percent without feeling antagonized from the modern world.

One of these biographies is of Rabbi Eliyahu Hazan who, you write, was the first rabbi to institute a *bas mitzvah* ceremony in the Sephardic world.

Yes, this was in the beginning of the 20th century in Alexandria, Egypt. He saw that there was a need for it due to the strong European influence in Alexandria. So Rabbi Hazan designed a ceremony and preparatory course in which the girls would learn more about Judaism. The ceremony consisted of the recitation of some prayers, and a test – answering questions dealing with the basic principles of Judaism. I think for his time it was revolutionary. [But he did it] so that girls would be stimulated to have a deeper knowledge of Judaism.

In another post on your website, you write about Rabbi Refael Aharon ben Shimon (1847-1928), who issued an interesting ruling regarding suicide.

He was a rabbi in Cairo at a time when there was, what he described as, an epidemic of suicides "because of small problems, illusory matters of honor, or frustrated romantic expectations." So what he did was ban people who committed suicide from a normal burial [even though standard halachic practice is to be lenient on this matter]. And it worked.

But he didn't only discuss suicide. He discussed and ruled on so many things, and it's unfortunate that he's not better known in the halachic world.

What's your family's background?

I'm half Syrian, half Moroccan. I was born in Argentina to Argentinian parents. My grandparents, though, came from Tetouan, Morocco, and Damascus, Syria.

How would you describe your present synagogue?

Ohel David & Shlomo mainly serves the Syrian community in Manhattan Beach. It is a very special, warm, highly organized, and very traditional and knowledgeable community. People love to study Torah, people come to shul every *Shabbat*, and practically every Syrian family sends its children to Jewish schools. The community is also extremely active in *chesed*.

Sometimes people claim that whenever Sephardim live as a minority among Ashkenazim, they tend to slowly lose their identity. Do you find that to be true?

No, absolutely not. The Syrians are extremely strict in keeping the traditions of their ancestors, and they've developed the means to perpetuate those traditions. They have schools, publications, and websites, and they instruct the youth in synagogue. The synagogues are the best schools. It's not rare to see in most Syrian communities young people in charge of leading the prayers and the Torah reading.

They are very conscious of the importance of the heritage they've received and they feel responsible to bequeath that legacy to the next generation.

— originally published September 17, 2013

Postscript: *In April 2017, Rabbi Bitton told me that the book he planned on writing on "the appearance of life, evolution, and dinosaurs" is now complete. Called "Dinosaurs and the Bible," it will soon be available in Portuguese, with an English translation hopefully appearing before the end of the year, he said.*

Douglas Axe

A Scientist Who Dares Question Evolutionary Orthodoxy

"Religion vs. science" conflicts are generally depicted in popular culture as battles between narrow-minded bigots and tolerant truth-seekers. From the Galileo Affair to the Scopes Monkey Trial, religious authoritarians are cast as forces of darkness attempting to stifle the light of science.

In recent decades, though, this narrative has arguably been turned on its head. Instead of religious authorities persecuting free thinkers, today, more often than not, it is "free" thinkers who persecute believers who dare challenge the popular consensus on such hot-button issues as evolution or global warming.

Douglas Axe, director of the Biologic Institute in Seattle, experienced this persecution first-hand. As a post-doctoral researcher at the prestigious Medical Research Council Centre in Cambridge in 2002, he was experimenting on protein structures when his superiors discovered that his research was being funded in part by an intelligent design organization. The science was solid – he later published his findings in a highly-regarded journal – but his association with intelligent design was considered unacceptable. He was asked to leave.

In his first book, *Undeniable: How Biology Confirms Our Intuition That Life Is Designed* – published two weeks ago – Axe recounts his experiences at the Medical Research Council Centre and presents his objections to the theory of evolution as it currently stands.

Axe holds a PhD from Caltech and has published in such scientific journals as Nature, Proceedings of the National Academy of Sciences, and the Journal of Molecular Biology.

The Jewish Press: You write in *Undeniable* that you harbored doubts about evolution even as a college student. What were those doubts?

Axe: I perceived there to be a deep contradiction between the materialist worldview – which is the idea that everything is matter and energy – and our notion of human free will. If we are nothing but large machines made out of atoms and molecules, all of which are slaves to the laws of physics, how is it that we can decide to do this or do that?

You write that you were convinced at the time that if you could prove the evolutionary theory was flawed, scientists would admit their error since they value truth above all. You now say you were naïve to believe this. Please explain.

It's a utopian view of science. It's this idea that although scientists have their own personal preferences, when they put on their white lab coats, they're ultimately about the truth – and nothing else – and if their theories are proven wrong, they will concede.

But scientists are 100 percent human, and all the things that other humans find hard – like admitting you're wrong – are hard for scientists too. Also, scientists survive in their profession by getting the approval of other scientists, so that gives rise to peer pressure.

You write that philosophical hindrances might also be holding scientists back from acknowledging the flaws with evolution.

Yes. I start the book with the question "Where did we come from?" and lay out the two possibilities: Either we're cosmic accidents or we're the product of purpose. If we're cosmic accidents, we basically end up with this nihilistic position – that there's no moral right and wrong and we're here today and gone tomorrow, so live how you want to live. But if that's false and instead we're a product of purpose and intent [conceived by a Creator], then you have a completely different view of who we are as human beings and how we ought to live our lives.

What experiments were you conducting at the Medical Research Council Centre that ultimately led to your ouster in 2002?

I was working on a class of proteins called enzymes. Proteins are the molecules responsible for most of the cellular activities of life, and they consist of long chains of amino acids. I was testing the idea that was prevalent at the time that proteins can do their function even if you monkey with their amino acid sequences. Now, that turns out to be true to a degree, but if you push that to its limit, you ruin them. And that gives you a probabilistic problem for evolution because in order to find one of these working sequences, you have to imagine a blind unguided search landing on an extremely rare functional sequence.

How rare?

Well, my Journal of Molecular Biology paper published in 2004 came up with the number of one in 10^{74}. And then if you need a particular function, it's going to be even worse. I estimated it to be about one good sequence in 10^{77} sequences. So, roughly, one in a trillion, trillion, trillion, trillion, trillion, trillion – which is not very good odds.

Why is your research problematic for evolution?

Because if evolution is unguided, then the whole process has no idea what sequence it needs in order to get to a particular function. Yet somehow it ends up finding these functions. Well, that's only plausible if the targets are large enough that a blind staggering walk can land on them. But if the targets are one in a trillion, trillion, trillion, trillion, trillion, trillion small, then no blind search is ever going to find them.

Wouldn't proteins develop properly just by accident given enough time, say 15 billion years, which is what scientists estimate the age of the universe to be?

If you have 10 billion chances for a one-in-10-billion event to occur, then it could very easily occur. But when you have a number like 10^{74}, it turns out that even when you take into account the age of the earth, that's not enough to solve this problem.

Do you reject the entire theory of evolution? Or just the notion that it was unguided?

I'm not arguing against common ancestry or some form of descent with modification. What I'm saying is that accidental processes cannot possibly have invented these things.

You write that the limits of natural selection are actually well-known to scientists and are not terribly controversial.

There's nothing controversial about saying that natural selection has been proven to be much less potent than Darwin thought it was. There have been mathematical challenges to natural selection since the 1960s. For example, Motoo Kimura, a great Japanese population geneticist, among many others, showed that it's far from a sure thing that a more genetically-fit individual will give rise to a more genetically-fit species. More often than not, that more genetically-fit individual will die and not have progeny. So it's a very hit-and-miss thing. But very few people take that conclusion to the extent that I have and say the entire theory is false.

One popular response to any type of design argument for the existence of God is to posit the existence of trillions upon trillions of parallel universes. If there are these alternate universes, it isn't surprising that one of them would contain working proteins – as well as plant, animal, and human life. How do you respond to this argument?

If there's an infinite number of universes and it's physically possible for everything we see here to evolve – and I don't grant that – the question would then be: Why are we in that special universe? We should find ourselves on a minimal planet where there's nothing except that which is necessary for us to think. Instead we find ourselves in a rich biosphere with biological diversity beyond our wildest imagination.

Why do you need to explain why we happen to be in this universe as opposed to another?

Because the whole problem is to explain the astonishingly improbable. If you say, "I'm not going to explain it," you might as well just say everything poofed into existence by accident. In other words, the claim of materialists is that we can explain life as we see it, not as something that's exceedingly improbable, but as something that's expected. The multiverse doesn't do that once you show that Darwinism doesn't work. It's highly *unexpected* for there to be all this life around us. That's my point.

Another argument against the multiverse is that positing the existence of myriads of parallel universes doesn't seem more plausible than positing the existence of God.

I totally agree with you. I think it's a stretch in the best of situations.

Last question: You argue that the scientific community would actually conduct better science if it believed in God. How so?

For example, you may remember when a human genome sequence was published many years back, it was thought that most of our DNA is junk – that it's not doing anything and it's just left over from this very inefficient evolutionary process. That idea caused scientists to write off 97 percent or so of our genome as not worth studying.

But that idea has turned out to be false. We now know that the vast majority of our DNA *is* functional in some way. So that's an example of how the wrong philosophy can lead us down the wrong road for decades.

— originally published July 27, 2016

Postscript: *In a January 2017 e-mail to me, Douglas Axe wrote that he has "a growing number of opportunities to discuss the basic message of 'Undeniable' – that common-sense reasoning justifies our intuition that life is designed. Radio and podcast interviews continue, as do speaking engagements, and I've taken up tweeting as well (@DougAxe)."*

Rabbi Natan Slifkin

Advancing "Rationalist Judaism"

(original interview, published here for the first time)

Rabbi Natan Slifkin's first books on Torah and science contained approbations from Rabbi Shmuel Kamenetsky and Rabbi Yisroel Belsky. Today, following a controversial ban, most of his books – including those Rabbi Kamenetsky and Belsky praised – are considered heretical by much of the charedi world.

To learn more about Rabbi Slifkin, and the views that caused such an uproar in the Orthodox world, this writer called Rabbi Slifkin in Israel.

Resnick: What's your background?

Rabbi Slifkin: I grew up in Manchester, England, but left when I was 17 and went to Israel to learn in yeshiva for a bunch of years.

Which ones?

Well, I've disowned them and they've disowned me – but I ended up in the Mir.

So you didn't go to college?

My parents wanted me to go to college, but I refused to go because I was brainwashed by *yeshivos* into thinking it was *treif*. I had a big fight with them.

Much later in life, though, I realized it was a good idea, so I finally went. I did my Master's at Machon Lander and my PhD at Bar-Ilan.

You don't mean you were literally brainwashed, do you?

Well, it depends what you mean by brainwashed. But it was drilled into me every day that going to college would mean failure as a *ben Torah*.

You're soft-spoken by nature and your books on science and Torah have *haskamos* from prominent charedi rabbis. How did you become so controversial?

It's a good question. The approach I presented in my books – which is what I learned from my mentor, Rav Aryeh Carmell – was considered reasonably normative in the circles I was in. But I was in a very particular part of the yeshiva world. What happened is certain people brought my books to the attention of the more right-wing [element] of the yeshiva world and stirred up this big controversy. So the views I presented in my books – which until then had been kind of tolerated in the yeshiva world as a minority view – suddenly became unacceptable.

A straightforward reading of the Torah suggests that the world is 6,000 years old while the scientific community believes it to be 15 billion years old. How do you reconcile the two positions?

In my book *The Challenge of Creation* I present a variety of different approaches. The one I favor is that of Rambam and others, such as Ralbag, which is that *Ma'asei Bereishis* is not to be interpreted literally.

Considering that evolution is a somewhat problematic theory even from a scientific perspective, why not just accept the Torah's account at face value?

I used to focus on all the *kashes* on evolution when I thought it was religiously problematic. But when I learned it wasn't, I realized that although there are questions, evolution answers a lot more questions than it raises. Certainly, if you're looking at two different models of how life appeared on earth – either gradually over millions of years or at the same time a few thousand years ago – what we see in the natural world fits much better with the evolutionary picture.

You've written that geology makes the case for evolution. How so?

People say, "Show me *one* thing that proves evolution," and then they try to argue with it. But there isn't one thing that proves evolution. It's a convergence of lots and lots of things – one of which is that there are different layers of rock in the world and each layer has fossils that are unique to it. For example, there are layers where the only thing you find is dinosaur fossils. You don't find fossils of people or dogs or lions or bears. So that shows very clearly that dinosaurs did not live at the same time as contemporary creatures.

The most common rejoinder to evidence of an old universe is that Hashem made a ready-made world. What's your response?

If people want to believe that, *gesunterheit*. But I think it's bizarre. You find all these skeletons of animals that died. Are you going to say God created the world with skeletons and creatures that never lived?

Why is that so farfetched?

C'mon. There's a mitzvah of *eglah arufah*. You find a dead body with a knife in it. You don't know how the murder took place, so you have this *mitzvah* of *eglah arufah* to atone for the unsolved murder. You don't say, "How do you know there was a murder? Maybe God just created a dead body with a knife in it."

There are reasonable assumptions we make when we see the world. If you see a body of a person with a knife in its back, it's reasonable to assume he was murdered. If you find the skeleton of an animal, it's reasonable to assume it lived and died.

Clearly, though, if Hashem made a ready-made world, there would be stars sparkling whose light would appear to be many light years old even though the world had just been created. Why can't you explain the existence of dinosaur fossils in a similar fashion?

You can find certain support [in Midrashic literature] for saying God created things in a mature state. But there's a difference between the world being in a mature state and it showing evidence of eras that never took place.

In other words, people want to say that man was created as a 20-year-old man. Fine. But was he created with memories of his childhood that never happened? Was he created with scars from childhood injuries that he never had? I don't think people are going to go that far. By the same token, why would the world be created with physical memories of eras that never took place?

Some people are reluctant to accept evolution because they think it diminishes God.

Yes, that's a common reason, but it's also very strange because people don't say that about any other area of science. We accept that God works through medicine, meteorology, and history. We talk about the miracles of the creation of Israel and its success in war; that doesn't mean God didn't work through historical processes.

So there's no reason why biology should be any different. The same way that God works through medicine, weather, and human history, God can work through evolution.

You seem to be echoing a point Rav Samson Raphael Hirsch made. He wrote that if evolution were proven to be true, "Judaism in that case would call upon its adherents to give even greater reverence than ever before to the one, sole God Who, in His boundless creative wisdom and eternal omnipotence, needed to bring into existence no more than one single, amorphous nucleus, and one single law of 'adaptation and heredity' in order to bring forth, from what seemed chaos but was in fact a very definite order, the infinite variety of species we know today..."

After the ban of my books, it took me two years to figure out it was about two different worldviews going back at least 800 years: the rationalist worldview and the mystical worldview. The rationalist view – of the

Rambam and the great Torah scholars of Spain – is that the laws of nature are God's greatest creation and He should work through them. The mystical approach is that the greatness of God is seen in supernatural miracles. It's two completely different ways of looking at the world.

Those who consider your books heretical point to your views on *Ma'asei Bereishis* as well as your approach toward scientific statements in the Gemara and *Midrash,* which you contend are sometimes inaccurate. How can you say *Chazal* were wrong?

The first thing is *Chazal* say it. The most clear discussion of this topic is a Gemara in *Pesachim* where there's a *machlokes* between the *chachmei yisrael* and the *chachmei umos ha'olam* about where the sun goes at night. The *chachmei yisrael* say the sun goes behind the sky and the non-Jewish scholars say the sun goes on the other side of the world – and Rav Yehudah Hanasi says the non-Jews are correct. So there you have a Gemara that *Chazal* were not omniscient about the natural world, and almost all the *rishonim* interpret the Gemara that way.

You argue that they were wrong about the animal world too.

That's another topic, right. Many different *sugyos* in the Gemara speak about different creatures born, not from parents, but from dust, dirt, fire, or mud. So you have lice that come from dirt, a salamander that is generated from fire, and mice that are generated from mud. These statements, though, are not surprising, because until a couple of centuries ago, the greatest zoologists in the world believed in spontaneous generation. So, as Rav Hirsch says, *Chazal* were unimaginably great Torah scholars, but when they spoke about the natural world, they relied on whatever was the common knowledge [of their era].

Who else says that besides Rav Hirsch?

The idea of *Chazal* not being experts in science is something Rambam says, as well as Rambam's son Rabbeinu Avraham and many, many other *rishonim* and *achronim*. And it didn't cause a religious crisis for them.

Jews nowadays don't assume that Rav Aryeh Leib Steinman knows more about nuclear physics than MIT professors. These same Jews, though, assume *Chazal* knew more about the animal world than the greatest scientists of their day. Why?

Because there's a general approach that everything *Chazal* said was said *b'ruach hakodesh* even though there's virtually no basis for that in the Gemara. But because we learn Gemara with such reverence, for many people it's very hard to revere the Gemara and yet believe that *Chazal* were not infallible. So I understand for some people it could be shocking or destabilizing to their Judaism if they're told that not everything in the Gemara is scientifically correct.

But on the other hand, you have a whole other crowd of people who know that not everything is scientifically correct, and if you tell them it's unacceptable to say that, they're going to be disenfranchised from Judaism. If you show them, though, that there were plenty of *rishonim* and *achronim* who said that too, you're helping them.

Some people believe that once you say *Chazal* are wrong in one area, people will start wondering if they were wrong in another area – i.e., the *mesorah* – which can lead to the breakdown of Judaism.

Well, none of the *rishonim* and *achronim* who said *Chazal* were wrong on science were worried about that point. It's actually kind of juvenile. Just because people are wrong about some things doesn't mean they're wrong about everything and that it should just be a free-for-all.

Plus, there's a difference between *halacha* and theology. In other words, *halacha* is what *Chazal* say it is. And that's why a *zaken mamrei* is put to death. The Chasam Sofer writes that if the *zaken mamrei* says a certain food is *treif* and the rest of the Sanhedrin says it's kosher, the *zaken mamrei* might be correct. And yet, says the Chasam Sofer, the *zaken mamrei* should still eat the food, and if he doesn't, he is put to death. Why? Because you can't undermine the system of halachic authority.

And that's the story of *tanur shel Achnai* – even though Hashem says

Eliezer is correct, the rest of the *rabbanim* say, "*Lo bashamayim hi,*" and you follow the majority. Ultimately, *halacha* is not about who's correct. It's about following a certain system of halachic authority, so it doesn't make a difference if there's an occasional mistake.

You are in midst of writing *The Torah Encyclopedia of the Animal Kingdom* and also operate The Biblical Museum of Natural History in Beit Shemesh, Israel. You strive in both these projects to steer clear from controversy and thus cater to everyone. Do these projects represent a return to your pre-controversy life in which you combined your love of Torah with your love of the animal world?

I'm trying to divide my career. The science and philosophy stuff is very important for some people, but it's not suitable for everyone, whereas the animal and Torah stuff is inspirational and suitable for everyone across the board.

So I still have my blog [www.RationalistJudaism.com] and books on Torah and science, but I don't get into any issues of Torah and science in the encyclopedia or the museum. And *baruch Hashem,* the museum draws visitors from across the religious spectrum, and everybody loves it.

Hitler's Inferno

Peter Ross Range

Chronicling the Year That Launched Hitler

How a man like Adolf Hitler managed to seize power in Germany and plunge the world into war is a question that still baffles people today. In his recently-released book, *1924: The Year That Made Hitler*, journalist Peter Ross Range adds his own perspective. A specialist on Germany, Range has written for such publications as The New York Times, Time magazine, and U.S. News and World Report, where he served as a national and White House correspondent.

The Jewish Press: The subtitle of your book is "The Year That Made Hitler." How did 1924 make Hitler?

Range: Hitler said he thought about revolution every day for four years – from 1919 to 1923. He did not participate in elections and didn't let any of his party members run for office. He thought the only way he could ever gain power in Germany was by overthrowing the Weimar Republic. And that's what he tried to do in November 1923 with the Beer Hall Putsch. He came closer to success than many people realize – it was not a comic opera as it has sometimes been described – but it failed for various reasons.

So Hitler ended up in prison, hit bottom, and went into suicidal depression. When he came out of that, though, he started preparing for his treason trial, which became a great political platform for him. He was able to get the Nazi brand out into the world in ways that had never been done before because the national press covered the trial.

You argue that the half year Hitler spent in prison following the trial was crucial to his later political rise. How so?

Because that's where he wrote *Mein Kampf*, and by the time he came out, he was a new man. His self-belief and self-confidence were soaring.

In addition, it was during this time that he realized that being a revolutionary was not going to work and that the only route to power was the electoral way. He said, "It will take us longer to outvote them than to outshoot them, but at least we will win by their rules, which will guarantee the outcome." He also said, "We will take the parliament in order to destroy it." So that was his thinking when he left prison.

Why was Hitler so set on revolution in 1923?

Because Germany was a mess, and 1923 was the worst year of the Weimar Republic. In January, the French and Belgians invaded the Ruhr area and occupied it, and inflation was out of control. The exchange rate was four trillion marks to one dollar. There were hunger strikes and the police were shooting at hungry Germans.

So conditions were indeed awful, and Hitler blamed all of this on democracy. He thought democracy was a terrible form of government and parliamentary decisions were weak decisions because they were by definition compromises and sometimes done by bare majorities. He thought only a strong man and a dictatorship could save Germany.

During his treason trial in 1924, the presiding judge, Georg Neithardt, indulged Hitler endlessly, at one point letting him speak continuously for four hours. Why?

The political atmosphere in Bavaria at this time was sympathetic to the direction Hitler was going, and his was just one of many far-right movements at the time. Hitler was also a dramatic speechmaker and held the court room in total thrall. People loved hearing what he had to say, so it was big entertainment for everybody and big news as well.

But it is widely agreed that this judge let him go way too far. Judge Neithardt later claimed he couldn't interrupt Hitler because of the flood of words, but that's a pretty lame excuse.

Even though Hitler was being tried for treason, you write that the most shocking moment of the trial was not anything he said about overthrowing the government but rather his accusation that General Otto von Lossow broke his word of honor. Even Judge Neithardt called it "an impropriety without precedent." Why was this accusation considered so shocking?

In Germany at the time, one's word of honor was taken very, very seriously, and breaking one's word of honor was essentially the highest possible offence you could commit, especially in military culture. So when Hitler accused Lossow of that, it was – you're right – the most dramatic single moment in the trial. Lossow stared at Hitler, grabbed his stuff, bowed to the judge, and walked out – never to return. So even though in the moment it appeared that Hitler had committed a horrible offence, he got away with it.

The copyright for *Mein Kampf* – held by the Bavarian government since World War II – expired on January 1, 2016. In preparation for that date, Munich's Institute for Contemporary History, with funding from the government, prepared a critical edition of *Mein Kampf* with extensive footnotes. You argued in an op-ed for The New York Times last year that this publication should be welcomed. Why?

For educational purposes. *Mein Kampf* is a central document to the study of Hitler, the Third Reich, and the Holocaust, and you can't really claim to know much if you haven't read it.

At the same time, though, a whole mythology has built up around *Mein Kampf* partly because it was out of reach, especially to Germans, since World War II. They could find it on the Internet or if they dug around in the back of some used bookstore, but it was not out in public to see or examine.

Furthermore, what the Institute for Contemporary History did was produce a commentated edition with footnotes and annotations that are about 1,200 pages long. Hitler's text itself is about 800 pages long. So there are one and a half times as many footnotes as there are words by Hitler, and it is very hard to read as a [regular book]. You're interrupted constantly by these footnotes, and they're fascinating because they give you background and context. They tell you where Hitler was lying or telling a half-truth and they cross index each other because Hitler was repetitious and confusing. So it's very useful.

This critical edition is the only modern version of *Mein Kampf* currently available in Germany. With the copyright now expired, though, can't any publisher print the original version without footnotes?

They can, but I was talking with a very knowledgeable person in Germany recently and he doubts any commercial publisher will jump on this because the critical edition kind of sucks all the air out of the room and the market for an edition [without commentary] would probably be fairly small.

There is also a legal threat against anybody who wants to do that. The conference for justice ministers of Germany – that is to say, the attorney general of each state in Germany – has said that they would prosecute anybody who publishes an uncommentated edition under Germany's hate speech laws. Now, we don't know if they would succeed in that prosecution, but it's a strong disincentive to anybody thinking of making a quick buck by publishing a pulp paperback of *Mein Kampf*.

— originally published March 2, 2016

Postscript: *Peter Ross Range is currently writing "The Unfathomable Ascent: Hitler's Climb to Power, 1925-1933," which is set to be published by Little, Brown and Company in 2018. Ross Range also informed me that a neo-Nazi publisher in Leipzig has since produced a non-critical edition of "Mein Kampf" (a facsimile of the 1943 edition), which is being sold mainly online.*

Dr. Michael Berenbaum

A Holocaust Historian Who Doesn't Hate FDR

Dr. Michael Berenbaum is one of the world's foremost experts on the Holocaust. From 1988-93 he oversaw the creation of the United States Holocaust Memorial Museum in Washington; from 1993-97 he served as director of its Holocaust Research Institute; and from 1997-99 he headed Steven Spielberg's Survivors of the Shoah Visual History Foundation, which currently possesses a collection of nearly 53,000 Holocaust testimonies in 40 languages.

Berenbaum is also the author and editor of numerous works on the Holocaust, including *Anatomy of the Auschwitz Death Camp*, *The Holocaust: Religious and Philosophical Implications*, and *The Bombing of Auschwitz: Should the Allies Have Attempted It?* Berenbaum currently heads the Sigi Ziering Institute for the Study of the Holocaust and Ethics at American Jewish University and consults for Holocaust films and museums.

The Jewish Press: FBI Director James Comey recently said, "In their minds, the murderers and accomplices of Germany, and Poland, and Hungary...didn't do something evil. They convinced themselves it was the right thing to do, the thing they had to do." Poland was outraged by these comments and demanded an apology. What's your reaction?

Dr. Berenbaum: Poland was occupied by Germany. Therefore, there were no Nazi death camps in Poland; there were Nazi death camps in *German-occupied* Poland. The Poles could have never pulled off anything like the scope and scale of the Holocaust. Anti-Semitism in Poland was sporadic rather than systematic.

Why do Jews, then, sometimes feel more intensely about Polish anti-Semitism than they do about German anti-Semitism? The reason is because we expected better treatment by the Poles – by people we had gone to school with, by people who knew us, by people who had bought in our stores. That expectation led to a feeling of betrayal.

Another point: Imagine returning home and finding somebody sleeping in your house and eating at your table. That's an act of *absolute* betrayal and many survivors experienced that. Contrast that with the behavior of the Danes who protected and preserved Jewish property; many Danish Jews who came back found a table that was set and food in the refrigerator. One is *mentchlichkeit* and one is taking advantage of the ill fate that befell your neighbor.

So I would say the Poles are less innocent than they would like to believe but also less guilty than many Jews emotionally feel them to be.

You wrote in 2013: "The easiest way to get booed by a Jewish audience is to tell them that President Franklin Delano Roosevelt's record regarding the Holocaust is less vile than they have been accustomed to hearing." Is it less vile? If yes, how so?

Let's begin with *lishvacho* [praise] and then *lignai* [criticism]. *Lishvacho*: Roosevelt got America into World War II, prepared America to fight World War II, and did not allow Britain and the Soviet Union to go under when they were fighting the Germans alone. So you have to give Roosevelt enormous credit. Without America in World War II, Hitler would have triumphed. That's not an insignificant accomplishment.

Regarding his record on the Holocaust, the most positive thing you can say is that Roosevelt was ungenerous toward the Jews. But if you're ungenerous at a time of greatest need, you're turning your back.

So if I weigh the evidence, I have to say Roosevelt was horrific by his inaction, horrific by his insensitivity, and ungenerous to the extreme. But I also have to balance those criticisms by his undeniable achievements.

You are the co-editor of *The Bombing of Auschwitz: Should the Allies Have Attempted It?*. What are your thoughts on why America didn't bomb Auschwitz?

June 11, 1944, the Jewish Agency held a meeting in Jerusalem under the chairmanship of David Ben-Gurion at which it voted not to request that Auschwitz be bombed. They said we don't know enough about the situation on the ground that we should ask in the name of the Jewish people that innocent civilians be killed.

So that means as a historian you have to say – presuming for a moment that David Ben-Gurion was not an anti-Semite – that a non-anti-Semite interested in the Jewish question could as late as June 11, 1944 say we don't know enough to request that Auschwitz be bombed.

Let's follow the trail. July 7, 1944, Chaim Weizmann and Moshe Shertok – who later became Moshe Sharett – ask Anthony Eden to bring a request to Winston Churchill to bomb Auschwitz. Now, you have to ask yourself the question: How is it that June 11, 1944, Ben-Gurion and the cabinet vote not to request that Auschwitz be bombed and July 7, 1944 – 26 days later – Chaim Weizmann and Moshe Shertok request that Auschwitz be bombed?

Two explanations are possible. One is that they acted contrary to instructions. The second is much more interesting, and that is that something came to their attention which made the policy decision non-operative with such clarity that they didn't need to have a [formal] meeting [to officially change it]. What could that piece of information have been? It was the famous Auschwitz Protocols – what's called the Vrba-Wetzler report – that was compiled in Slovakia and gave a total picture of what Auschwitz was like, including maps.

That documentation did not reach the United States in its entirety until November 1944. And by that time the gassing at Auschwitz had ended so the bombing would have been irrelevant.

For many people, Auschwitz has become a symbol of absolute evil. Some historians, however, point out that a Nazi camp like Belzec was arguably even more horrific, and the only reason relatively few people know about it is because almost no Jew survived Belzec to tell the tale.

I curated the museum at Belzec. 500,000 Jews were killed at Belzec in 1942 – all of Galicianer Jewry. It did more damage per day than any other camp. There are only two known survivors. And only one of those survivors ever gave testimony.

Auschwitz was actually three camps: a prison camp for Poles, a slave labor camp, and a death camp. Belzec was only a death camp. There were three camps which had only death as its mission: Belzec, Sobibor, and Treblinka. To give you an idea of the statistics:

• 500,000 Jews killed in Belzec, 10 months. One of those months they were reconstructing the place. Two known survivors.

• Treblinka: between 850,000-925,000 killed from *Tisha B'Av* 1942 to August 4, 1943. 67 known survivors.

• Sobibor: 250,000 killed between the spring of 1942 and November 1943. Less than 100 survivors.

You've been teaching on university campuses for several decades now. How do your non-Jewish students react to learning about the Holocaust?

More intensely than Jews. And the reason is because Jews grow up with it. You've seen the imagery, you've spoken to survivors. For many non-Jews, though, it's all brand new – it's a new horror – and the intensity of it overwhelms them.

— originally published April 29, 2015

Postscript: *Dr. Berenbaum has since consulted for Holocaust museums in Dallas and Skopje, Macedonia, and for two films that premiered in 2017, "The Zookeepers Wife" and "The Escape Tunnel of Vilna."*

Dr. Rafael Medoff

Revisiting the Life of a Notorious Rabbi

Dr. Rafael Medoff is the founding director of The David S. Wyman Institute for Holocaust Studies and author of 16 books about Jewish history and the Holocaust. His latest is *The Anguish of a Jewish Leader: Stephen S. Wise and the Holocaust.*

The Jewish Press: Why did you write *The Anguish of a Jewish Leader*?

Medoff: Stephen Wise's supporters tend to defend everything he did, while some of his detractors condemn him as almost treasonous. I thought it would be useful to take a more nuanced look at the historical circumstances and probe deeper into the reasons for Wise's relationship with President Roosevelt and Wise's attacks on Jewish activists.

Jews today, by and large, think of Stephen Wise as a timid leader. You write in the book, though, that in his younger years Wise was something of a militant.

Correct. Wise was a Zionist at a time when most of his fellow Reform rabbis were anti-Zionists, and he created the American Jewish Congress in 1918 as an activist alternative to the conservative and cautious American Jewish Committee.

Sometimes, however, Jewish leaders start out as firebrands and then gradually get tired, or even co-opted. Sometimes – and this is true of some leaders today as well – they start to really enjoy the "*kavod*" of having their photo taken with prime ministers and become reluctant to risk losing that by speaking out on controversial issues.

There were a number of proposals to save Jews during the Holocaust, including two that would have brought several hundred thousand Jews to Alaska and the Virgin Islands. Wise opposed these plans. Why?

I interviewed the leader of a group of rabbinical students who met with Wise in 1942. He told me they asked him about these two proposals and Wise told them the Virgin Islands were "too hot" for Jewish refugees and Alaska was "too cold." That was ridiculous. Jews whose lives were in danger would gladly have gone anywhere, regardless of the weather, and Wise knew that.

The real reason he opposed these proposals was that he was unwilling to challenge President Roosevelt, and Roosevelt's position was that letting Jews enter even those remote American territories would give them a springboard to try to get into the mainland United States.

Wise also opposed the famous Rabbis' March on Washington in October 1943. Why?

Wise had two problems with it. The first was that the march highlighted the Roosevelt administration's abandonment of the Jews, and that was something Wise wanted to downplay. The other issue was that Wise was personally uncomfortable at the thought of these very Jewish-looking Jews marching through the streets of Washington. That's why he wrote an article denouncing the march as a "parade" and a "stunt." He found it both politically and personally embarrassing.

Many Jews today regard Peter Bergson (also known as Hillel Kook) as a hero for his unconventional campaign in America to rescue European Jewry. You write, though, that Wise greatly disliked Bergson. Why would he dislike someone trying to save Jews?

Some historians claim that Wise opposed Bergson because Bergson had been connected with the Revisionist Zionist leader, Ze'ev Jabotinsky, and the Irgun. But I concluded from my research that two other factors were much more significant. One was sheer jealousy – Bergson's group was making headlines and Wise didn't like sharing the spotlight. The second was Wise's fear that the Bergson Group's loud protests would cause anti-Semitism.

Wasn't this fear valid considering the unprecedented level of anti-Semitism in America in this time period?

Yes, his fear was valid – but only until the evidence showed that there was no reasonable basis for it. Jewish leaders worried that a march on Washington might cause an anti-Semitic backlash, but once the march took place and there was no backlash, it was unreasonable for Wise and his colleagues to continue opposing such marches.

At one point, Jewish leaders warned Bergson that a particular newspaper ad he was planning was so strongly worded that it might cause pogroms. Well, the ad was published in The New York Times and it didn't cause any pogroms. So, at that point, Wise and other Jewish leaders should have acknowledged that their fears had been unwarranted.

You also write that Rabbi Wise believed that, as an American, it might not be right to ask a government at war to take a special interest in the Jews of Europe. Isn't there some validity to this argument as well?

Sure – except that during the Holocaust there were many things President Roosevelt could have done to help the Jews that wouldn't have involved taking special action or detracting from the war effort. For example, the immigration quotas were largely unfilled; he could have simply let them be filled. Or troop-supply ships that were returning empty from Europe could have carried Jewish refugees.

Likewise, on the question of bombing Auschwitz, American planes were already flying within a few miles of the gas chambers in 1944 when they were bombing German oil factories nearby. It would have required a very minimal effort to drop a few bombs on the gas chambers or at least on the railway tracks leading to them.

At the end of *The Anguish of a Jewish Leader*, you quote several of Wise's colleagues who said he was essentially a good man taken in by FDR's enormous charm. Can you elaborate?

It's true that President Roosevelt was remarkably skilled at gland-handing – telling people what they wanted to hear and making them feel as if he agreed with them even if he had no intention of doing what they wanted. There is an anecdote about FDR calling Wise "Stevie," which may or may not be true, but there is no doubt Roosevelt understood how to disarm Wise by stroking his ego.

It's also true that Wise's admiration of Roosevelt was extreme. I found correspondence in which Wise referred to the president as "the All Highest" and similar expressions. The combination of FDR's smooth talking and Wise's weakness for flattery definitely made it harder for Wise to muster the courage to criticize the president's policies.

But that's exactly why he should have recused himself – if he didn't have the political or personal courage to challenge Roosevelt's abandonment of the Jews, he should have resigned.

What will your next book be about?

It's called *Cartoonists Against the Holocaust* and it brings together political cartoons about the plight of the Jews in Europe which appeared in American newspapers in the 1930s and 1940s. The reader follows the history of the Holocaust through the eyes of political cartoonists, including Dr. Seuss and the famous "Herblock" of The Washington Post.

— originally published December 23, 2015

***Postscript:** "Cartoonists Against the Holocaust" was published in 2015-2016 (the "publisher did several roll-outs of the book," Dr. Medoff explained). His next book, "We Spoke Out: Comic Books and the Holocaust," is set to be released in early 2018.*

Ingrid Carlberg

Investigating Raoul Wallenberg's Disappearance

Raoul Wallenberg saved the lives tens of thousands of Hungarian Jews, but he couldn't save his own.

In January 1945, the 32-year-old Swedish diplomat approached the Red Army as it liberated Hungary to discuss his humanitarian plans for the post-war period. The Soviets immediately arrested him, but subsequently denied knowing anything about his whereabouts. In 1957, after German prisoners of war, recently released from Soviet prisons, testified to having conversed with Wallenberg while in captivity, the USRR changed its tune, admitting to having arrested Wallenberg. It claimed, however, that Wallenberg died of a heart attack in prison in 1947 – even though the Swedish diplomat was only 34 at the time.

The true story of Wallenberg's fate may never be known. Some believe he lived for several more decades while others think the Soviets murdered him in 1947. A new biography of Wallenberg by journalist Ingrid Carlberg spends more than 200 pages (a third of the book) on this subject, chronicling the efforts – or lack thereof – of the Swedish government to bring Wallenberg home.

Carlberg's book, *Raoul Wallenberg: The Heroic Life and Mysterious Disappearance of the Man Who Saved Thousands of Hungarian Jews from the Holocaust,* originally appeared in Swedish in 2012 and won Sweden's prestigious August Prize for non-fiction. An English translation was published this month.

The Jewish Press: How did Wallenberg wind up in Hungary in 1944 with a mission to save Jews?

Carlberg: After the German invasion of Hungary in May, there was an initiative taken by the American War Refugee Board to finance a rescue mission in Hungary. The United States couldn't act in Hungary since they were part of the war, so they asked their diplomatic envoy in Stockholm – Herschel Johnson – to persuade the Swedish government to help.

It so happened that the firm where Raoul Wallenberg worked was situated in the same building as the American legation in Stockholm, so even before the American envoy suggested this rescue mission to the Swedish government, there had been a lot of discussions in the building about it. Furthermore, Raoul Wallenberg's boss was Jewish and his family was in Hungary, so it didn't take long before all these things came together, and it was Hershel Johnson who actually suggested Raoul Wallenberg to the Swedish government.

You write that the War Refugee Board sent requests to several countries to intervene to stop the extermination of Hungarian Jewry. Sweden, though, was the only country to respond positively. Why?

I think the American diplomats in some of these countries felt it was really strange for them to ask their host governments to increase diplomatic work in Hungary at a time when the German army had invaded Hungary. So some American ambassadors didn't even ask their host countries. Other countries just didn't want to.

Sweden at this time, though, had a great need to please the Western allies because the neutral policy Sweden took during the war meant a certain German-friendly attitude that the Western allies thought had passed the limit of the acceptable. So now that the war had turned and it was obvious that the Germans were facing defeat, Sweden sought to improve its reputation among the Western allies.

Once in Hungary, how did Wallenberg go about saving Jews?

There's a myth that Raoul Wallenberg walked around the streets distributing protective papers and thus personally saved tens of thousands of Jews. That's not the truth. Raoul Wallenberg's heroic deed was the huge organization he managed to build to help Hungarian Jews. There were nearly 350 people employed in his organization, and they delivered food to tens of thousands of people, ran a hospital, and had their own security police which was sent out by Wallenberg to save Jews who were being taken away.

It was an immense organization, and the basis for all of it was the distribution of Swedish Schutzpasses, which Wallenberg designed. It was a fake passport, but it looked so credible that it was the most credible protective paper in Budapest that autumn, and it saved many people.

How many lives in total did Wallenberg save?

It's really hard to say. He himself mentions in his last letter back to Sweden the number 20,000. That includes 15,000 people saved from forced labor due to his intervention with [the Nazi-supported Hungarian] Arrow Cross and 2,000 people saved by his security police patrol in street-saving actions. And then there were the death marches ordered by Eichmann in November 1944 when 35,000 Jews had to walk from Budapest to Hegyeshalom. Wallenberg and his security police managed to save up to 1,000 people from those marches.

In the end, it was enough just to mention the name Raoul Wallenberg to save people. In January 1945, General Gerhard Schmidthuber gave the order to destroy the central ghetto in Budapest, which had between 70,000 and 100,000 Jews in it. Wallenberg was no longer in town, but he had a companion in the Arrow Cross police force who had switched sides at the end of 1944 – Pal Szalai – and Szalai told Schmidthuber that he had been ordered by Wallenberg to remind him that he would face prosecution for war crimes if he destroyed the ghetto. Schmidthuber backed off.

You write that to a certain extent it was Wallenberg's acting abilities that helped him save Jews.

Yes, he spoke German fluently and he was a very creative and artistic person. So he often played theater with German officers and Arrow Crossers, shouting at them in German and giving orders. And it worked. Many times he gained respect when he acted like that.

During the Holocaust most people either didn't care about the extermination of European Jewry or didn't want to endanger themselves by getting involved. How do you explain Wallenberg being such an exception?

In December 1942, when knowledge of the Holocaust started to be very clear, Sweden began stretching out its hand to Jews fleeing neighboring countries. In 1943, Sweden's borders were totally open to all 8,000 Danish Jews threatened with imminent deportation. Earlier Sweden had closed its borders and even asked Germany to stamp Jewish passports with a clear "J." But Sweden changed – and quite early compared to other countries – so when Wallenberg was sent on this rescue mission he was acting with the Swedish government's consent.

The second thing to keep in mind is that Wallenberg was not an ordinary Swede. He had lived abroad for five years, including three and a half years in the United States and four or five months in Haifa in Palestine. That's crucial because in Haifa he lived in a colony of German Jews who had fled persecution. So when he came back to Sweden in 1936, he had insight into what was going on in Germany that was different from that of most Swedes.

He also looked upon himself more as a world citizen. His friends at the time described him as a person with a special international flair, and it's clear that he saw what was happening to the Jews in Germany in a way that the ordinary Swede maybe did not. Most people saw a problem, but it wasn't *their* problem. Raoul Wallenberg was inclined to automatically see the "us" in the problem. He identified with European Jews because he had been in Haifa, had a lot of friends there, and had searched his own heritage and found a small microscopic part of his blood that was Jewish. He was one-sixteenth Jewish, but in the 1930s he told his friends he was a quarter Jewish or half Jewish. He was very proud of that.

After a half year in Hungary saving lives, Wallenberg in January 1945 approached the invading Soviets, who promptly arrested him. Why?

I'm not so surprised they arrested him. I'm more surprised they never let him go. There were a lot of suspicions surrounding Raoul Wallenberg's actions in Budapest. To start with, his mission was a collaboration between Sweden and the United States, and Stalin had started to become very suspicious of the United States. He thought the Western allies had tried to make a separate peace with Germany without the Soviet Union, and the name Wallenberg had been linked to those peace negotiations because Wallenberg's father's cousins had been secret messengers between the German opposition and the Western allies. This is, I think, a very important reason for the arrest.

Additionally, Soviet spies in Budapest saw the enormous size of this rescue mission and reported back home that Wallenberg was not a normal diplomat and that there were strange things going on with all those Schutzpasses. Also, from a diplomatic point of view, Wallenberg overstepped a lot when it came to contacts with the Arrow Crossers and the Nazis. He had three telephone numbers for Adolf Eichmann in his telephone book, for example. Because of his goal to save people, he allowed himself contacts that were looked upon by the Soviets as very suspicious.

According to the Russians' current version of events, Wallenberg died in prison of a heart attack in 1947. But in your book you argue convincingly that they are lying. Interestingly, when you asked the archivist of Russian intelligence services in 2011 if Wallenberg died of a heart attack in 1947, he said, "Yes, at least for now" – which is a peculiar answer.

[Laughs] Yes, very Russian.

There's an interesting internal document from 1956 in which officers at the Foreign Ministry in Moscow are ordered to look through the archives of prison hospitals to find some kind of disease that the Swedes could be told Wallenberg died from. Originally the suggestion was to tell them Wallenberg had *pneumonia* and died in *Lefortovo* prison in 1947. Later they came up with another answer – that he died of a *heart attack* in *Lubyanka* prison.

But why didn't the Soviets just let him go? Why did they need to kill him or imprison him for decades as some people believe they did? Was it just too embarrassing to release him at a certain point?

We don't know for sure, but I think the answer is to be found in the Swedish attitude toward Stalin at the time. The Swedish diplomats were the first to believe the Soviet disinformation campaign, so already in 1945 there was an informal conviction inside the Foreign Ministry in Stockholm that Wallenberg was dead – that he died in Budapest in an accident or something like that. And that influenced the way the Swedish government acted.

You could say the Swedish foreign policy after the war was to keep Stalin in a good mood, and to ask questions about Raoul Wallenberg was of course not to please Stalin. And in the end this lack of action or lack of will was interpreted by the Soviet government as Sweden not wanting Wallenberg back. And if Sweden didn't want him back, what could they do? He had already seen too much.

To end on a happier note: What do you consider to be the lesson of Raoul Wallenberg's life?

He was a person of action. When faced with what was happening to the Jews, he was not satisfied with formulating beautiful words on what needed to be done. He went into action and made things happen. So the lesson is that when there's a crime against humanity, the world has a responsibility to take action, but that responsibility needs to be taken up by individual people.

— originally published March 30, 2016

Postscript: *Ingrid Carlberg is currently working on a new book on Alfred Nobel and the Nobel Prize.*

Andrew Nagorski

Profiling Nazi Hunters

Major Wilhelm Trapp, who led one of the most notorious Nazi killing squads in Poland, once said to his driver, "If this Jewish business is ever avenged on earth, then have mercy on us Germans."

Most Nazis never did meet justice on this earth. That even a few did is largely thanks to a small group of individuals – both Jews and non-Jews – who refused to forget and forgive. They are the subject of a new book, *The Nazi Hunters*, by award-winning journalist and author Andrew Nagorski. The book will be available in bookstores on May 10.

The Jewish Press: What was the immediate reaction of Jews to their Nazi tormentors after the Holocaust?

Nagorski: Many people had a natural urge to seek vengeance. But that pretty quickly transformed into an impulse, not for vengeance, but for justice. They felt there had to be individual accountability and there had to be a record of what had happened because the greatest fear of many survivors was that the world would quickly forget or even deny its existence.

The Allies tried a number of Nazi leaders after World War II but soon soured on holding trials and even commuted the sentences of several Nazis who had already been convicted. Why?

At first there was the question: What do you do with these people? Stalin suggested we take out a whole bunch of them and have them shot. Then there was talk of trials, but Churchill was reluctant because he was afraid they would be show trials. The Americans, though, said we have to show that these people are responsible.

So that was implemented in the Nuremberg and Dachau trials. But with the advent of the Cold War, both the Soviets and the Americans were much more concerned about recruiting German scientists and getting West Germany or East Germany lined up on their side, so there was a lot of pressure to commute some of these sentences and stop some of the trials.

In the book you write about the Adolf Eichmann trial at some length and note that some prominent individuals – Isaiah Berlin and Erich Fromm, for example – were morally opposed to Israel trying him. What was their argument?

Many people said it was going to look like vengeance. But Ben-Gurion's government felt it needed this for internal consumption as much as anything else. Gabriel Bach, who is the last surviving member of the team that prosecuted Eichmann, told me there was almost a feeling of shame about the Holocaust in Israel, especially among the younger generation. They didn't understand how Jews could go "like sheep to the slaughter."

The Eichmann trial gave Israel a chance to educate a whole generation about how the Holocaust transpired – how Jews were deceived at every turn, how it was impossible in most cases to resist, and how when there were possibilities to resist, people did.

Several years after the Eichmann trial, Israel pursued and killed Nazi-collaborator Herbert Cukurs, who was known as the "Butcher of Riga." Why didn't they try him like they did Eichmann?

Cukurs had escaped to Latin America, and in 1965 someone posing as an Austrian businessman lured him to a house in Uruguay where a group of Mossad agents standing only in their underwear – so that no blood would get on their clothes – killed him. They then left a note saying this was vengeance for what he did.

This operation has always been cloaked in mystery since this was not the way the Mossad normally operated. When I talked to Rafi Eitan, who was the Mossad agent on the Eichmann case, his only explanation was that it must have been something personal. Maybe the parents of someone high up in the Mossad died at the hands of Cukurs.

After Eichmann, number one on the list of many Nazi hunters was Dr. Josef Mengele. He somehow managed to elude their grasp, though. Can you talk a bit about Mengele and the efforts to find him?

He was known as the "Angel of Death" and was a particularly vicious person who sent countless Jews to their deaths and conducted really horrible experiments on people, especially twins.

After catching Eichmann, the Israelis made some efforts to find Mengele. A couple of agents were on his trail – one of them thinks he may have even seen Mengele walking on a country path – but then they were called away to work on a child custody case [the Yossele Schumacher affair].

Mengele drowned off the coast of Brazil in 1979, and his remains were definitively identified in 1985.

In addition to describing Israel's forays into Nazi hunting, you profile a number of individual Nazi hunters in your book, including Simon Wiesenthal. Wiesenthal is somewhat of a polarizing figure among Nazi hunters, with some regarding him as a hero and others as a publicity-seeking hound. What's your take?

Even those who quarreled with Wiesenthal – including, most famously, Isser Harel, the head of the Mossad – give him credit for pressuring governments to put Nazi war criminals on trial, especially in the 1950s and '60s when most governments were turning away from this whole issue.

He kept up the momentum when it could've died and, with it, the whole era of Nazi-hunting. The fact that we have trials of elderly Auschwitz guards in Germany today is to a large extent the product of the early efforts of Nazi hunters – Wiesenthal foremost among them – not to allow the public to forget.

Perhaps the most interesting Nazi hunters featured in your book are Serge and Beate Klarsfeld. Can you talk a bit about them?

They are a fascinating couple. Beate, who isn't Jewish, was born in Germany. Her father served in the Wehrmacht, and when she was growing up, her parents didn't speak much about the war or the Holocaust. When she was about 20, though, she went to Paris to strike out on her own and met her husband, Serge, whose father had died in Auschwitz. At that point, Beate started discovering what had happened during the war and became this really radical Nazi hunter.

One of her more brazen actions took place in 1968 when she was so outraged that the German chancellor – Kurt Georg Kiesinger – had been a member of the Nazi party that she got a press pass to the Christian Democrats' convention, walked up to the chancellor, and slapped him in the face.

Later, as a couple, the Klarsfelds went after top Nazis – most prominently Klaus Barbie – who had served in occupied France and was responsible for the murder of [tens of thousands of] Jews. They personally tracked Klaus Barbie down in Latin America and kept up the pressure on the French government to have him extradited and put on trial. He was, in fact, ultimately put on trial and died in prison.

A 94-year-old Auschwitz guard, Reinhold Hanning, is currently being tried in Germany for his role in the Holocaust. Some people wonder if putting such an elderly man on trial for crimes he committed 75 years ago makes sense. How do contemporary Nazi hunters see it?

Each of these cases is seen as a way to bear witness to what happened. And since there are only a few of these people left – just as there are fewer and fewer Holocaust survivors left – these cases become even more important. Individual testimonies are the most powerful tool to educate the world about what happened.

It's interesting, by the way, that the German courts have finally accepted something they did not accept before. Today, you no longer have to prove that an individual Nazi killed or tortured a specific person. It's enough just to show that his role was essential for the mass killing. So if you served as a guard in Auschwitz, for example, you were part of the killing machinery and can be held accountable.

Once this legal principle [was accepted in 2011], Germany started looking through the records of Auschwitz guards and other guards to see who was still alive, who was mentally capable, and who was in Germany. That's where the Reinhold Hanning trial originated.

— originally published April 27, 2016

Postscript: *Andrew Nagorski is currently conducting research for a new book whose working title is "1941: The Year Germany Lost the War." If all goes well, it should be out in 2019, he said.*

As for Reinhold Hanning: He was convicted in June 2016 and sentenced to five years in jail. He appealed, however, and died on May 30, 2017, never having served a day behind bars. Nonetheless, Nagorski told me in April 2017 that Hanning's conviction "was a very positive thing" as it "reinforced the point that living to an old age doesn't absolve you of guilt."

God vs. the USSR

Rabbi Hillel Zaltzman

Recalling Years of Terror Behind the Iron Curtain

"Persecution of the Jewish people." When young Jews hear these words, they tend to think of events like the Crusades, the Inquisition, and the Holocaust. If you were to tell them fierce oppression of millions of Jews occurred during the 1950s and '60s as well, many would no doubt regard you with a certain degree of puzzlement.

And yet, the fact is that while Jews in postwar America were living in the lap of luxury, their brethren in the Soviet Union were still being terrorized for such "sins" as keeping Shabbos and teaching Torah. In his memoir, *Samarkand: The Underground With a Far-Reaching Impact*, Rabbi Hillel Zaltzman, a 76-year-old Lubavitcher *chassid*, provides insight into the struggles he and other Jews experienced trying to observe Judaism under a government that considered the practice of religion counter-revolutionary.

Rabbi Zaltzman, who left the USSR in 1971, is currently president of Chamah, an organization devoted to helping Jews from the former Soviet Union. He is being honored this week in Washington, DC, as part of American Jewish Heritage Month.

The Jewish Press: You grew up Samarkand, the third largest city in modern-day Uzbekistan. How did your family wind up there?

Rabbi Zaltzman: I was born in Kharkov, Ukraine, but when the Nazis approached Kharkov in World War II, we were told on the radio that we should escape. So my parents decided to go to Samarkand and Tashkent, which is where many Jews found refuge.

You write that your defiance of the Soviet Union began as a boy when it came time to attend school. How so?

The schools in the Soviet Union wanted to build a personality. They used to call it a "Homo Sovietica," a Soviet personality. No religion, no beliefs, no parents – if you saw your parents practicing religion, you had to tell the school. There was no private education. The whole Soviet Union was based on Marxism and Leninism, which is against any religion.

My father was scared I would lose my *Yiddishkeit* if he enrolled me in school. So he hid me and my brother at home so that the neighbors shouldn't see us and tell the government. For years, I'd walk out with a school briefcase in the morning and go to a friend's house and then come back in the afternoon after school.

How long did that last?

Until I was nine. Local school officials used to go from house to house looking for children, and one day the neighbors reported there was a child in our home. The government found out I wasn't going to school for religious reasons, so they told my father, "We'll take away your son and send him to a foster home for reeducation."

So my father went to a school in a neighborhood with no Jews and told the teacher, "My son is a sick boy who must relax two days a week – Saturday and Sunday." He also gave her a gift, and that worked for a year until they realized something was wrong and demanded that I come to school on Shabbos.

Did you?

No, never. My father tried to convince me. He said, "You're not bar mitzvah yet. They're going to arrest me and take you to a foster home. It will be much worse. Just go. You won't be forced to write."

But I didn't want to go. I woke up early Shabbos morning and went to a friend's house. So my father decided to take me to another school. It's a long story, but after a few years I managed to stop attending school without the government noticing.

The heart of your memoir revolves around the secret Jewish community you belonged to in Samarkand. Can you describe this community?

As an example, we had a secret *minyan* on Shabbos. There was an official shul in Samarkand, but I never went to it. We weren't allowed. If a child under 18 went, they would close it up. Bringing up children in the Jewish faith was considered religious propaganda. They would arrest you. Most of the people in that shul were KGB agents.

So we would *daven* secretly. We would select a house situated in a non-visible area – but never the same place two weeks in a row because the amount of traffic would be suspicious. When I approached the house, if I saw a neighbor nearby, I wouldn't enter. I'd walk around the block. If I saw another member of the *minyan* nearby, I'd also walk around the block, or he'd walk around, and then come back two or three minutes later.

You write that you wouldn't even tell your closest friends or relatives about some of the underground Jewish activities in Samarkand. Why not?

Because you never knew who would be called to the KGB. We had a yeshiva at my brother's house. When my father came to the house, though, they tried to hide it from him. We had a rule growing up: What I don't have to know, please don't tell me. The KGB can't get something out of me that I don't know. People say this was heroic, but we didn't feel heroic. This was the regular way of life we were used to from the day we were born. When I met Rav Moshe Feinstein after I left the Soviet Union, he asked me, "How were you able to live like that?" I said, "Did we have another choice?" and Rav Moshe broke out crying. He understood. He was a Russian Jew himself.

You write that the overwhelming majority of Orthodox Jews in the Soviet Union ultimately succumbed to the communist campaign to stamp out religion from society.

Yes, there was persecution, and there was no community structure in the Soviet Union. Parents were afraid to educate their children at home because they would tell their friends. When I was in Kiev in the 1960s and asked some older Jews where I could *daven*, they were shocked that someone my age *davened* and spoke Yiddish. It was unheard of.

You write that you visited a *chassid* in the 1960s who was so isolated from Jewish life that he didn't know – *in the mid-1960s* – who had succeeded the fifth Lubavitcher Rebbe who had passed away *in 1920*. Were there no Jewish newspapers at all? Was the persecution that total?

That was Reb Itche Garelik, who was one of the first teachers in the yeshiva in Lubavitch. He didn't know anything going on in the Jewish world.

I remember I once managed to get hold of an Agudas Yisroel magazine in Moscow and was stopped by a government official in Lvov. I thought it was the end of me since the magazine was published in America. It was an open miracle that he didn't find the magazine in my suitcase.

You have a fascinating story in your book about a *chassid* named Reb Berke Chein who hid in your house for five years, separated from his wife and children. Can you share?

He tried escaping the Soviet Union in 1946 with false papers, but was caught and fled to Samarkand. My parents told us a Jew was coming to the house who didn't have a place to sleep and no one should know he was there. And this is the way he lived in our house for five years. My mother told him, "Berke, your wife doesn't know you're alive. You have to tell her." He said, "No, never. Maybe she'll be called by the KGB and interrogated. She doesn't want to know, believe me."

For five years, he never left the house except at night – even to go to the bathroom, which was outside the house. He used a chamber pot, which my mother would discreetly empty while he was *davening*.

You lived during Stalin's infamous Doctors' Plot of 1953. What was the atmosphere like at the time?

It was a very terrible time. Stalin was crazy. He announced that a group of Politburo doctors planned to kill the highest Soviet rulers, and every day there were articles in the newspaper identifying the doctors as Jewish. People would beat up Jews in the street and police would say, "Don't touch them, we'll soon kill them all."

The plan was to hang the doctors in Red Square in March 1953, after which the people would vent their anger against "the enemies of the Soviet Union" – the Jews. Then Stalin, "the father of humanity," would step in to protect the Jews and send them to Siberia. There were three million Jews in the Soviet Union. One million would be killed in pogroms, one million would die on their way to Siberia, and one million would stay there. But then Stalin suddenly died on March 5.

Were Jews really scared?

We thought this was the end! My father bought some china for *Pesach*, and my aunt said, "What are you doing? We have to buy food for the road to Siberia. How will we survive?"

How did you finally get out of the Soviet Union?

There was already a little more freedom in the late 1960s. I tried to leave for 14 years and finally in 1971 the government said yes.

Why did they say yes?

Nobody knew their policy. Some they let go, some not.

What's your view of Russia today?

The whole world is against Putin, but I am 100 percent for him. He's a dictator, but I would say he loves Jews. In his book he writes about his Jewish karate teacher, and he's the hero in the book. You see how much freedom he gives the Jews, how he invites the chief rabbi of Russia, Rabbi Berel Lazar, to the Kremlin. Nobody can deny his good relationship to the Jews. What else should we ask for? That Russia be a democracy and some anti-Semite be elected?

— originally published May 25, 2016

Rabbi David Hill

Stoking Embers Under the KGB's Watch

With almost all of world Jewry located in liberal democracies today, it's easy to forget that a mere 25 years ago, 1.5 million Jews lived under a totalitarian Soviet regime that suppressed Judaism. In the Soviet Union, even procuring a *siddur* or Jewish calendar could be a clandestine affair filled with fear.

This history is not unknown, but in a recently published memoir, *Serving the Jewish People: My Message to the Generations*, Rabbi David Hill adds his personal perspective as an American Soviet Jewry activist. A nonagenarian today, Rabbi Hill served as vice chair of the National Conference on Soviet Jewry and ran Operation Lifeline, which sent American Jews behind the Iron Curtain to teach Torah and distribute religious articles.

Rabbi Hill also headed the National Council of Young Israel from 1961-1965 and was president for several decades of the Real Kosher Sausage Company, popularly known as "999."

The Jewish Press: How did you get involved in helping Soviet Jewry?

Rabbi Hill: Around 1960, I met with Golda Meir, and she wondered why nothing was being done in America about Soviet Jewry. I told her I would make it my priority.

And that led to Operation Lifeline?

Operation Lifeline started after I met the Lubavitcher Rebbe a few times. I was the first person whom he allowed his followers to give names and addresses. After all, you just couldn't go to Russia and say, "Who's a Jew? I want to help you." But Lubavitcher *chassidim* were spread throughout the entire country. They were the only ones who kept any sort of *Yiddishkeit* alive from the time of the Bolshevik Revolution. The Lubavitcher Rebbe instructed his *chassidim* to keep working and build an underground until help came from the outside.

Was it dangerous to send American Jews to the Soviet Union to teach Torah?

Absolutely. If the KGB caught them teaching Torah or anything that had to do with the history of our people, they could be arrested. Whatever we did in visiting the refuseniks was illegal, but we were extremely fortunate in that no harm was done to those we visited.

The KGB wasn't stupid. It must have known what you were doing. Why, then, did it allow your people to come into the Soviet Union?

Because they were hungry for the dollar. They knew what we were doing, but somehow from all the years that I sent travelers to Russia, on only one occasion did they [kick] someone out.

When you visited the Soviet Union in 1981, you met Rabbi Abraham Meller, whom you describe as the last student of the Chofetz Chaim. What were your impressions of him?

He could not teach Torah publicly, so he would walk with his students on the street and teach them as they walked. He was a person with a great amount of not only knowledge but also humility. The only thing he wanted from me was more paper and pens and kosher food so he could have something kosher for *Shabbat*.

In all your years of activism on behalf of Soviet Jewry, which American president would you say was the most helpful?

Ford was helpful. But Reagan, with Secretary of State George Shultz, was the most helpful. When Reagan first met with Gorbachev, human rights was on the lower part of the agenda. But it eventually became the number one issue, and that was due to Secretary Shultz. Gorbachev said to Reagan, "Let's address arms," and Reagan said, "No, human rights first."

You have an interesting story in your book – albeit unrelated to your Soviet Jewry activities – concerning President Carter's national security adviser, Zbigniew Brzezinski. Can you share?

When Carter was signing the Panama Canal Treaty, he wanted the clergy in this country to give him support, so I was invited. When I met Brzezinski in the White House, I asked him, "Do you believe in the Old Testament?" He said, "Of course." I said, "Well, in the Book of Genesis you have the boundaries of the state of Israel." The minute I said that, he picked himself up and walked away.

Many years later when we invited Brzezinski to a national conference on Soviet Jewry in Washington, he came over to me and said, "Were you the one who asked me that question?" I said, "I didn't think you remembered." He said, "I never forgot it."

You were president of the National Council of Young Israel from 1961-1965, yet you write in the book that you are displeased with the organization today. Why?

Because they turned to the right. When I was president, and even a short time thereafter, we had national conventions that attracted over a thousand people. Prior to Lubavitch, it was Young Israel in the 1930s, '40s, and early '50s that did work in *kiruv,* attracting young people.

In what sense did Young Israel move to the right?

I'll give you an example. There was a rally that was called for by the OU in the 1990s, and they asked Young Israel to participate. To bring in greater numbers, they also asked Agudah to participate, but Agudah insisted that no prayer for Israel or the soldiers be made. And as much as I objected, Young Israel gave in. That was unforgiveable.

As someone who is, thank God, over 90 years old, what would you say has been the most important value you've carried through your life?

The concept of *hakaras hatov* – to recognize that when something good is done to you, you should have the ability to say thank you. My thank you was to the Almighty God who rescued my family from Europe, and, at a very young age, I decided that I had a debt to pay back.

Is there any message you would like to impart to the younger generation?

Read Jewish history. If you do, you will find that more miracles have happened to the Jewish people in the last 70-odd years than in the previous 2,000. Our prophets proclaimed in the name of God, "I will gather you amongst the nations and bring you back home." We are the generation [referred to in that prophecy] – mine, yours, and the ones to come. Young people must understand the beauty and history of our people to see what they can contribute to the future.

— originally published July 3, 2013

Rabbi Avi Weiss

Reminiscing on the Struggle to Free Soviet Jewry

Rabbi Avi Weiss is best known today for his controversial religious views and activities. Until 1999, however, it was his political activism that defined him, landing him in jail dozens of times – perhaps most famously in 1989 after he and fellow activists donned concentration camp clothing and scaled the walls of a convent that had been erected at Auschwitz.

In a new book, *Open Up the Iron Door: Memoirs of a Soviet Jewry Activist,* Rabbi Weiss reminiscences about his two decades fighting to free Soviet Jewry. The Jewish Press recently interviewed him on this topic.

The Jewish Press: In *Open Up the Iron Door,* you write, "Some of my proudest achievements as an activist were accomplished because I was naïve." What do you mean by that?

Rabbi Weiss: When you stand up for causes that are right but which are not popular at their inception, it takes a certain naiveté to really believe you're going to be victorious.

Also, in regards to the Soviet Jewry movement, only someone with youthful naiveté, vitality, and idealism could believe that he or she could go toe to toe with the powerful Soviet Union and win.

You were on the front lines protesting for Soviet Jewry. What do you

say to those who argue that public protest was counter-productive – that it only made the Soviet Union less inclined to allow its Jews to emigrate?

Whatever we were able to accomplish was with God's help. But on the human level, public protest played a very central role. And that's not my position – it's the position of historians who are experts in this area.

In the book, I talk about the differences Soviet activists had with Agudah and Chabad in particular. I also write about a debate I had with Rabbi Pinchas Teitz – one of the most important figures in Agudah – who was very much opposed to public protest. But on Solidarity Day, when hundreds of thousands of people gathered every year, Rabbi Moshe David Tendler would read a statement from his father-in-law, Rabbi Moshe Feinstein, sending his blessings. So even in Agudah there were those who believed public protest was important.

Fully one-third of your book is devoted to Natan Sharansky's wife, Avital, whom you call "the greatest activist of the latter half of the twentieth century." What makes her so great in your eyes?

One of the major goals of an activist is to inspire others to become involved, and that's exactly what she did. And she did it in a very unusual way. Most activists and leaders are loud and, frankly, pompous. Avital is the reverse. She's very humble, and her leadership reflects the teaching in *Tanach* that God's voice is not in the thunder or the lightning or the earthquake. It's in the *kol damama daka,* the still small voice. Avital would speak softly, and precisely because she spoke softly, sincerely, and humbly, her voice had the strength to inspire millions of people to become involved.

Avital was also able to work with the establishment while, at the same time, refusing to become co-opted by the establishment. That was quite extraordinary.... It hurts me to say this, but, in the beginning, the Israeli government was not pro-Sharansky. There were even those in the government who encouraged Avital to split from him after he was sentenced.

Why?

Because Natan was not only a great Zionist; he was also the head of

Helsinki Watch, which spoke out for human rights in the Soviet Union. The Israeli government felt that the person representing the Soviet Jewry movement should be someone who was committed only to Zionism.

At the end of the book, you argue that the Jewish community honored the wrong people for freeing Soviet Jewry. How so?

When communism fell, there was a tremendous push to honor Gorbachev. But honoring Gorbachev is like giving an honor to Pharaoh for letting *Am Yisrael* go.

Henry Kissinger was also honored. Kissinger is on tape in the '70s saying that even if Jews in the Soviet Union were put in gas chambers, it's not an American problem. My parents were close to people who knew Kissinger's parents. And they were quoted as saying, "We have much respect from our son, but little *nachas*."

The Soviet Jewry cause was a movement of all of *Am Yisrael* who stood up for their brothers and sisters behind the Iron Curtain. But the real heroes were those in the former Soviet Union itself – people like Natan Sharansky, Yosef Mendelevich, and Boris Kochubiyevsky.

As an activist, you often clashed with the Jewish establishment. Can you elaborate?

We believed in non-violent civil disobedience. There was a whole campaign at one point for rabbis to get arrested on behalf of Soviet Jewry, called Operation Redemption. The establishment, by and large, opposed that.

There were also many in the establishment who opposed Yaakov Birnbaum [founder of the Student Struggle for Soviet Jewry] when he introduced the idea that the American government should be criticized for not doing enough to pressure the Soviets.

Another major difference had to do with the Jackson-Vanik amendment, which linked freedom of immigration to better trade with the United States and was critical in freeing Soviet Jewry. There were some key establishment leaders who were opposed to it.

Why?

Those closest to President Nixon were opposed to it because the American government feared it threatened détente. And when you're close to the president, you're vulnerable to pressure. The president says, "I don't want this amendment" or "Listen, I know what's best, I'm telling you that the Jackson-Vanik amendment is going to hurt Soviet Jewry." One of my rules of activism, though, is: Never trust someone who says, "Trust me."

Are you still involved in political activism?

Yes, very much so. If somebody asks what my life was about, I hope people will answer, "This was a man who loved Jews." If you love Jews, how can you not be involved in political activism? And that's one of the reasons I wrote this book. I hope people will read it and say to themselves, "You know what? I can make a difference, too, with God's help."

— originally published July 8, 2015

Skewering the Left

David Horowitz

Exposing Terrorism-Friendly Universities

Many Jews know that anti-Israel sentiment is rampant on American university campuses. Few, however, would call these universities "terrorist-friendly." Conservative activist David Horowitz has no such compunctions. Last month he released a report through his David Horowitz Freedom Center on the "Ten Top American Universities Most Friendly to Terrorists." The list includes Brandeis, Columbia, and Harvard.

In addition to heading the Freedom Center, Horowitz – who once identified as a radical leftist – is the editor of FrontPage Magazine, the director of Discover the Networks, and the author or co-author of some 60 books, including *Unholy Alliance: Radical Islam and the American Left*, *Indoctrination U.: The Left's War Against Academic Freedom*, and *Destructive Generation: Second Thoughts About the '60s*.

The Jewish Press: When you call a university "friendly to terrorists," what do you mean?

Horowitz: We have groups on American campuses led by Students for Justice in Palestine – which is a Hamas front – and the Muslim Students Association – which is a Muslim Brotherhood front – that are promoting terrorist propaganda.

Muslim Students Association and Students for Justice in Palestine sponsor Israel Apartheid Week and erect giant apartheid walls which pay tribute to terrorists like Sheikh Yassin, who was the founder of Hamas and responsible for over 390 murders. They also feature a four-panel map created by Hamas, which shows the entire Israel in green – calling it Palestine and dating it 1947 – and then purports to show how Jews infiltrated the Palestinian state, which is of course a big lie.

They also chant, "From the river to the sea, Palestine will be free." Well, the river is the Jordan and the sea is the Mediterranean. Those are the east and west boundaries of the state of Israel. So what they're really chanting is, "Death to Israel."

This wouldn't be tolerated by universities if it were directed against a black African state or a Muslim state. But because it's Jews, it's okay. And that's what our campaign is designed to confront. These groups are funded by the universities. They get student funds, and they have offices in the student union buildings.

You've pointed out that the heads of these groups have sometimes gone on to become actual terrorists. Anwar al-Awlaki – an al Qaeda leader in Yemen killed by the U.S. in 2011 – is perhaps the most famous example.

Anwar al-Awlaki was the president of the Muslim Students Association at Colorado State University. There are a dozen former presidents of Muslim Students Association who have gone on to high-level careers in al Qaeda and other terrorist groups.

On your list of terrorist-friendly universities is Brandeis, which some people might find surprising considering its reputation as something of a Jewish university.

Well, if you've been to Brandeis as I have several times, you would know it's a left-wing university and the political left is a supporter of terrorists and Jew haters. The main source of anti-Semitism in this country is the Left and its Muslim allies. So Brandeis is not a pleasant place politically. Like most universities, its liberal arts faculty is imbued with this anti-American, anti-Israel, anti-Western, anti-white, anti-Christian mentality.

I've been on 400 campuses. I can tell you, it's the same everywhere. I did a speaking tour last spring and I was confronted by people cheering Hamas. Hamas is a Nazi organization. In its charter, it calls for the extermination of the Jews. So we have open supporters of genocidal Nazis – and I include Fatah in that too. The Palestinians are worse than Nazi Germany because Hitler hid the Final Solution and many Germans didn't know his intentions. But the Palestinian leaders shout it from the rooftops, and yet there's no outrage.

We're really the only group that's been willing to conduct a campaign like this. Hillel defends the Muslim Students Association.

Why?

You have to ask Hillel. Even conservative Jewish groups are afraid to confront Students for Justice in Palestine and the Muslim Students Association the way I do because they're afraid of being denounced as Islamophobes and racists, and that will hurt their college careers.

Intimidation is a very powerful weapon. There's a professor who admitted that he won't be as critical of Muslims as he is of other groups because he's physically afraid for his family. Not that he's been directly threatened. He doesn't have to be. You see these people; they love violence. You have Jews being stabbed in the street in Jerusalem and Students for Justice in Palestine is cheering the terrorists on.

Some of the entries on your terror-friendly university list are not surprising. For example, you have three universities from California, which is the home of many liberals...

...They're not liberal! *I'm* a liberal. I believe in two sides to a question. They're not liberals. They're leftists, they're totalitarian. When I go to a campus, I have to face down demonstrators inside the lecture halls trying to shout me down and shut me up. I'm a liberal. I believe in liberty. These people don't. They want to suppress any opposition to their genocidal agendas.

How did the University of New Mexico get on your list? New

Mexico doesn't seem a likely place for radical Muslim activism.

The liberal arts faculties of all these universities are communists, and I say that advisedly – my parents were communists. I know what a communist is. They believe in suppressing opposition. That's why 90 percent of professors on liberal arts faculties are on the Left. How is that possible in a country which is pretty evenly divided? It's because they're totalitarian. They don't want a conservative voice on campus.

Columbia and Harvard are also on your list. How do you explain students at such high-IQ universities believing such blatant lies about the Jewish state?

Because it's a religion. There are lots of smart members of the Muslim Brotherhood too. Smarts have nothing to do with being moral or politically astute. You can be brilliant and be a Nazi.

You mentioned that your parents were communists. How did you go from being the son of communists to where you are today?

I wrote a book called *Radical Son,* which describes it all, but it came down to a murder. The Black Panther Party murdered a friend of mine and the Left defended the murderers. And then I saw how we succeeded – "we," meaning the Left, since I was a leader of the New Left – in getting America to withdraw from Vietnam, and then the communists, who are the Left's friends, slaughtered two and half million Cambodians and Vietnamese with no protests. That's how I got off the boat.

What do you want readers to do with the information you provide in this report on terrorism and universities?

Well, I wish more people had the courage to stand up and start calling things by their right names. I think it was Confucius who said that in order to start rectifying the world you have to call things by their right names. These groups are mouthpieces for terrorists on our campuses, and they're being supported by the universities.

I want people to have the courage to confront these universities, confront their board of trustees, confront the heads of alumni organizations. America is a free country. As I said, I'm a true liberal and I believe that people have the right to say even hateful things. But the university has no obligation to provide offices for these groups or to provide funding out of student funds for their genocidal attacks on Jews. No university would do that if it were blacks, Hispanics, or Muslims who were the targets.

— originally published November 18, 2015

Postscript: *David Horowitz has since published three more books, including "Progressive Racism" and "Big Agenda: President Trump's Plan to Save America."*

Stephen Norwood

Unmasking the Left's Anti-Semitic Past

On September 5, 2012, at the Democratic National Convention, chairman Antonio Villaraigosa asked those assembled if they approved of an amendment to the Democratic Party platform affirming Jerusalem as Israel's capital. Half the crowd – if not more – shouted, "No!"

This reaction surprised many American Jews, but, as Stephen Norwood documents in his new book, *Antisemitism and the American Far Left* (Cambridge University Press), antipathy toward Jews and Zionism on the political left has a long history, dating back more than a century. Norwood, a professor of History and Judaic Studies at the University of Oklahoma, recently discussed this topic with The Jewish Press.

The Jewish Press: How do you explain the popularity of anti-Semitism and anti-Israel sentiment on the far left?

Norwood: There's a long tradition of it going back to the middle of the 19th century. Oddly, a lot of the far left outlook closely resembles traditional Christian theological anti-Semitism in the sense that Jews are perceived as an archaic group rigidly adhering to an outmoded sterile religion and speaking languages that are obsolete.

There's also the issue of accusing the Jews of being excessively materialistic and exploitative of non-Jews. You see a lot of that in far-left propaganda – that the Jews are overwhelmingly concentrated in the petty bourgeoisie, which in itself is an archaic class form, and thrives on tricking people and squeezing money out of them through illicit methods of trade.

If you look at the Christian Bible, you see a very similar type of outlook. And this Christian theological anti-Semitism is so deeply embedded in Western culture that the far left has really never escaped its influence.

Nowadays, the far left often portrays Israel as the aggressor in its fight with Arab terrorism. You write in your book that this practice actually hails all the way back to the 1929 Chevron massacre, which American communists apparently supported.

Yes, the Communist Party endorsed the pogroms. The Daily Worker, which was the Communist Party newspaper in the United States, not only endorsed them but printed cartoons that reflected Christian theological anti-Semitism stereotypes of Jews – like a cross in the background with bodies of Arabs hanging and a fat, smiling capitalist in the foreground labeled "Zionist."

The Morgen Freiheit, which was the Yiddish-language communist newspaper in the United States, initially reacted by calling the attacks "pogroms," but because the Soviets ordered the communist parties to view them as progressive anti-colonial revolts, it switched.

The Daily Worker, though, right off the bat, viewed them as a revolutionary Arab uprising against Zionist exploiters. The Jews were labeled bourgeois imperialists and tools of British imperialism.

Despite the Soviet Union's anti-Semitism, Joseph Stalin amazingly supported the creation of the state of Israel. Why?

That was during a brief period running from 1945 or 1946 up through the end of 1948 when the Soviet Union supported the partition plan in the United Nations. Their support was critical because they brought the Soviet bloc in with them, and it helped achieve the vote total needed for the General Assembly to pass the partition resolution.

The reason for this is that the Soviets were intent on pushing the British out of the Middle East and they thought this was the best way to do it. They continued to ban Zionism within the Soviet Union, but they supported the partition plan. In 1947 and 1948, they came out openly for it and were even more supportive than the United States, which was equivocating. In fact, the most sympathetic presidential candidate to Israel in the 1948 election campaign was Henry Wallace, who was the Progressive Party candidate – and the Progressive Party was highly influenced by the communists.

You write that Wallace even criticized Harry Truman for his Middle East stance, claiming that he "talks Jewish and acts Arab."

Truman didn't support de jure recognition, only de facto recognition. He also imposed an arms embargo so Americans could get arrested for running guns to the Haganah or Irgun. So Truman was kind of equivocating....

In 1947, the Haganah had almost no weaponry to speak of – no heavy artillery, no heavy machine guns, and so on. The armaments they acquired came – with Soviet approval – from Czechoslovakia. These were obsolete weapons that the Haganah had to pay a good deal for, but nonetheless they were helpful.

In fact, many Jewish pilots, veterans of World War II from around the world, went to Czechoslovakia for flight training since Israel had no air force to speak of. English was the major language within the Israeli air force in 1948 for this reason, since these pilots were largely from America and British Commonwealth countries.

You also write interestingly that American communists aggressively protested anti-Semitism in the United States after World War II – almost at the same time that Stalin was embarking on an aggressive campaign against Jews in the Soviet Union. How do you explain that?

The communists after World War II believed that a fascist takeover was imminent in America. This was what they called the "five minutes to midnight line," and they felt they would have to go underground. They also believed that anti-Semitism was a feature of a new fascism and that they had to combat it.

So when the film "Oliver Twist" was released in the British zone of occupation in Germany in 1948, the communists protested vehemently and even aggressively demonstrated at theaters where it was being shown, saying that it was offensive to Jews. They also denounced the U.S. government for being too slow in moving Jews out of the DP camps, many of which were former Nazi concentration camps where they were held behind barbed wire. And they also picketed the movie "The Desert Fox" in 1951, which they saw as glorifying the Nazi general Rommel. They took the lead in some places in doing that.

At the same time, they claimed there was no anti-Semitism in the Soviet Union because the Soviet Union had made it illegal, as if that were the end of the discussion. They also pointed out that the Soviets had established an autonomous Jewish region, Birobidzhan, which they claimed was a bountiful area where Jews could thrive when, in fact, Birobidzhan was this remote, swampy, heavily-forested area off on the border of Manchuria that never amounted to anything.

In 1958, in an interview with a Paris newspaper, Khrushchev finally admitted that Birobidzhan had not been a success but that was because – he said – the Jews were unable to organize themselves collectively. They were too strongly individualistic to live in a functioning society together, and, besides, they were too intellectually oriented. They argue too much, and so on.

You write a lot in the book about anti-Zionism on the American left over the last 50 years or so. Why is there so much more anti-Zionism on the political left than on the political right?

That's a very good question because it used to be the reverse. When I was growing up, it tended to be liberal Democrats who were more sympathetic to Israel, not conservative Republicans. As late as 1968, the major liberal Democrats – Bobby Kennedy, Eugene McCarthy, and Hubert Humphrey – were all very staunchly pro-Israel.

The whole civil rights leadership was also strongly supportive of Israel: Roy Wilkins, Whitney Young, Martin Luther King, A. Philip Randolph, Bayard Rustin – all solid supporters.

All of that changes really after 1968 when liberals abandon Israel. To some degree, it's the influence of Black Nationalism that was always hostile to Israel. The black nationalists didn't want any coalition with whites ("You can't trust whites"), and a way of expressing that view was to say, "The Jews" – whom everyone knew were among those most solidly behind civil rights – "are no different than other whites, or they're even worse and more racist than other whites."

And so, that outlook penetrates into the mainstream – that race is everything and people who are non-white are progressives. And somehow, the Arabs are seen as non-whites and the Israelis as white even though half of Israel's population comes from Africa and Asia.

Arabs are not exactly black, either.

No, they're not. And on top of that, when Eldridge Cleaver, the Black Panther leader, went to Algeria, he became very disillusioned, and his views changed radically when he saw a slave market in an Arab country. This goes on in Mauritania, in the Sudan – it's well documented. Everyone knows that black people are enslaved by Arabs and bought and sold as if they're animals. The Simon Wiesenthal Center had a big symposium on this in 1999 at which black people who had been slaves testified about their experiences. It's a scandal that this is going on and that people aren't paying very much attention to it.

Israel, in the meantime, has airlifted a significant population of dark-skinned Jews out of Ethiopia. In fact, I think Israel is the only country in the world that has brought black people out of Africa other than as slaves.

Ignorance is one of the big problems here. The propagandists present everything in very simplistic terms: that Arabs are non-whites – that's good

– and Israelis are whites – that's bad. But it's mystifying to me because Israeli society is very committed to principles that you would think liberals would admire: like egalitarianism, providing services to people, being committed to civil liberties, etc. That's not the case anywhere else in the Middle East. So I'm at a loss to understand why liberals have abandoned the state of Israel. But they have.

— originally published February 12, 2014

Postscript: *Dr. Norwood is currently completing a book on American and British responses to Nazism from 1930-1935.*

Ben Shapiro

Beating Liberals at Their Own Game

Call him the conservative movement's whiz kid. At age 17 he was the youngest nationally syndicated columnist in the United States. Today, 13 years later, he is a popular talk radio host, the author of six books – including a New York Times bestseller – and the editor-at-large of Breitbart.com, a major conservative news outlet.

Ben Shapiro is also an Orthodox Jew. "My parents became Orthodox when I was about 11 and, as you know, the Orthodox community tends to be disproportionately more conservative politically than the non-Orthodox community," Shapiro told The Jewish Press.

Shapiro is a graduate of Harvard Law School and has appeared numerous times on television defending Israel and conservative principles. Last year, he started his own media watchdog group – TruthRevolt.org – in an effort to "unmask leftists in the media...destroy their credibility with the American public, and devastate their funding bases."

Shapiro's latest book, published earlier this year, is *The People vs. Barack Obama: The Criminal Case Against the Obama Administration*.

The Jewish Press: Some people are struggling to write their first book at age 60. You're 30 and have already written six. How do you do it?

Shapiro: Writing always came naturally to me, thank God. From the time I was very young, I was reading incessantly, and because I was reading incessantly, I began writing incessantly. I remember trying to start my first novel on my mom's typewriter when I was maybe seven. Truth be told, if I go through a long period of time without being creative, I start to get depressed.

How do people in conservative circles react when they see your yarmulke and realize you're an Orthodox Jew? Are they fascinated? Shocked? Hostile?

There's always a bit of fascination. People are so used to hearing that Jews are leftists that they're not used to the idea of Jews being right-wing. And that's the fault of the Orthodox community, which has not taken a leadership role in defining Judaism to the public mind. The Orthodox community is more likely to shy away from political debate than leftist Jews who have no compunction about speaking out – and speaking out qua Jews – even though they really have nothing to do with Judaism and Torah....

I've never experienced anti-Semitism with folks on the Right. They're very warm and interested. I remember I was once speaking in Iowa for a Christian group and before I spoke, I was *davening* in my room. They called and asked, "How is it going?" I said, "Just give me three minutes, I have to finish *davening*." And they said, "Oh, do you have phylacteries? Can we come up and see them?" I said, "Sure." So here I was in the middle of Iowa showing evangelical Christians how to wrap *tefillin*.

You're friends with Ann Coulter, Sean Hannity, and many other conservative icons. Who among this crowd impresses you most?

I don't like the word impress with regard to my peers because it makes it sound like I'm patting them on the head, which is ridiculous since most of them are my seniors and most of them helped me when I was getting started.

But I *appreciate* people on the right side of the aisle for a variety of reasons. I appreciate Ann for her wit; I appreciate Sean for his stalwartness in the face of enormous personal attacks and his willingness to continue to maintain a certain sunny optimism despite the state of the country; I admire Mark Levin because he's a very smart guy; and I admire Rush Limbaugh for continuing to weather the storms and continuing to maintain his principles.

You were also very close with the late conservative pioneer Andrew Breitbart. What was he like?

Andrew had a whole different way of doing politics, which influenced me in certain ways. He embraced the notion that culture was an "upstream of politics." In other words, people's politics are defined by the culture – not the other way around – and therefore, he said, focusing on culture is not only not a waste of time but is actually the crux of the matter.

On that note, you argued several years ago that religious Americans should try to shape popular culture rather than shun it. But you also said in an interview with Glenn Beck that the one time you tried writing a pilot for a TV show, Hollywood producers slammed the door in your face after a Google search revealed that you were a conservative. How can conservatives shape popular culture when Hollywood is overwhelmingly liberal?

We have to build alternative methods of distribution. This is something that folks on the Right – forget religious or non-religious – have a deep problem doing. They don't believe culture is important even though they participate in it by watching it. They would prefer to sign a check to a politician – even if the politician loses – than sign a check to invest in an entertainment property even though millions of people will watch an entertainment property and nobody will remember the candidate who lost in the first congressional district in Iowa.

So it's imperative that people begin to understand the value of culture and understand they have to put their money where their mouth is. The problem is not lack of talent. There are talented people in the conservative and religious communities. It's a problem of Republican and conservative funders sitting around all day twiddling their thumbs and wondering why they're losing and then they dump another $400 million into Karl Rove's latest idiotic Super PAC, as opposed to saying, "Okay, if we spend $400 million on making some movies, or making some TV programming, or buying up some media outlets, maybe we'll shift the culture and have a shot at actual victory."

So you're talking about bypassing Hollywood?

Yes, the Internet has changed everything. I mean, look at Netflix, YouTube, and Hulu. Look at all these various online distribution mechanisms. That means the necessity for a network is dropping rapidly. The only reason my wife and I have cable is to get Fox News. For a very long time we didn't even bother with that. We had Hulu and Netflix and that was plenty for us. And that's going to be increasingly the case.

As technology moves forward, bundled cable and satellite service is going to end. You're going to be able to specifically pick which channels and programming you want to watch. You're going to be able to watch it on demand and that means you don't need to get greenlit by a network. All you have to do is pay Netflix a carriage fee basically.

In an interview on Fox News last year, you condemned ethnic studies in college – Jewish studies, black studies, Latino studies, etc. Why?

Because they're a waste of time and they fragment society along racial and ethnic lines. Most Jewish studies courses also have nothing to do with the study of actual Judaism. They tend to evolve into anything that anybody Jewish ever did at one point. I don't find that valuable. I especially don't find it valuable when these courses are funded by the state.

Orthodox Jews are generally more politically conservative than non-Orthodox Jews. Why do you think that is?

Because Jewish law and Jewish philosophy are both significantly more in line with conservatism than they are with leftism. Judaism has very strong social standards, Judaism has very strong expectations for behavior, Judaism has very strong beliefs about the values of hard work and playing by the rules, and liberalism doesn't tend to believe in any of those things. It tends to believe that consequences must be alleviated for people who make bad or immoral decisions and it tends to justify such decisions by appealing to lack of free will.

The Rambam writes that free will is the basis of all human morality as well as the Torah. That's a deeply conservative principle.

Why did you go to Harvard Law School? Was it just so that you could say, "I spent three years as a conservative in a liberal lion's den"?

If you get into Harvard Law, you don't pass it up. I finished school and I considered whether I wanted to go directly into politics or business, and my mom – who runs a television company and always regretted not getting a law degree – suggested it might be valuable to go to law school. So I took the LSATs, did well, applied to Harvard, got in, and once you get into Harvard Law, you don't say no.

Has it been an asset in politics? Of course it has because the Left only has three attacks on people on the Right in politics: you're stupid, you're corrupt, or you're evil. When you put Harvard Law on your resume, it makes it very difficult for them to use stupid, so they have to turn to corrupt and evil.

You have written that the "age of civility" in politics is over. Can you elaborate?

I'm not sure there ever was an age of civility. I think we have a tendency – politically, religiously, all over the place – to create these golden years in the past that probably didn't exist.

But the reality is that civility is less important than clarity, and, right now, only very few people on the Left are interested in having a civil conversation about the merits of particular policy solutions. They're interested in attacking you as a racist, sexist, bigot, or homophobe if you disagree with them. And you cannot deal with folks who are uncivil in a civil fashion. That's a recipe for losing. That's why Mitt Romney lost in 2012 and that's why John McCain lost in 2008.

You've also said that liberals often harbor an "undeserved sense of moral superiority." What do you mean by that?

Most people on the Left have never actually done anything to help folks they claim to have helped. The black community, for example, which the Left has claimed to have helped over the last 50 years, has not in fact been helped. The poverty rate of the black community is basically the same as it was before the War on Poverty, the illegitimacy rate is almost four times as high as it was before the War on Poverty, and the education levels are actually slightly elevated but lag dramatically behind those of other races over the past 50 years.

People on the Left will say if you oppose their education or welfare policies, you must be anti-black. Well, that's creating a sense of unearned moral superiority, and you have to strip them of that, because the reality is that not only is the Left not morally superior to the Right, in most cases the Left is morally *inferior* because of the results of the philosophies they've touted for so long.

You're on the radio six hours day. If someone wanted to listen to you, what station should he turn to?

In the morning I'm on KRLA 870 in Los Angeles from 6:00-9:00 a.m. That's a three-person show. And then I host a radio show in the afternoon in Seattle on KTTH 770 from 3:00-6:00 p.m. You can download podcasts from both shows on the Internet.

— originally published November 5, 2014

Postscript: *Ben Shapiro does not host a radio show anymore, but he does produce a daily podcast, "The Ben Shapiro Show," available on The Daily Wire, a conservative news site he founded in 2015 where he serves as editor-in-chief. Shapiro quit Breitbart in March 2016 after the news organization didn't sufficiently defend one of its reporters who had been pushed aside by then-Trump campaign manager Corey Lewandowski.*

In November 2016, he wrote his first novel, "True Allegiance."

Anti-Semitic Diversity

Dr. Manfred Gerstenfeld

Fighting 150 Million Anti-Semites in Europe

Many Jews know that Europe has witnessed a resurgence of anti-Semitism in the past decade. But how bad is it? Which countries pose the greatest threat? To what extent are Muslim immigrants influencing their host countries?

These questions and others are addressed in Dr. Manfred Gerstenfeld's latest book, *Demonizing Israel and the Jews*. In it, 57 journalists, academics, and politicians address various aspects of anti-Semitism – one chapter per person – under such headings as "The BBC: Widespread Antipathy toward Israel" and "Distorted Dutch Views of the Jews."

The Jewish Press recently spoke with Dr. Gerstenfeld.

The Jewish Press: You open your latest book by citing several polls that indicate that 40 percent of Europeans – over 150 million people – are anti-Semitic. That's an extraordinarily high figure. Can it possibly be accurate?

Dr. Gerstenfeld: I am merely quoting the numbers. The University of Bielefeld [which conducted one of the polls] has published first-rate research on discrimination for many years. There's no reason to assume its poll is not accurate. The polls done in Norway, Switzerland, and Germany also showed similar figures.

All these polls asked either, "Do you agree that Israel is conducting a war of extermination against the Palestinians?" or, alternatively, "Do you agree Israel behaves toward the Palestinians like the Nazis do?"

The belief that Israel is attempting to exterminate the Palestinians seems rather illogical. Israel, after all, is not a weak country. If it wanted to exterminate the Palestinians, it could have easily done so many years ago in a matter of days.

My conclusion from this is that large percentages of the European population are as irrational as their ancestors were 600 or 700 years ago when they thought the plague broke out because the Jews poisoned the wells.

People generally like to think we've made progress since then.

Yes, people like to think that. But this proves that we are living in a world that has a totally wrong perception of itself. I think there's no structural development in the irrationality of people in the Western world.

Is there no hope, then, for mankind?

Of course there's hope. But basically, we should be very skeptical of optimists and many liberals. In fact, you find many racists among these so-called anti-racists. For example, the NGOs who condemned Israel at the United Nations' anti-racism conference in 2001 in Durban were racists dressed up as anti-racists. The United Nations Human Rights Council is a racist body even though it says it protects human rights.

Bias against Israel is so obvious sometimes that even a Spanish translator at the United Nations recently reacted to a flurry of anti-Israel resolutions by blurting out to her colleague – while her microphone was accidentally still on – "It's a bit much, no? ... There's other really bad [things] happening [around the world], but no one says anything about the other stuff."

Look, what do you want? Even the United States speaks about the illegality of the settlements even though it isn't clear at all that settlements are illegal. There were a thousand lawyers and jurists who recently signed a statement that Israel has full rights to settle in the West Bank. But a man like John Kerry makes statements which have no substance in law. Kerry says many things which aren't logical at all.

Jewish activists often argue that Israel needs better PR to combat statements from people like Kerry. Others, however, argue that the root of the problem is Israel's refusal to announce forthrightly to the world, "The land is ours." It always highlights the victims of Arab terror, but that doesn't address the heart of the dispute – which is, "Whose land is it?"

The problem is much deeper. The problem is that Israel is the subject of a new type of propaganda war. All propaganda wars in the past, such as in World War II, played out in what we call modern society. People said straightly what they thought. If you listened to Hitler you understood clearly what he wanted. Today, we live in a post-modern society. So while many Arabs say exactly what they want, Europeans and Americans are far more confused and very often speak from behind masks.

Israel's government hasn't understood how to deal with a propaganda war in post-modern society. Israel should establish a body which analyzes this war and develops answers. For example, if Israel is attacked militarily, Israel has an instrument – the IDF. It's a very advanced military. If Israel is attacked by spying, or terrorists, we have the Mossad and a domestic intelligence agency which is very sophisticated. We are now working on a cyber-war unit which probably, within a few years, will be the most sophisticated in the world.

But in the propaganda war, which is part of the total war against Israel, Israel is totally backward. Its government doesn't understand that it should develop new tools and a new unit which oversees the propaganda battlefield. That's why Israel is losing the propaganda war.

Don't you think stating explicitly "The land is ours" would help too – something that Israel almost never says? As matters stand now, the world hears the Arabs claiming the land is theirs and the Jews responding,

"Maybe, but we can't give it to you as long as you're violent." Is it so surprising, then, that many people back the party that claims the land actually belongs to it – even if it is using violent means to acquire it?

We're dealing with a very complex issue. What you said is one aspect of it....

But you will also never hear an Israeli politician, or a liberal American Jewish leader, say that criminality in the Muslim world is much greater than the criminality and violence of any other religion. That sort of statement is taboo even though it's the simple truth. At least 70,000 Muslims will be killed this year for religious, ethnic, or political reasons – by other Muslims. You will hardly hear anybody, though, tell you that.

Can you talk a bit about Christian anti-Semitism, which is one of the topics addressed in your book? Because of the strong evangelical Christian support for Israel, some Jews are unaware that sizable numbers of Christians, especially liberal Protestants, still oppose Israel.

We always get to the same point. In the blood libel of the Middle Ages, they said the Jews needed blood for baking *matzos*. Today, you get people who say Israel goes into Gaza because it likes killing children and women. You had the largest paper in Sweden saying that Israel was killing Palestinians because it needs its organs. You had the third largest paper in Norway featuring a cartoon on how bloody *brit milah* is. Leading English papers a few years ago showed Prime Minister Sharon eating a child.

These are all blatant anti-Semitic ideas which Catholicism and Lutheranism, for instance, have for hundreds of years pumped into Western society. They are part of European culture.

What would you say to people who might react to your book by saying: "Yes, we know all about anti-Semitism; it's a tired subject and there's nothing we can do about it"?

These are lazy people – that's what I would say. There are many ways of fighting anti-Semitism. There are many ways of embarrassing anti-

Semites. There are many ways of exposing anti-Israelis. But if you are lazy, you don't do anything.

What, for example, can a person do?

First of all, you can show how the Durban conference of the NGOs was a racist conference. You can show what they said about Israel and then show the criminality going on in the Muslim world which they said nothing about.

If you apply a double standard to things, you're an anti-Semite. If you treat Jews and Israel differently than you treat Saudi Arabia or Syria, you're structurally an anti-Semite because according to the United Nations' Human Rights Declaration all people are responsible for their acts. If you say Palestinians who want to commit genocide are not responsible for their acts, you're treating them as animals and you're a racist.

So expose anti-Semites...

...Expose them, attack them, take away their mask. There are all kinds of liberal organizations and NGOs that attack Israel which are much less aggressive toward very criminal states. You should expose them and say, "You are not human rights people; you are racists masking as anti-racists." And if you do that a sufficient number of times, you will get them off your back.

What's your background? How did you get involved in this line of work?

I have been a business analyst and adviser to some of the largest corporations in the world, at the highest levels, for decades. So when I became, by chance, chairman of a leading Israeli think tank – the Jerusalem Center for Public Affairs – in 2000, it so happened that I gradually got into the emerging explosion of anti-Semitism, and I applied to it the same analytical techniques I applied to complex business problems.

How about your upbringing? You've written books in Norwegian, Italian, and Dutch...

...Let's get this clear: Some of my books I can't read. I speak Dutch, German, French, Italian, Hebrew, Yiddish and English, but I don't speak Norwegian or Greek in which I've published books.

I was born in Vienna in Austria. As a baby I came to the Netherlands in 1938. My parents and I were hidden [by a non-Jewish family] in Amsterdam for two years, and I lived and studied there until 1964. Then I lived for four years in Paris, and in 1968 I came to Israel.

For Zionistic reasons?

I was always a Zionist. I was the chairman of the World Union of Jewish Students from 1963-1967. I was the chairman of the Zionist student organization in Amsterdam, and I was the chairman of one of the Zionist youth movements in the Netherlands.

What was your aim in publishing this book? What do you hope to accomplish?

I want to expose the reality, and I hope this book will be used by others for that purpose. It has already been used by the Simon Wiesenthal Center. They raised the issues in my book with the pope. They also sent the book to a number of senior archbishops and cardinals in the Western world so that people can't say, "We don't know."

— *originally published December 18, 2013*

Postscript: *In 2015, Dr. Gerstenfeld published "The War of a Million Cuts: The Struggle Against the Delegitimization of Israel and the Jews, and the Growth of New Anti-Semitism."*

Professor Edward Alexander

Focusing on the Enemy Within

"This book is about the new forms taken by Jewish apostasy in an age when Jewish existence is threatened more starkly and immediately than at any time since the Nazi war against the Jews."

Thus begins Edward Alexander's latest work, *Jews Against Themselves.* Published last month, the book is comprised of 18 essays Alexander penned over the last 30 years with titles like "Noam Chomsky and Holocaust Denial" and "Choose Your Side: The New York Times or Judaism."

Now retired, Alexander formerly taught English at the University of Washington. His previous works include *The Jewish Idea and Its Enemies* and *The Holocaust and the War of Ideas*.

The Jewish Press: In *Jews Against Themselves,* you call Jews who hate Israel "anorexics." What do you mean by that?

Alexander: Anorexics express their resistance to growing up and managing their own affairs by starving themselves. Jewish "anorexics" want the Jewish people to live without a national body – a state – because having one forces them to manage their own affairs instead of counting on the gentiles.

You write that such Jews lead secular private lives but often publicly identify as Jews in order to lend greater weight to their anti-

Zionist activities. You call them "men at home, Jews in public."

It's a reversal of the slogan of Jewish *maskilim*: "Be a Jew at home and a man in public." In a 1942 Hebrew short story by Haim Hazaz, a character says, "When a man can no longer be a Jew, he becomes a Zionist." Nowadays, in countless instances, the slogan is: "When a man can no longer be a Jew, he becomes an anti-Zionist."

How do you explain Jews joining Israel's enemies in denouncing and boycotting the Jewish state?

It would be risky to assign a single motive to what I have called "modern Jewish apostates." Some of them – forgetting, if they ever knew, Zionism's rejection of chosenness – reject the Jewish state because, in their view, far from being a "light unto the nations," it exhibits many of the flaws of other nation-states and isn't a light even unto Jews. So if it isn't that, it shouldn't exist at all in their view.

Some people argue that without a strong basis in Torah and tradition, a Jew is less likely to understand why he's different from other people and, as a result, becomes increasingly uncomfortable, defensive, even self-hating. Do you agree with this analysis?

Only up to a point. I don't think it can explain everything.

In your book, you quote author Ian Buruma who wrote a decade ago that the "Palestinian cause has become the universal litmus of liberal credentials." How does supporting a people seeking the destruction of another people make one a liberal?

Modern liberals, of course, don't admit that. It goes against the liberal unwillingness to credit the existence and tenacity of evil. Recall the liberal failure, embodied in The New York Times, to publicize the German massacres of Jews during the Holocaust. Today, the Times and the numerous Jews who view it as their *Shulchan Aruch* hold Israelis responsible for the 67-year-old Arab refusal to accept Israel.

For the liberal mind, each Arab atrocity against Jews only serves to confirm the lurid accusations made against the Jews themselves. The viler the atrocity, the greater the Jewish guilt. As Abba Kovner once acidly wrote: "There is always someone more guilty – the victim, the victim."

Is there anything we can do about Jews who work against Israel?

Stop treating them with conciliatory gestures, honors, flattery, and oily sycophancy. Do not assume that every liberal fad must at once be called up to the Torah. Remember that *exclusion* is as much a function of human intellect as *inclusion*. And view them as apostates – Jews who, in Maimonides' words, are indifferent to their people when they are in distress and therefore have no share in the World to Come.

What's your Jewish background?

My father and grandfather marched me off to Rabbi Z. Harry Gutstein's Talmud Torah Beth Israel – located, providentially, at 500 Herzl Street, Brooklyn – when I was a young boy. There I was a better than average student in Hebrew, Yiddish Reading and Writing, Prayers, Bible, and Laws and Customs.

Both my grandfathers were central figures in their Brooklyn shuls – one located in the basement of Beth-El Hospital, the other on Kingston Avenue near Eastern Parkway. My father, a shoemaker, and my mother presided over a strictly observant Jewish home.

What were your experiences like at the University of Washington as a pro-Israel professor?

Very lonely after the mid-1970s. I was disliked but never "punished" academically by colleagues – unless one counts being dropped down the memory hole by the current Jewish Studies faculty whose official history of the program at my university begins after I departed the chairmanship, which I held for its first decade.

— originally published August 19, 2015

Postscript: *In a May 2017 e-mail to me, Professor Alexander blasted yet* *another Jew with less than warm feelings for Israel: Senator Bernie Sanders. He noted that Sanders "did not flinch" during his presidential campaign from accepting support from people like Cornel West and Al Sharpton who have "demonstrated a venomous hostility towards Jews and Israel." He also noted that Sanders said he would look to J Street and James Zogby of the Arab-American Institute for foreign policy advice should he become president – which, Alexander argued, "would make Israel and her supporters long for a return to the Obama administration."*

Gloria Greenfield

Exposing a Lethal Hatred

Although it was released in 2011, "Unmasked Judeophobia: The Threat to Civilization" is still playing to audiences across the world. As the title suggests, "Unmasked Judeophobia" examines the history of anti-Semitism and its alarming resurgence in the form of anti-Zionism in the late 20th and early 21st centuries. On February 6 and 7, the film is screening at Manhattan's Park East Synagogue and the Museum of Tolerance New York, respectively – both at 7 p.m.

The Jewish Press recently spoke with the film's director and producer, Gloria Greenfield. Greenfield has previously worked as strategy manager for the Partnership for Excellence in Jewish Education, director of the Adult Learning Collaborative for Combined Jewish Philanthropies, and executive director of The David Project.

The Jewish Press: Many recent articles, books, and films have highlighted the increasing hatred against Jews and Israel around the world. What's new about your film?

Greenfield: Many people don't necessarily know about the speech in 1946 that Hassan al-Banna, the founder of the Muslim Brotherhood, made articulating a commitment to continue the work of Hitler and the SS. Many people don't know the strategy that the Muslim Brotherhood utilized in founding itself – that it realized it could get Muslims to stop killing each other, at least partially, by focusing on killing Jews and fighting Zionism. Many people don't know about the daily broadcasts delivering Nazi propaganda into Arab countries throughout World War II.

Your film starts with the history of Christian anti-Semitism. Hasn't this topic already been covered exhaustively?

If the film didn't start with that, it wouldn't have integrity. But, in a sense, it's also an example of hope. Lethal Jew-hatred started in the Christian world, but it no longer resides there because of reformations within the church. [In other words,] if people decide they want to stop being genocidal murderers, it's possible.

Your film is frightening in the amount of virulent anti-Semitism it depicts around the world. Suppose someone watches your film and wants to do something about anti-Semitism but doesn't know where to turn: What would you tell him?

Doc Emet Productions has actually released a companion activist guide to go with the film. It's available on UnmaskedTheMovie.com. It gives about 65 pages of suggestions to fight hatred against the Jewish people – whether it's focusing on what's happening on university campuses, looking at textbooks [biased against Israel], lobbying elected officials, or watching media and writing letters to the editor and opinion pieces.

Some Jews, especially in the Orthodox community, see anti-Semitism as almost inherent in the state of nature and hence a waste of time to fight. What would you say to them?

My concern is *lethal* Jew-hatred. I'm not talking about discrimination. Do I think hatred towards the Jewish people and Jewish state will ever totally be eliminated? I wouldn't put my money on it. But I think it's absolutely urgent that we diminish the hatred to levels that don't threaten our lives.

At this point, I don't really care about jokes about Jewish noses or whether there's a country club that prefers not to have any Jews in it. My concern is genocide, and if one says that there's always going to be lethal Jew-hatred, that's a completely unacceptable thought for any decent person to have.

Some Jews, though, see anti-Semitism as a divine decree that's unalterable.

But it's a sin not to defend life. It seems like they're confusing their own theology with Christian theology. Jews are obligated to fight for their survival and beliefs.

The title of your film is "Unmasked Judeophobia: The Threat to Civilization." In what sense is anti-Semitism a threat to civilization?

Because when we look throughout history, a society that allows genocidal hatred toward the Jewish people falls apart. It becomes poisoned by that hatred. So it's a message to non-Jews that they, as members of society, become poisoned if they don't stand up and fight this.

You were once a radical feminist. How did you come to make a pro-Israel film?

I always liked Israel – even when I was a radical feminist. I was raised as a Zionist, and when I was a radical feminist, I was also a right-wing Zionist. I left the feminist movement because of its dogma and anti-Semitism. I could not invest any more energy in a movement that nurtured Jew-hatred.

What's your next film going to be about?

An examination of the historical connection between the land of Israel and the Jewish people – because many people today are denying that connection.

— originally published February 6, 2013

Postscript: *The film Gloria Greenfield mentions in her last response was released in 2014 under the title "Body and Soul: The State of the Jewish Nation." She is currently producing her fourth film, "The Fight of Our Lives: Defeating the Ideological War Against the West," which is scheduled to be released in late 2017.*

Daniel Jonah Goldhagen

Taking the Cudgel to Anti-Semites

Daniel Jonah Goldhagen has a way of upsetting people. "Exceptionally wrong," "worthless," "racist" are just some of the epithets his academic detractors used to describe his bestselling first book, *Hitler's Willing Executioners: Ordinary Germans and the Holocaust.* His second book, *A Moral Reckoning: The Role of the Catholic Church in the Holocaust and Its Unfulfilled Duty of Repair,* was criticized for "turning history into a kind of cudgel," having an "anti-Catholic agenda," and failing to "meet even the minimum standards of scholarship."

Goldhagen's critics would perhaps prefer to ignore him, but they can't. Formerly a professor at Harvard, Goldhagen has a knack for writing books on sensitive topics that grab public attention. When *Hitler's Willing Executioners* was published in 1996 Time magazine deemed it one of year's two best works of non-fiction and the New York Times called it "one of those rare, new works that merit the appellation 'landmark.'" Translated into 15 languages, the book sparked passionate debates in Germany and elsewhere on the German population's role in the Holocaust.

Goldhagen's latest work is *The Devil That Never Dies: The Rise and Threat of Global Antisemitism.* The book may be less controversial than some of his earlier works, but it still is "Goldhagenesque" enough for some to slam the book as "radically under-researched" (Wall Street Journal) and others to hail its author as a "prophet, offering the world an apocalyptic call to self-examination and repentance" (Washington Post).

Goldhagen recently spoke with The Jewish Press.

The Jewish Press: In *The Devil That Never Dies*, you write that a Martian who visited Earth would find anti-Semitism incomprehensible. Why do you think so?

Goldhagen: Because the Jews compose a tiny percentage of all humanity and yet they're hated worldwide even in countries where there aren't any Jews....

If a Martian looked at Israel, for example, he'd be flabbergasted that so much hatred is directed at it when there are so many other countries perpetrating colossal crimes which merit condemnation that dwarfs any reasonable assessment of Israel's policies. Sudan, for example, has been pursuing genocidal policies for more than two decades, with a mass murder toll of perhaps 2.5 million people.

People are often accused of being anti-Semitic for making generalizations like "Jews are good at business" or "Jews are communists." But Jews *are* apparently good at business and Jews *have*, historically, been overrepresented in various radical causes, including communism. Why is someone an anti-Semite for harboring stereotypes that are based in reality?

There are sociological statements you can make about Jews just as you can about other groups that may on the whole bear out to be true. But what anti-Semites do is reduce the complexity of people to their Jewishness. A person may be a man, may be an American, may be a businessman, may be a Jew, and may be a member of a local country club, but for the anti-Semite, everything he does – particularly the negative things – is attributed to his Jewishness.

Perhaps on the whole Jews are better in business than other groups, but why are Jews who are businessmen seen as *Jews* rather than simply *businesspeople* who do what businesspeople do – which is to try to make a profit, make goods, sell goods, and expand their markets? Why are they seen as Jews? What about what they do is *Jewish* as opposed to being just *business*?

And anti-Semites don't just say Jews are good at business. They say Jews have too much power in business. What does that mean? How could one demonstrate this? And if you say they have too much power in business, obviously you think they're doing something bad with that power. What exactly is that? What can anybody show that Jews do that's bad with their alleged power in business?

So we have to make a clear distinction between appropriate sociological generalization and prejudice.

Turning to your first – and most famous – book, *Hitler's Willing Executioners*: One of the criticisms leveled against it was that it's anti-German. In other words, while it's true that many Germans willingly followed Hitler, some people argue that the case can be made that a Hitler-like figure would have been just as popular in Poland or Romania, for example.

I'm happy to answer this critique, but it would be nice if it addressed what the book is about. In *Hitler's Willing Executioners,* I showed that ordinary Germans acted or supported actions against Jews because they were anti-Semites – not because they were coerced, duped, or just following orders, which is how it had been represented before.

I show this by studying the perpetrators of the Holocaust and drawing on their own words. Their prejudice was deep, their prejudice was broad, and they actually looked upon Jews as devils in human form who needed to be exterminated. One of the things I showed is they didn't just follow orders; they often did more than they had do. They acted with the zeal and energy of true ideological warriors.

Now, when this book came out in 1996, it turned the field of Holocaust studies upside down, and of course there was pushback from a lot of people. In Germany it was seen as a political issue and produced a societal conversation that lasted months and months. One of the things people said was that I argued that only Germans are anti-Semites. Well, I never said that. I focused on Germans because it was Germans who initiated the Holocaust. I have no doubt that a leader in any number of other countries who would have been dedicated to eliminating the Jews could have found many willing helpers.

So that criticism simply did not speak the plain truth about what my book said. They were attacking me for a position I never held.

Your book argues that ordinary Germans supported the Holocaust, but if so, why was Hitler so careful not to talk publicly about exterminating the Jews? Also, isn't it true that the Nazis built gas chambers because many German soldiers on the Eastern front felt uncomfortable shooting vast numbers of Jews?

To take your points one by one: That the Germans were killing Jews on a large scale was an open secret in Germany. We have a lot of evidence that shows that. The Nazi leadership did not want to broadcast this over the radio or print it in newspapers because it made people uneasy. It was a radical thing to do; it would have led to questions of "What if we lose the war? What will happen to us?" and it also would've handed the Allies a propaganda coup.

But it was an open secret. Millions of Germans had direct knowledge of what was taking place. We have a lot of evidence that soldiers coming back from the front told their family and friends about what was going on. People knew.

It's true that some Germans did find the killing unspeakably gruesome – that is, when they were shooting victims face to face at point-blank range – but one of the things I did was study those units where the men were given the option not to take part in the killing. I found that very few men availed themselves of the opportunity – even when they saw that those who refused to kill were just given other duties.

So you have to ask yourself the question: Why would someone shoot children at point-blank range if he didn't believe that what he was doing was right? And they didn't just shoot them. They brutalized them, subjecting them to all manner of cruelty. A common phrase that the perpetrators themselves used was, "Beating Jews was our daily bread." Why would they do it if they thought the Jews innocent and undeserving of their fate?

Now, even if you think you're killing a devil in human form, just the sight of blood, brain, and bones flying around and spattering on you can be unsettling. After all, many people who eat meat do not want to slaughter the animals themselves or will not go into a slaughterhouse, because it's gruesome. So the leadership did try to find a more cosmetic way of killing the Jews and that's why they eventually set up the gas chambers in the extermination camps. But it was definitely not because of widespread opposition.

In 2002 you wrote another controversial work, *A Moral Reckoning: The Role of the Catholic Church in the Holocaust and Its Unfulfilled Duty of Repair.* What exactly was the Church's role in the Holocaust other than a passive one?

In order for the Nazis to enforce the race laws, they needed access to church records to determine the lineage of people. The Catholic Church fully cooperated.

In Germany, France, and Italy, the Church supported the race laws. In Slovakia when the regime was about to undertake the deportation of Slovakian Jews – many of whom ended up in Auschwitz – there was a pastoral letter read by the priests in parish after parish, justifying in Nazi-like terms the deportation of the Jews. In Croatia some priests participated in mass murders, and so on and so forth.

So there's a lot the Church needs to answer for. It's not just whether the pope didn't speak out on behalf of Jews, which is what the discussion has typically been about. It's all the things Church members did, including national churches, to facilitate the persecution of Jews.

Now, I should add quickly that individual bishops, priests, and nuns probably saved more Jews than [members of] any other institution during the Nazi period because they, as individuals, acted upon their moral sensibility. But the overall record of the Catholic Church is quite bad.

In a country like Bulgaria, Christian leaders stood up for the Jews. How do you account for Christian leaders standing up for Jews in one country and not in another?

There was a systematic difference between the Catholic Church and most other Christian churches. From its perspective, the Catholic Church was mired in a foundational struggle with Jews. It claimed that it was the rightful heir of the Jewish tradition, that the Jewish bible was its bible, and that the Jews had become wayward. So it was more deeply anti-Semitic than many other churches, which were much more moderate.

A second reason is that the Catholic Church was profoundly anti-Bolshevik and it identified Jews with Bolshevism, which the Nazis called Judeo-Bolshevism. This view was not nearly as widespread among other Christian churches.

You write in the book that the Catholic Church must make amends for its misdeeds, but hasn't it already done everything it can? Didn't it drastically alter its basic beliefs regarding Jews during the Second Vatican Council in the 1960s?

I give the Church a great deal of credit for the advances it's made, but it still has a long way to go. Surveys show that between 20-35 percent of people from Catholic countries believe that Jews today – not just way back when, but today – are guilty for the death of Jesus.

So the Church has to address the falseness of such a damaging charge and teach Catholics that this is a form of anti-Semitism, which the pope has said is actually a sin.

What will your next book be about?

I have a bunch of projects underway, though I'm not quite ready to talk about them. I write every day, literally every day. I'm also working now with WNET on making a documentary based on *The Devil That Never Dies* for public television.

— originally published November 19, 2014

Postscript: *In April 2017, Daniel Jonah Goldhagen told me he is still working on the several projects he mentions at the end of the interview but does not like to talk about his work until it is pretty much complete. As for the documentary on WNET, he said it "died on the vine."*

Organizational Chiefs

Russell Robinson

CEO of the Jewish National Fund

Mention the Jewish National Fund (JNF) and the image of blue *tzedakah* boxes likely comes to mind. Starting in 1901, Jews throughout the world dropped coins into these blue boxes, helping the JNF buy and develop land in Palestine on behalf of the Jewish people. The JNF today still owns 13 percent of the land and has planted 250 million trees in its 111-year existence.

JNF's CEO, Russell Robinson, recently spoke with The Jewish Press.

The Jewish Press: The JNF's original purpose was to buy land in Palestine. What is its purpose today, considering that the Jewish people now possess most of Palestine?

Robinson: Well, the purpose wasn't to buy land just for the purpose of buying land. The purpose was to develop the state of Israel for the Jewish people everywhere. It was about bringing people home and having a place to call home. It was about establishing the Technion, it was about establishing Tel Aviv University.

And today?

Today that continues because the 13 percent of the land which is owned by the Jewish National Fund is held in perpetuity for the Jewish people everywhere. So whether you're in Israel or here, you're still a landlord, you're still part of that development of the land. So that connection continues.

It's also still about creating. The Negev comprises 60 percent of Israel, yet only holds nine percent of the population today. The Galil comprises 17 percent of the land but only holds 13 percent of the population. So if you want to be a 21st century pioneer, the opportunity to create the land of Israel for the Jewish people is still in front of us.

The JNF, in other words, tries to settle Jews in the Negev and Galil?

Absolutely. That's been our biggest thrust in the past 10 years. We have an objective: 500,000 more people in the Negev and 300,000 more in the Galil. A town like Yerucham in the Negev was established in the 1950s by immigrants that came from Arab countries. We put them in Yerucham, not because it was a great place to live, but because we needed them strategically to live there. We put them in tents and tin shacks and told them, "We'll come back."

Well, in 60 years, we never did, and Yerucham is still a town of less than 10,000 people. So the opportunity to bring prosperous opportunities for all the people of Israel throughout all the land of Israel is still in front of us.

How many Jews currently live in the Negev?

You have 215,000 Jews in Be'er Sheva, another 110,000 Jews outside of Be'er Sheva, and about 200,000 Bedouins.

And you want to bring a half million *more* people to the Negev?

Absolutely. When we started working in Be'er Sheva 10 years ago, it had 193,000 people and losing three percent of its population every year. Today, it has 215,000 people and is one of the fastest growing communities in Israel. Be'er Sheva should have 450,000 people.

Why is a population increase in the Negev necessary?

A place like Yerucham was established in 1950 with 10,000 people. Today, it's a community of 9,500 that still has high unemployment. Yerucham needs to have 30,000 to 50,000 people. You can't make it with 10,000 people.

Why not?

Because the tax base has to go up. You have to fix roads, you have to have education, you have to have schools. And if your population is small, you'll never have enough. You'll always be on the brink of not having. You'll have to add 10 kids to this class and move three kids from that class. In the meantime, you don't really have a teacher, so you have to drive in a teacher....

The magical number for urban development is between 30,000-50,000. With that, you're able to have the community stand on its own and develop itself. People in Yerucham don't deserve to be poor just because they don't have a population.

Can you talk a bit about the JNF's efforts to solve Israel's constant water problems?

We have added about 12 percent water availability to Israel. We've built 240 reservoirs and developed technology to use recycled and brackish water, making Israel a country that recycles almost 80 percent of its water. Spain, which recycles the most after Israel, recycles less than 20 percent. Almost 50 percent of the farming in Israel today is done without fresh water. So water is a very important component of what we do.

Why is the JNF doing all this? Shouldn't the Israeli government be in charge of such matters?

You can say the same thing about The Salvation Army or a soup kitchen. The fact is that philanthropy is able to make things happen because it can take risks that a government can't.

In recent years, there's been talk of privatizing some of Israel's publicly-owned land, which amounts to 90 percent of the country. Is the JNF considering relinquishing some of the 13 percent it owns?

No, we have a covenant with the Jewish people who bought land in 1901, 1905, 1910, etc. They did it based upon hopes and dreams. We have a covenant that our land is to be held in perpetuity for the Jewish people everywhere.

In the past decade, the JNF has faced criticism for its policy of only leasing land to Jews. How do you address this criticism?

I have an organization called the Jewish National Fund. If I had an organization called the Catholic Church, it would be different. I think the Catholic Church should be giving services for people who are Catholic.

So I have no problem. If people want to say, "Does the Jewish National Fund help the Jewish people?" the answer is yes, and I'm proud of it.

Can you talk a bit about your background? Is it true that you're a sixth-generation American?

Yes, my family was one of the first Jewish settlers in Virginia. They came in the late 1700s, and after all these generations I'm still a proud Zionist Jew.

Robinson, at first blush, sounds like a non-Jewish name.

It's a French derivative. They came from Alsace Lorraine and it's a derivative of Robinsohn. If you go to the cemetery in Petersburg, VA, our section of the cemetery is the Robinsohn section.

Does the JNF still sell blue *tzedakah* boxes?

Yes, we send out about 100,000 blue boxes a year. If people go on JNF.org they can order one. It's one of the great icons of the Jewish world.

Imagine, this was before faxes and e-mails. It was about somebody from the Jewish National Fund asking people to take money off of their plate and put it into a blue box. Somebody would collect it and we would buy land. Now that is what I call the real vision and dreams of the Jewish people. Not to be cynical but to be so unbelievably visionary. And that's why we're in the land of Israel today.

— originally published November 14, 2012

***Postscript:** In May 2017, Adam Brill, JNF's director of communications, told me his organization is still focused on all the goals mentioned in this interview. In particular, he highlighted JNF's activities in the Negev, where, significantly, the IDF plans on moving its technology and intelligence units in 2021. The move should prove to be a boon for Be'er Sheva, he said.*

Daniel Mariaschin

Executive Vice President of B'nai B'rith

Daniel Mariaschin can boast of a rich career in Jewish organizational life. In his over four decades of activity, he has served as community relations associate for the Jewish Community Council of Boston; director of the New England office of the American Zionist Federation and Zionist House in Boston; director of the ADL's Middle East Affairs Department; assistant to ADL national director Nathan Perlmutter; and director of the Political Affairs Department of AIPAC. Along the way, he also somehow found time to serve as press secretary for former secretary of state Alexander Haig during his 1987-88 presidential campaign.

For the past 25 years, though, Mariaschin has worked for B'nai B'rith International and today is the organization's executive vice president. He recently spoke with The Jewish Press.

The Jewish Press: Broadly speaking, how would you describe B'nai B'rith's activities, and what distinguishes B'nai B'rith from other Jewish organizations?

Mariaschin: The first distinguishing factor is that B'nai B'rith is the oldest of the Jewish organizations – we're now into our 172nd year. We're also an international organization made up of members in nearly 50 countries around the world.

We concentrate on three main areas: One is pro-Israel advocacy and fighting global anti-Semitism. We've had credentials at the United Nations since 1947, and we spend a good deal of our time there fighting bias against Israel.

The second area is senior housing and advocacy. The Jewish community has probably the largest proportion of senior citizens of any ethnic group in this country, so for more than 40 years now we have been sponsoring affordable housing for seniors in conjunction with the Department of Housing and Urban Development. We're also involved in senior advocacy – issues like Social Security, Medicare, etc.

The third area is disaster relief. We help victims of hurricanes, earthquakes, tsunamis – all kinds of natural disasters around the world.

You were recently involved in fighting HarperCollins for expunging Israel from atlases it sold in the Middle East. Can you talk a little about that?

This is only the latest in a long series of these kinds of omissions. We've seen it particularly with airlines omitting Israel on route maps, for example. But HarperCollins' omission was especially egregious because it is a major general and educational publisher. And if we're going to talk about peace and a peace process, it's not only for diplomats – it's for everybody. When a major publisher leaves Israel off a map, what kind of message does that send to schoolchildren in the Arab world?

You won this fight with HarperCollins.

Yes, HarperCollins decided to call the atlases back and pulp the rest. Hopefully it will serve as a lesson for others because this was just a microcosm of the larger issue of the delegitimization of Israel. It doesn't necessarily have to be a speech at the United Nations; it can be a decision made in an editorial office somewhere to say, "Look, we don't want to offend our readers so we think we'll just leave Israel off." Hopefully, the firestorm around this story will send a message to others that a) it's unacceptable and b) there are people out there watching who will raise the red flag if they do this kind of thing.

What kind of work does B'nai B'rith do at the UN?

We were actually present in 1945 when the UN was founded in San Francisco, and we received our first credentials as an NGO in 1947.

What has happened over the last 25 years, unfortunately, is that much of our UN activity relates to the demonization and delegitimization of Israel. We feel very strongly about trying to keep the UN honest on this issue. So, for example, in March every year we go for a week to Geneva where the UN Human Rights Council is based and meet with ambassadors. We're also in Paris at UNESCO.

So B'nai B'rith will meet with various ambassadors?

Yes. There are 194 member states of the UN. Of course we're not meeting all of them – some of them we don't want to meet – but many of them have relations with Israel and should know better. In the UN there's a lot of "go along to get along." Many countries will say, "Well, this country voted that way, so we're going to vote the same way." They hide behind the vote of the bloc. So there's a lot of work to be done.

In August, you wrote an op-ed column in The New York Times arguing that the UN should recognize Yom Kippur as an official holiday on its calendar. Why is that important?

Because there are Christian and Muslim holidays on the UN calendar and there should be at least one Jewish one.

When the UN started back in the '40s, the first two days of *Pesach* were actually on the UN calendar, but then they disappeared. So we don't think it's asking too much for there to be a Jewish holiday. We've contributed so much to the betterment of the world in so many ways.

When you meet with world leaders and ambassadors, what's your sense of their feelings toward Israel? To many Jews, anti-Israel bias in Europe and elsewhere seems so obvious that it's hard to believe others don't see it. Are these leaders just playing along for political reasons or do they truly believe that Israel deserves, for example, to be repeatedly

singled out in the UN as the world's worst violator of human rights?

There are some who rationalize their behavior to kind of cover what they know is the right thing, and then there's a large category of countries that are simply out to do Israel wrong – starting with Iran. So it's mixed. But the most disappointing thing are the folks in the first category – people who know that Israel is being targeted all the time, who know that the line between criticizing Israel and anti-Semitism is very thin – sometimes non-existent – but who act against Israel anyways because politics trumps the right thing. That's the most frustrating.

Which ambassador or world leader is B'nai B'rith scheduled to meet next?

We have a diplomatic luncheon series, so this week we're having the ambassador of Latvia. Until June 30, Latvia holds the presidency of the European Union, so when the ambassador comes here we'll have questions for him about European Union policy vis-à-vis Israel. If you remember, the European Court of Justice dropped Hamas from the terrorism list, and now the European Union has to reapply to get Hamas back on it. So that will be a question for him. This is something we do constantly.

B'nai B'rith spends millions of dollars helping victims of natural disasters. While doing so is obviously an enormous *chesed,* some people argue that Jewish organizations should spend all their resources on Jewish causes. What's your response?

These funds are spurred by the natural disasters; they're not coming out of our general budget. In other words, when there's a tsunami or a hurricane, B'nai B'rith members want to help. So that's the reason for it, and we've been doing this kind of relief since the 1860s. We're very proud of what we do.

But what need is there for a *Jewish* organization to do this? Why not just direct your members to the Red Cross?

Look, we're a Jewish organization and much of what we do is work inside our own community obviously. But *tikkun olam* as a value of Jewish life is extremely important to who we are as a people. To help others and to feel that *rachmanut* for others has been a hallmark of our community, so if we can make life better for those in need, we should do that.

You've been active in Jewish organizational life for over 40 years now. The one blip on your radar screen is the time you spent working for Alexander Haig when he ran for president in 1987-88. How did you get involved in his campaign and what was that experience like?

As a young person, I was deeply involved in local and state politics in New Hampshire, and even though I chose a career working in the Jewish community, politics has always been of great interest to me. When I was working for the Anti-Defamation League, I met General Haig at one of our annual meetings and I stayed in touch. He was a good friend of Israel and the Jewish community, so when I was offered the opportunity to be his press secretary, I immediately accepted.

I was on that campaign for 13 months. It was a great experience. He was a great American, and it was an opportunity for me to see our presidential electoral process from the inside out – campaigning, preparing issue briefs, fighting to get media time, preparing for presidential debates, etc. It's a uniquely American experience and I feel very fortunate to have had it.

— originally published February 4, 2015

Postscript: *Now in its 174th year, B'nai B'rith continues to promote its agenda, including defending Israel at the United Nations and around the globe. In one of its latest lobbying efforts, Daniel Mariaschin and B'nai B'rith President Gary Saltzman led a mission to Azerbaijan and Georgia where they met with the two countries' prime ministers, among other officials.*

Allen Fagin

Executive Vice President of the OU

The OU – or, more formally, the Union of Orthodox Jewish Congregations of America – is one of the oldest and most widely known Jewish organizations in the United States. Founded in 1898, the OU today consists of numerous departments servicing Orthodox Jews in a variety of ways. Its most famous department is its Kashruth Division, which certifies 800,000 products and ingredients in 92 countries. But the OU also, for example, lobbies on behalf of Orthodox Jews through its Advocacy Center; helps adults find employment through its Job Board; organizes programs for teenagers through NCSY; and publishes books through OU Press.

Currently heading all these divisions is Allen Fagin, the OU's new executive vice president. Formerly an attorney at the prestigious law firm Proskauer Rose for 40 years – six of those as its chairman – Fagin holds degrees from both Columbia and Harvard. He retired in 2013 to devote more time to the Jewish community. Appointed in April, Fagin is the first non-rabbi to serve as executive vice president of the OU.

The Jewish Press: Did the decision to appoint you, a layman, to head the OU cause any controversy?

Fagin: I don't think so. I don't think the focus, frankly, was on having a rabbinic or a non-rabbinic figure. I think the focus was on finding someone who knew and understood the community and who also had significant management background.

What's your vision for the OU?

To try to expand the resources that are available to the OU in carrying out the multiple missions it has within the *frum* community. These all require enormous resources, so a large part of my job is to see to it that those resources are available, to make certain that programs and activities are functioning cohesively with one another, that we stay true to our mission, that we be as cost-effective as we can be, and that we pay attention to the development of our professional staff and the ways in which we deliver services to our communities.

In Rabbi Berel Wein's recently published autobiography, he recalls his days as the OU's executive vice president in the 1970s. After listing the OU's main departments at the time, he writes, "In theory, I was to coordinate and administer these divisions so they would form a harmonious whole. In practice, this proved impossible, since each operated as an independent fiefdom supported by different personalities and forces within the OU." Have things changed at all since the 1970s?

I think things have changed very substantially. We see, daily, terrific examples of inter-departmental cooperation. For example, just recently, there were sweeping changes within the New York City Department of Education for families with children with special needs. The OU was at the forefront in fighting for those changes both in Albany and at the municipal level. This was a joint effort between OU Advocacy, which is our political action arm, and Yachad, the National Jewish Council for Disabilities.

Another example: Last month we sponsored a rally in front of the Israeli consulate in support of the three teens in Israel who were kidnapped. The rally was spearheaded by NCSY, the publicity for the rally was orchestrated in large measure by our web department, and the many political figures who came to the rally were there at the invitation of our advocacy arm.

You told the OU's Jewish Action magazine last month that the OU could accomplish much more if it had additional funds. What did you have in mind when you said that?

I think every single one of our programs is resource-constrained. NCSY, for example, will send 1,100 teens to Israel this summer. About 500 of them are teens from public schools, all across the country. We provide substantial scholarship assistance to enable those teens to get to Israel and to participate, many of them for the very first time in their lives, in meaningful opportunities to learn Torah.

But there is a limit to the assistance we can provide. If we had greater resources, we would double or triple or quadruple the number of teens we send. That's true in almost every aspect of our programming.

The OU runs a Jewish Learning Initiative on Campus (JLIC). What is its purpose? Aren't Chabad and Hillel already on campus?

First, I should point out that every campus we go to – and this fall we'll be on 21 campuses across the United States and Canada – we go to at the invitation of, and in partnership with, the campus Hillel.

The other major difference is that the JLIC program is designed for Orthodox students on campus. While there is some measure of outreach to others, the emphasis is providing educational opportunity and infrastructure to Orthodox students – a structure that they really wouldn't have were it not for our couples.

As an organization that lobbies in Albany and Washington, the OU undoubtedly has to take a position on such hot-button issues as gay marriage, abortion, etc. Some Orthodox Jews believe we have a duty to be active in the culture wars, acting as an *ohr la'goyim* by fighting for morality in this country. Others maintain we should only concern ourselves with the needs of the Orthodox Jewish community and otherwise mind our own business. What's the OU's position?

We are not here to impose legislatively our Torah obligations on others. What we seek to accomplish is preventing legislation or regulation that would make it difficult or impossible for the *frum* community to be able to live in a manner consistent with our values. So our posture has been primarily defensive.

You talk of imposing our values on others. But isn't all moral legislation an imposition? Aren't public indecency laws an imposition by one group on another?

There clearly are some values that have been legislated that are universal in nature. But many others aren't.

But opposition to homosexuality was pretty much universal in the West until very recently.

I think there's a difference between communicating our Torah values – making clear where we stand – and seeking to impose those values on others. It's a difficult balance. We don't oppose legislation that provides civil rights. At the same time, we are always vigilant to try to preserve our own right to live the way we believe is appropriate.

You told the Jewish Action that Rabbi Joseph Grunblatt of the Queens Jewish Center and your in-laws, Max and Liesel Rosenberg, were significant influences in your life. How so?

My father-in-law, *a"h,* was for many years the chairman of the board of Yeshiva Rav Samson Raphael Hirsch. My mother-in-law, *a"h,* was also enormously involved in the Breuers *kehillah.* I'm not sure I can identify a couple as dedicated to, and involved in, their *kehillah* as they were, and that's been a tremendous influence on me.

And Rabbi Grunblatt?

Rabbi Grunblatt was the consummate pulpit rabbi. He was a tremendous *talmid chacham* and also one of the most sensitive and caring individuals I've ever met.

Just watching him day and night do what he did – most of it under the radar with very few people even knowing the extent of his *maasim tovim* – was a huge inspiration to generations of congregants. He was just a remarkable human being and a remarkable rabbi.

He asked you to become president of the shul, correct?

Yes, it's something he asked me to do and you didn't say no to Rabbi Grunblatt. But I was very hesitant, since becoming president would mean my inability to sit next to my two young sons during *davening*. And his response to me was that it would be a more important lesson for my sons to see me sitting at the front of the *shul* and all that that entailed than my sitting next to them during *davening*.

It's interesting he said that because many people today believe spending time away from one's children, even for a worthy cause, is deleterious.

I think one of the most important lessons we can teach our children is the importance of being an *osek b'tzarchei tzibbur*. Not to the exclusion, by any means, of family obligations or our obligations to be *kovei'a itim*. But the importance of communal activity, especially in the times we're currently living in, is enormous.

Can you elaborate?

Look at the shocking statistics of the Pew Report. It is a huge motivation for us at the OU, recognizing how American Jewry is being decimated right before our eyes.

And if there is a fundamental mission on the non-*kashrus* side of the OU, it really is in many respects to reverse, or at least to minimize, the effects that are represented in the conclusions of the Pew Report.

The vast majority of our program dollars go to NCSY and to its *kiruv* and *chizuk* activities. We're dealing with thousands and thousands of teens all across the country with really significant success. This past December, we had a *yarchei kallah* that was attended by about 300 public school teens who gave up their winter break to come to the East Coast and learn together for a week. For many of them it was the first taste of Torah they had ever had.

We're now the third or fourth largest Birthright provider in the

United States. And we supplement it with OU funds to make certain that it is not just seeing the sites. We have a strong educational component, and a large percentage of the teens we bring on Birthright programs stay in Israel to participate in learning programs.

And yet, the statistics in the Pew Report portray a very dim future.

True, but we must never lose hope. The Gemara in *Yoma* relates an incident involving Shimon HaTzaddik, who was the *kohen gadol*. One year, he gathered all his students and told them he was going to die that year.

How did he know? The Gemara explains that each year on Yom Kippur, when Shimon HaTzaddik entered the *Kodesh Hakadashim,* he would see a vision of a man dressed solely in white accompanying him into the *Kodesh Hakadashim* and exiting with him. This year, he explained to his students, the vision was absent and in its stead he saw a man dressed in black burial shrouds. Based on this vision he knew he was going to die.

But what exactly did Shimon HaTzaddik see in the *Kodesh Hakadashim* that convinced him he would perish? Rav [Yoshe Ber] Soloveitchik explained that each year when Shimon HaTzaddik entered the *Kodesh Hakadashim* he experienced a feeling of optimism. But that year he experienced a feeling of despair regarding the continued existence of the Jewish people due to their religious and spiritual decline. When he experienced that feeling, Rav Soloveitchik explained, he knew he could no longer serve as a leader of the Jewish people.

In other words, when we lose hope, we perish. We must never lose hope.

— originally published July 9, 2014

Postscript: *The OU's Kashruth Division now certifies approximately a million products and ingredients in 104 countries and JLIC operates on 23 campuses. The OU's Job Board has ceased operations.*

Miscellaneous

Yoram Hazony

Selling the Bible to Intellectuals

An intellectual with truly fresh ideas is something of a rarity. An intellectual with an activist's sense of mission is even rarer. An intellectual who doesn't consider himself too sophisticated to have nine children – well, that's almost unheard of outside of rabbinical circles.

But Yoram Hazony is one such person. President of the Herzl Institute in Jerusalem, he is also the director of the John Templeton Foundation's project in Jewish Philosophical Theology and a member of the Israel Council for Higher Education committee on Liberal Studies in Israel's universities. He currently is filming "The Story of God" with Morgan Freeman for National Geographic.

As an author, Hazony has written *The Philosophy of Hebrew Scripture*, the widely-acclaimed *The Jewish State: The Struggle for Israel's Soul*, and, most recently, *God and Politics in Esther*, which is a revised edition of his first book, *The Dawn*.

The Jewish Press: In your third book, *The Philosophy of Hebrew Scripture*, you argue that the Torah should be read to some degree as a philosophical work. What do you mean by that?

Hazony: There are many people who have this view of the *Tanach* that you're just supposed to believe – even if it doesn't make any sense. I don't think that's a very Jewish view. Moshe says the Torah is "our wisdom and understanding in the eyes of the nations." In other words, you're supposed to be able to look at the Torah and say, "Wow, that's so wise, that's so brilliant. We should do that."

I'd like everybody – Jewish and not Jewish – to be able to look at the Torah and see the incredible beauty and how much sense it makes and how it's the best way for people to live.

You lament in *The Philosophy of Hebrew Scripture* that universities do not currently see the Bible the way you do.

It's a very tragic story. Many professors aren't even aware that the modern university was created to toss the Bible – and Jewish sources in general – out of being legitimate intellectual pursuits.

In the introduction to *The Philosophy of Hebrew Scripture* I provide some of the history – and people find it absolutely shocking. Essentially, the major thinkers who founded the modern research university 200 years ago in Germany were open anti-Semites and the goal of a university education – as they understood it – was in part to discredit Jews and Judaism, to prove how ridiculous, absurd, and meaningless the *Tanach* and Talmud are, and to demonstrate that they contributed nothing to the creation of anything good in the world.

Two hundred years have passed, and most of the anti-Semites are gone from the universities, but the same ideas are still being taught.

Can you give an example?

If you're teaching an introduction to ethics and for a whole semester you teach Aristotelian ethics and Kantian ethics and utilitarian ethics, but you don't even mention the Torah once, then your course is kind of a fraud. You can't untangle the history of ethics in the West from the impact of 2,000 years of the Jewish Bible on Christianity. But our universities pretend you can.

And so we send our children to universities and they come out thinking that basically the Bible is totally irrelevant to being an educated human being. We're raising up an entire culture of people who don't have the faintest idea where we came from or where we're going. And then we're surprised that the entire West is drifting away from the biblical values on which it was built...

But you want the Bible examined not only in ethics courses, but in philosophy courses as well, correct?

Yes. It's especially important, for example, to notice that the Jewish Bible is full of political theory. And I'm not the first person to notice this. Throughout Western history there were important Christian thinkers who turned to Jewish sources in order to understand the political ideas of the Jews – in part because the New Testament is really not a very political book.

So in the 17th century, for example, Christians in Protestant countries like Holland or England who wanted to break away from the Catholic Church went back to the Bible to try to figure out how they should set up governments. And because the New Testament has so little politics in it, they went back to what they call the Old Testament, and in some cases the Talmud.

John Locke's two treatises on government, for instance, are among the most influential books of political theory ever written. People know that, but they tend not to notice that Locke's philosophy relies to an extraordinary degree on his reading of the Hebrew Bible. There are several hundred references to the *Tanach* in Locke's political theory while virtually nothing from the New Testament. But in universities it's usually taught as though Locke was just a liberal thinker who made it all up. The fact that he's taking so much from the Bible is not even a subject considered worth mentioning.

I'll give you another example. The idea that the world should not have one world government but rather should be divided into nation-states is a biblical idea. You cannot find it anywhere in Greek or Roman sources. It enters Western civilization only through the Jewish tradition. And yet, when people talk about the nation-state, they talk about it as though it was some kind of modern idea.

In your most recent book, *God and Politics in Esther*, you aim to uncover the central ideas of *Megillas Esther*, one of which, you argue, is that human beings must act if they wish to effect change. Can you explain?

It says in *Sefer Shoftim* that God "raised up" Ehud to fight Israel's battles. Yet, everything that takes place seems to be something that Ehud did and planned himself. So who's making the decisions here? God or Ehud?

Or let's say at the waters of the Red Sea. God says to Moshe, "What are you calling on me? Take your staff, place it over the waters, and divide the sea!" And then it says that God divided the sea because Moses put his staff over the waters. Why do you have both God and Moshe acting?

So the proposal I make in this book is that these two levels of causation are very basic in understanding how the *Tanach* is written. The *nevi'im* saw human beings as standing in relation to God the same way a chief of staff stands in subordinate relation to his president. The president doesn't expect him to do everything, but he expects him to constantly take initiatives to make his will come true in the world.

How does this relate to *Megillas Esther*?

I don't read the story of Esther as though it's full of coincidences. There are no coincidences in the story. Everything that happens is directed by human actors and human decisions. But at the same time, God is supposed to be hidden there somewhere, so how can that be? The answer I propose is that Esther's actions are God's actions. God's actions depend, to an extent, on our actions.

In your 2001 book, *The Jewish State: The Struggle for Israel's Soul*, you write at length about post-Zionism – a worldview that would like to see the removal of the Star of David from Israel's flag and the abolishment of the Law of Return, for example. Is post-Zionism still a problem today?

In the 1990s, right after the Oslo Accords, Israel's intellectual and public leadership were in kind of a crazy euphoria thinking that peace was going to come to the Middle East any minute, and many of them were willing to give up on Zionism and Judaism because they thought that would help bring peace more quickly.

Since then, the Middle East has turned into a gigantic slaughterhouse where hundreds of thousands have been killed. That's a terrible tragedy, but it has had one positive effect in Israel, which is that most of the leadership elites are no longer willing to throw Judaism away in order to bring a kind of "instant peace."

But that doesn't mean post-Zionists aren't a problem. They are. They have a huge influence in the media and the courts, and they dominate the universities, raising up a future generation of students who don't understand the connection between their country and being a Jew. But for the moment, all of that is kind of on hold, and it's given us a grace period where we have time to fix things.

You dedicate *God and Politics in Esther* to your father, who, you write, is a bit of a gadfly in the world of quantum mechanics. It's fascinating that both you and your father are champions of unconventional views.

I learned from my father to think that wherever you see experts overwhelmingly agreeing with one another, chances are it's because they're copying ideas from one another without thinking too deeply about them.

And this is something that goes all the way back to the *Tanach,* which records that there were 400 prophets saying that the Baal is God and only one prophet, Eliyahu, saying that [Hashem] is the true God. So the *nevi'im* also understood that wherever you see some kind of huge consensus – where all the experts are agreeing – it doesn't mean they've found the truth. It means they've entered this herd mentality where they don't even criticize themselves anymore because they think they must have the truth since they all agree.

So once you understand that, you quickly become a very good critic of all sorts of things that are accepted as true and wise. In my father's particular case, he is defending a small minority view of Einstein and a figure named David Bohm who believed that quantum mechanics is likely to be a limited part of physics rather than the universal theory that almost everybody thinks it is today. And it's a great honor to watch my father do experiments and write papers, challenging what almost everybody thinks is the truth. I hope some day he's proven correct.

— originally published February 26, 2016

Postscript: *Two seasons of Morgan Freeman's "The Story of God" ultimately aired on National Geographic. Professor Hazony appeared in two episodes. He is now working on a new book – titled "What Is Nationalism?" – in the wake of Brexit and Donald Trump's victory in the 2016 U.S. presidential election.*

Rabbi Yaakov Dov Bleich

Leading an Anxious Ukrainian Jewry

A year has passed since Russia annexed Crimea, but Vladimir Putin is not done thumbing his nose at the West. Despite sanctions and condemnation from the EU and the U.S., Putin continues to arm pro-Russian separatists in eastern Ukraine and some analysts believe he may even bring nuclear weapons into Crimea in the near future.

No one knows when Ukraine will settle down and what its borders will look like when it does. In the meantime, Ukraine's population and its 300,000 Jews are trying to weather the storm as best as possible. For an insider's view of the turmoil, The Jewish Press recently spoke with Rav Yaakov Dov Bleich, one of Ukraine's chief rabbis (the title is claimed by several people). Rav Bleich is a Karlin-Stolin *chassid* and lives in Kiev together with his wife and eight children.

The Jewish Press: What is daily life like for Jews in Ukraine today? Do they feel secure? Do they feel nervous?

Rabbi Bleich: Jews don't feel any more nervous than others. The situation today is that in eastern Ukraine you have Russian terrorists and Russian-backed terrorists fighting and killing indiscriminately. They're trying to pretend they're a separatist movement, but they're being armed to the teeth by the Russians.

Now, where do we Jews stand in all this? The Jews are only part of this fight insofar as they are citizens of Ukraine. In the beginning the Russians were trying very hard to make this a Jewish thing. They said, "We're coming to Ukraine because we have to help the Jews who are in danger from Ukrainian fascists." But we were able to stop the propaganda machine, and that was very important – that Jews not be schlepped in and made to blame for this war.

How many Jews live in eastern Ukraine where the fighting is now concentrated?

We estimate approximately 20,000 Jews lived there before the Russians attacked a year ago. Now there are probably between 6,000-10,000. Many of them are elderly, many are infirm, and some are young people who don't want to start their lives again.

Of those who left, something like 2,000 Jews made *aliyah*, and the rest can be anywhere in Ukraine or Russia. We call them IDPs – "internally displaced persons."

In an interview last year you said that there's a greater sense of security among Jews in Ukraine than in France. Is that really true?

One thousand percent. Jews are not afraid to walk around as Jews in Ukraine. We walk the streets with yarmulkes and are not attacked. There are no Islamic fundamentalists here, thank God.

A cease-fire agreement was signed in Minsk, Belarus last month between Ukraine, Russia, and pro-Russian separatists. Do you think it will hold?

It's a hard question to answer because it isn't even really holding now. The terrorists are still shooting, and we know there's a lot of regrouping going on. NATO has said they've seen a lot of weaponry still being transferred from Russia to the terrorists. In the Ukrainian press, if a day goes by that no one is killed, it's very big news.

[You can argue that] the cease-fire is nominally holding, but the question is: Will it hold enough to go to the second stage? – which is legal elections and some sort of deal under which [areas coveted by pro-Russian separatists] will have some sort of autonomy but still be part of Ukraine. At this point, we don't think that's going to happen. At this point, it looks like the Russians may be trying to create what we call a "frozen conflict" like they did Moldova and Georgia.

What's Putin's endgame?

In Yiddish, there's a saying, *"Tracht nisht vas die ferd tracht veil die ferd tracht nicht* – Don't try to try to figure out what the horse is thinking because the horse is not thinking."

That said, I think Putin's endgame may be to keep Ukraine destabilized enough so that the people of Russia never want to do what the Ukrainians did – which is sign an association agreement with Europe – because that would destroy his dictatorship in Russia. Putin is afraid that if Ukrainians' standard of living goes up because they're part of Europe, it will cause him trouble. He's afraid of an uprising.

It's interesting that for Jews in Ukraine, Putin is the enemy while many Jews in Russia regard him as a great friend.

Let me tell you something: This is not a Jewish fight. The Jews have no side here. The Jews in Ukraine are siding with Ukraine, and the Jews in Russia are siding with Russia. It's very important to understand that.

The Jews in Russia have their president who for whatever reason does whatever he does for them. There's a court Jew, there's a government rabbi – it's a different type of society, and if it works for them, fine. But in Ukraine the Jews want democracy. We believe a democratic society is the best for Judaism to thrive.

What is Judaism like in Ukraine? How many communities are there? How many rabbis?

There are approximately 40 rabbis serving the 300,000-350,000 Jews of Ukraine. The biggest community is in Kiev, where there are three big shuls and another five smaller shuls where Jews *daven*. There are also five day schools. There's an *ivrit b'ivrit* school where kids learn in Hebrew, a school for religious kids, and *kiruv* day schools for kids who are not religious.

There's a lot of kosher food available throughout Ukraine. There are *shechitahs*, there's kosher milk, kosher milk products, etc. It's a really great community with many successful rabbis. In Dnepropetrovsk, there's Rabbi Kamentzky, who is a very famous Chabad rabbi. In Odessa, there's Rabbi Bakst, who has Tikva schools and orphanages for kids. In Kharkov, there's Rabbi Moscowitz, who's a very successful Lubavitch rabbi. In Lvov, there's Rabbi Bald, who's a Stoliner with a beautiful community. In Zhitomir, Rabbi Wilhelm has a very successful community.

So we're not just talking about elderly Jews who are survivors of Soviet communism.

No, not at all. There are many young Jews.

You have to understand that Ukraine was really a very, very Jewish place for many years. It's true that there was a lot of fighting between Ukrainians and Jews throughout the generations, but usually the way it went is like this – let's take, for example, the pogroms that took place from 1648-54 during Chmielnicki's times: There were six years of pogroms, but after that the Jews lived very well with their Ukrainian neighbors.

If you ever read Shalom Aleichem, you'll see a true portrait of what Jewish life looked like in Ukraine. There was a love-hate relationship. They would be very friendly and tight, and then suddenly there would be anti-Semitism. Right after World War I, for example, there were many pogroms in Ukraine, and during World War II many Ukrainian nationalists sided with the Nazis. But if you look at 400 years of history in Ukraine, the overwhelming majority of the time Jews lived well with the Ukrainians.

The reason I'm telling you this is because I hear all the time, "Oh, the Ukrainians are anti-Semites." It's true there was a lot of anti-Semitism, but if you consider what the Jews went through in Russia – which was 400 years of non-stop anti-Semitism – it's not a comparison.

I'm not justifying any anti-Semitism. All I'm saying is that Jews and Ukrainians lived well together most of the time, and today what we're trying to do is build a new pluralistic democratic society where everyone feels comfortable. That's what the Jews of Ukraine want.

You mentioned many Lubavitch and Stolin rabbis serving the Jews of Ukraine. Are there any non-chassidic rabbis in the country? If not, is that because Jews in Ukraine respond better to the chassidic temperament?

The only non-chassidic rabbi is Rabbi Bakst in Odessa. Historically, Ukraine was the bedrock of *Chassidus*. *Chassidus* started in Ukraine. Over the years I've been asked to compare Judaism in Russia and Ukraine and I find it goes along those historical roots. Most Jews in Russia are there because they left the shtetl searching for integration into society. The Jews in Ukraine, by contrast, grew up more in a shtetl – more with chassidic warmth and the environment of *Chassidus*.

So I find that when you speak to Jews in Ukraine, they're more willing to accept warmth and the basis of Judaism in that way than Jews in Russia. In Russia the Jews question, they study, they want to understand. It's a different approach to Judaism.

— originally published April 8, 2015

Postscript: *The number of Jews from eastern Ukraine who have made aliyah is now between 7,000-8,000, Rabbi Bleich told me in April 2017. The Jews of western Ukraine meanwhile are suffering economically from the country's instability. Putin's intentions for the future – and thus the fate of Ukraine – are "very unpredictable," he said.*

Rabbi Joseph Telushkin

Chronicling the Life of the Lubavitcher Rebbe

When Rabbi Menachem Mendel Schneerson assumed the position of Lubavitcher Rebbe in 1951, Chabad was a relatively tiny movement that sometimes struggled to get a *minyan* at its headquarters in Crown Heights. Today, it is the most widely known chassidic group in the world with over 4,000 Chabad emissaries spanning the globe.

How did the Lubavitcher Rebbe build such an empire? What about him inspired so many? What drew people from all walks of life to seek his advice?

In a new 600-page book on the Rebbe, Rabbi Joseph Telushkin attempts to answer some of these questions. Published earlier this month, *Rebbe: The Life and Teachings of Menachem M. Schneerson, the Most Influential Rabbi in Modern History,* is already a New York Times bestseller.

Rabbi Telushkin is also the author of such books as *A Code of Jewish Ethics, Jewish Literacy,* and *Why the Jews?: The Reason for Antisemitism,* which he co-authored with Dennis Prager.

The Jewish Press: How does someone like yourself come to write a biography of the Lubavitcher Rebbe?

Rabbi Telushkin: I have very strong family ties to Chabad. My father, Shlomo Telushkin, *a"h,* was the accountant for the Rebbe and the Previous

Lubavitcher Rebbe from the time Chabad came to the United States, and my grandfather had a strong relationship with both Rebbes. So I grew up with tremendous affection and admiration for Chabad.

And then, for the 12th *yahrzeit* of the Rebbe, I wrote an article about the Rebbe which contained a very moving story about my father. In 1986, my father had a stroke and was unconscious for several days. Every day I would get two calls from the Rebbe's office – "The Rebbe wants to know how your father is."

My father finally came out of his coma, and a few days later I got a call from Rabbi Krinsky, the Rebbe's aide, who said to me, "The Rebbe has an accounting question for your father." I asked him, "Do you know how sick he is?" Rabbi Krinsky said, "Of course the Rebbe knows, but nonetheless he has a question."

So I asked my father the question, and he said to me, "The answer is obvious, you should do this and this," and at that moment I realized what the Rebbe had done. Sitting in his office in Brooklyn, dealing with the biggest issues facing Jewish life, he thought of my father lying in a hospital bed feeling his life perhaps was coming to an end, and he wanted to make my father feel useful and needed.

I was profoundly moved by that experience because it underlined what I came to understand in researching this book – that as much as the Rebbe dealt with world Jewish issues, he always remained focused on the individual.

In *Rebbe,* you write that the 19th-century clergyman Henry Ward Beecher once reportedly told his sister Harriet Beecher Stowe (author of *Uncle Tom's Cabin*) that he was too busy to get involved with the problems of individuals – to which his sister responded, "Even God is not that busy."

It's a great story. But you're right, the Rebbe seemed to find time for individuals, and part of it was because of his extraordinary work ethic. I have a chapter on his work ethic where I quote what his father-in-law said of him: "At 4 a.m., Menachem Mendel is either getting up or going to sleep."

You also mention that the Rebbe once responded to a rabbi who complained of being tired by saying, "I'm also tired, so what?"

That's a very important story because the Rebbe never complained, and you could think, "Okay, maybe he's superhuman. Maybe these things don't get to him." So when he said, "I'm also tired," we realize that he worked on himself to overcome it. The fact that you're tired doesn't free you from obligations.

In that same chapter, I tell of another rabbi, Rabbi Zev Segal, whom the Rebbe had asked to carry out a certain mission when he was in Eastern Europe. When he came back, he reported to the Rebbe that he was able to do it but it was much more difficult than he had expected. The Rebbe said to him, "Rabbi Segal, since when did you make a contract with the Almighty for an easy life?"

Going back to the Rebbe's focus on individuals, you also have a nice story about the Rebbe's response to a rabbi who felt disappointed with the turnout to his event. Can you share?

In Australia, an effort had been made to organize a class on *taharas hamishpacha,* and only one person came. Rabbi Chaim Gutnik, who helped arrange the event, was unhappy and wondered if the effort was worth it. The Rebbe told him, "Moshe Rabbeinu only had one mother."

The idea is that you never know how many more people you might ultimately be influencing when you influence one person. And even if you don't end up influencing other people, that one person himself is an *olam malei.*

What did you find most impressive about the Rebbe in researching this book?

The unconditional love he was willing to offer. He really was not judgmental....

When the Rebbe met Rabbi Israel Meir Lau when Rabbi Lau was still a young rabbi, he asked him what sort of work he was involved with. When he said, "I'm doing work in *kiruv rechokim* – bringing near those who are far away," the Rebbe said to him, "How do we know who's near and who's far? They're all precious in God's eyes."

The Rebbe influenced people from a variety of backgrounds, including such famous personalities as Prime Minister Menachem Begin, Senator Daniel Patrick Moynihan, and Rabbi Jonathan Sacks. How did he reach so many people?

Number one, he was known for being really smart. When people met with him, it wasn't just a photo op. Israeli generals and others would actually discuss strategy with him.

The Rebbe also became known through the *shluchim* he sent. He was [trying to do] something that, as far as I know, has never previously been attempted in all of Jewish history: He wanted to reach every Jew in the world. But in the course of doing that, the *shluchim* carried the Rebbe's message wherever they went, so the Rebbe started to become very known.

You write that the Rebbe also elevated the status of girls and women in Lubavitch. How so?

I mention that there was a Chabad magazine, The Moshiach Times, and the Rebbe was insistent that if there was a boy on the cover, there had to be a girl too. In one case, when they sent him a magazine cover to approve and there was no girl on it, he said, "Where is the girl?"

The other way in which he elevated the status of women – and this was unusual – was by making the wives of the *shluchim* as much a part of the *shlichus* as their husbands. In Tunisia, for example, the *shliach*, Rabbi Pinson, passed away in 2007, but his wife, who might well be 90 years old today, never left. She's continued to head the Chabad activities there because she understood the Rebbe as wanting her to stay as long as there were Jews in Tunisia.

You cite several stories in the book of the Rebbe being unhappy with his *chassidim* calling him Mashiach. You don't mention, however, that after his stroke in 1992, he seemed to give the opposite impression. Do you think he might have thought himself Mashiach at the end of his life?

It's possible the thought entered his head, but on the other hand, I'm more struck by the story that Rabbi Yosef Greenberg, the *shliach* in Anchorage, Alaska, told me. He said he addressed a note to the Rebbe as the Mashiach and handed it to Rabbi Groner, the Rebbe's secretary. When Rabbi Groner came out, Rabbi Greenberg said, "Well, how did the Rebbe react?" And Rabbi Groner said, "He sort of crumpled up the note, threw it on the table, and said, 'Tell him when the Mashiach comes, I'll give him the note.'"

And this happened very late – either late '91 or early '92 – within a couple of months of the Rebbe suffering his stroke.

And after the stroke?

If we are going to draw implications, they have to be drawn prior to the stroke. Once he was sick, we don't exactly know what he was thinking because he couldn't speak. And there's a difference of views. The neurologists, by and large, felt the Rebbe retained his mental faculties fully after the stroke. But Dr. Ira Weiss, who treated the Rebbe very closely and had a close relationship with him, told me the Rebbe's mental [faculties] were compromised.

To end on a positive note: You write in the preface that you are a better person as a result of having written this book. That's a rather unusual statement for a biographer to make.

But it's true. I became a more patient person, I became less judgmental, and I was particularly influenced by the Rebbe's usage of positive language. For example, the Rebbe never liked to use the term "*beit cholim*" because it means "house of the sick." He tried to get Israeli hospitals to call themselves "*beit refuah*."

My wife would often comment that when I came back from working at 770, I always seemed more upbeat and optimistic. The Rebbe really created an infectious, very positive spirit.

— *originally published June 25, 2014*

Russel Pergament

The Newspaper Whiz

When the Boston Globe was up for sale in 2013, former New York Sun managing editor Ira Stoll compiled a list of 25 potential buyers. One of them was Russel Pergament. "[I]f you were buying the Globe and wanted a business-side success," Stoll wrote, "you'd want him on your team, or at least not competing with you."

Pergament, 67, is the former publisher of amNewYork, Boston Metro, and the Tab – a chain of 14 free suburban weeklies outside Boston – as well as the managing partner of two wire services, News Service Florida and State House News Service. Widely acknowledged for his news business acumen, Pergament ventured into the world of Jewish publishing in 2011 when he founded JNS, a Jewish news wire service currently used by several dozen newspapers and websites.

He recently spoke to The Jewish Press.

The Jewish Press: What's your background?

Pergament: I grew up in Queens, NY, in a family that was distinctly unreligious, totally assimilated. I went to public schools in New York, a private high school in Massachusetts, and then Boston University. I became a Zionist, though, during the Eichmann trial. I was 12 at the time, and I was stunned by the trial. It made me realize how vulnerable Jews are, and it really has colored my understanding of history ever since.

How did you get into the newspaper publishing business?

When I was growing up in New York there were seven or eight different daily papers, so I saw a very vibrant press. And as I got older and started to work at different newspapers – Rolling Stone, Hearst newspapers, weeklies, underground papers, etc. – I quickly understood that you could obtain national and world news from half a dozen sources, but local news or news for a specific ethnic group could only be found in your local weekly – which gives these small papers an outsized influence.

So in 1979, my close friend Stephen Cummings and I decided to create a very ambitious local weekly in the Boston area with investigative reporting. That was the Tab, and it worked really well. We really shook it up and put seven other weeklies out of business which just did not work as hard as we did.

In 2003 you launched amNewYork, a freebie many New Yorkers are familiar with from their subway commute. What was your thinking in launching it?

The premise of amNewYork originally was to reach young professionals heading to work in Manhattan with a newspaper they could read in 20 minutes and get a quick scan of the world. We had a lot of world news and we had investigative reporting; our editor was a Pulitzer Prize winner who left the Daily News to lead the newsroom.

It was an energetic and fearless newspaper, and we started attracting advertising from Bloomingdale's, Macy's, Lord & Taylor – the top advertisers in the city – because the ads worked. But then in 2006 we sold our equity to the Tribune Company, and since then it looks like the paper has become more of a lifestyle and pop culture publication, which is a different approach than we had originally succeeded with.

How did you have the gumption to start a newspaper in a market like New York?

People said we were nuts, but we were too into it to even listen. We wanted to reach people in their 20s – and we succeeded. The average age of amNewYork readers was in the high 20s. It became the number-one paper in Manhattan with a circulation of 330,000.

The Sun, a conservative New York newspaper founded a year before you launched amNewYork, ceased publication in 2008 for financial reasons. As someone who leans right politically, did you ever say to yourself, "Maybe I should call up The Sun's publisher, Seth Lipsky, and help him save this paper"?

Before I started amNewYork, I was asked by some of the owners of the paper to look into how I might assist The Sun, but that didn't really go anywhere…

Look, I think The Sun was a remarkable newspaper with coverage that surpassed that of The New York Times. But the focus there always appeared to be content and not so much sales and distribution. They did not want to go free. I think they could have been very successful if they had made it a long-tab size and distributed it in appropriate areas in the city, but that never appealed to them.

Your latest venture is JNS, a Jewish news wire service you started in 2011. What drove you to enter the Jewish news business?

Well, I have a background in wire services. I'm one of the owners of a couple of wire services in Massachusetts and Florida that go to hundreds of newspapers, so I understand the business. I never had much to do with Jewish newspapers, but some of the board members at JTA asked me if I could look over their operation and offer some advice. I made some suggestions that didn't really grab them, and then some of the guys on the board said, "Look, why don't we start our own?"

There was a personal motivation as well. Media coverage of Israel around the world is not merely unfriendly but reflexively hostile. There almost is a conspiracy in the media to somehow delegitimize Israel and make it hesitant and ashamed to use its legitimate means of self-defense. In some ways, it's like liberal media are trying to impose a unilateral disarmament on Israel. That troubled me a lot.

Even more troubling is that in newspaper coverage there's very little context provided. Israel is the size of New Jersey, the armistice lines are only eight miles from Tel Aviv, it's been invaded four times by seven Arab armies, the Hamas charter calls for the destruction of Israel, and there are six million Jews in Israel versus 370 million Arabs around the world. When people understand that, it's much harder to envision Israel as a monolithic Nazi-like war machine.

How many news outlets use JNS stories on a weekly basis?

Probably 40 Jewish newspapers and websites. Some weeks a little more, some a little less. But I find now, for example, that some of our stories are running in the Times of India, which has a circulation of four million, or the Chicago Tribune or the Los Angeles Times.

I find some Christian websites are also taking us. And unlike some Jews, I don't fear evangelicals; I think they're some of Israel's greatest supporters and they should be appreciated, not insulted.

Do you find any newspapers reluctant to use JNS stories for one reason or another?

I'll tell you what surprises me: There are some editors who do not want to upset their readers so they'll publish a JNS news brief about someone in Israel inventing a new flavor of ice cream or an animal born in the Tel Aviv zoo, but they won't run anything that's kind of "scary." Obviously that's very troubling to me. I don't think they should be running a newspaper if they have to sanitize and eliminate such coverage. But I can't pick the editors.

Many people your age are ready to retire, but you seem to be working as hard as ever. One colleague a few years ago said about you: "It's like he drinks 30 Red Bulls every morning – and he never slows down." Do you ever think of retiring to Florida and taking it easy?

I see these people. They're sitting, playing cards, waiting for liver spots.... If you're doing important work and satisfying work, why would you stop?

Throughout your career, you seem to move from venture to venture, never staying put for too long. What's next for you after JNS?

I'm sort of a myopic guy. I'm not a big strategic thinker. I think there's going to come a time before long when JNS is not going to need my involvement anymore. At that point, we'll figure out what kind of trouble I can get into. Right now, I'm loving this.

— originally published October 22, 2014

Postscript: *In a May 2017 e-mail to me, Pergament wrote that "JNS has become one of the largest specialized news wires...and is distributed in every English-speaking nation in the world as well as several Asian and European nations where local editors translate the copy. In North America, JNS content is carried in 55 Jewish weeklies, digital publications, and close to 20 Christian news media outlets.*

"JNS's mission," he wrote, "remains what it was always: to assure objective coverage of Israel amidst the complexities of the Middle East's geopolitics."

Professor Marc Shapiro

Exposing Orthodox Revisionism

Marc Shapiro is one of the most popular and controversial writers in the Modern Orthodox world today, most famous perhaps for publicizing little-known – and often radical – positions in Jewish law and thought.

A professor at Scranton University, Shapiro has just published his fifth book, *Changing the Immutable: How Orthodox Judaism Rewrites Its History*. His first two works – *Between the Yeshiva World and Modern Orthodoxy* and *The Limits of Orthodox Theology* – were National Jewish Book Award finalists.

The Jewish Press: In the preface to *Changing the Immutable*, you quote Yugoslavian writer Milovan Djilas who said, "The hardest thing about being a communist is trying to predict the past." What's the relevance of this quote to your book?

Shapiro: Communist society kept rewriting the history books so you never knew what was going to happen. One day this person was an honored communist figure and the next year he was discredited. Likewise, Orthodox society is constantly rewriting the past. A rabbi can be regarded as an honored figure today, but 10 years later he isn't. An idea might be acceptable today, but 10 years later it might not be.

Your book is filled with examples of historical revisionism and

omissions. Let's go through a number of them. First: Rav Shlomo Zalman Auerbach's position on *lashon hara* between a husband and wife.

He thought if someone is having a bad day and has to get something off his chest, he can mention a certain individual to his wife. Under normal circumstances, that would be *lashon hara,* but he thought among spouses it is permissible because they're like one person. This *p'sak,* though, was removed in a later edition of Rav Shlomo Zalman Auerbach's work because it's not in accordance with the Chofetz Chaim's position.

The Vilna Gaon's comments on Greek philosophy.

The Vilna Gaon states that the Rambam was led astray by "accursed philosophy." But the people who published the Vilna *Shulchan Aruch* – the Romm publishers – were enlightened Jews who were troubled by the phrase "accursed." So they removed it. And until the recent Machon Yerushalayim printing, that's the way it appeared in standard editions of the *Shulchan Aruch.*

Rav Yosef Karo's view of *kapparos.*

He calls it a "*minhag shtut.*" That was removed for obvious reasons – because it was thought to be offensive to those who practice the custom. It appears in the first edition of the *Shulchan Aruch,* but it's not in the Vilna edition or any of the other standard editions.

The Chasam Sofer's position on the beginning and end of Shabbos.

There was a practice in Europe that Shabbos began after sunset, in accordance with Rabbeinu Tam's position. This is an old practice that has pretty much fallen out of favor, but for much of Jewish history Shabbos started after sunset.

What I quote in the book is a protest [letter] that criticized Jews in Williamsburg who were still observing this custom. [The main point of that letter, though, concerned] the end of Shabbos. When Rav Moshe Stern published a volume of the *teshuvot* of the Chasam Sofer, it was censored because the Chasam Sofer doesn't rule like Rabbeinu Tam. The Satmar Rav didn't want that to be known.

The *Kitzur Shulchan Aruch*'s comments about non-observant Jews.

In the original text, he says that you don't mourn for irreligious Jews, and you don't really have anything to do with them. They're wicked people, and we should rejoice when the wicked die. But if you look in later editions of this work, those comments are completely removed.

The Rema's *teshuvah* on *yayin nesech*.

The Rema [confronted] a situation where Jews were drinking non-kosher wine in Moravia. The water was not very healthy, so people started drinking wine. The question was: Can this be justified? In his responsum, Rav Moshe Isserles is very upset that they're drinking the wine. However, he attempts to justify them ex post facto so that they would not be viewed as sinners.

The censors, though, were worried that people would see the *teshuvah* and say, "We can drink non-Jewish wine," so they removed it. It was a valid concern because Israel Silverman from the JTS actually used Isserles' responsum to justify drinking non-Jewish wine today. He was attacked for that – and rightly so – because this was only an ex post facto justification.

The speech of the Belzer Rebbe's brother in 1944 when the Rebbe and his family escaped Hungary.

He said the Rebbe wasn't leaving because there was anything to be afraid of, and that the people don't need to be worried. When the *drasha* was reprinted in 1967 that was cut out – for obvious reasons, because the Nazis *did* move in to Budapest and destroyed as much of the Jewish community as they could.

Rav Kook's many *haskamos*.

In his day, Rav Kook was the greatest writer of *haskamot* and pretty much everyone in the Lithuanian Torah world wanted his approbation. Over the years, though, Rav Kook has fallen out of favor and therefore there's a problem: If Rav Kook is not an acceptable authority, what do you make of the fact that all these great rabbis were proud to have his *haskama* grace their works?

The solution has been a systematic campaign to wipe out Rav Kook's *haskamot* and wipe him out from the Torah world. There's been more censorship with Rav Kook than really any other figure.

Interestingly, you write that Rav Yosef Shalom Elyashiv – regarded by charedim at the turn of century as the *gadol hador* – was not happy with this censorship and that Rav Kook was even *mesader kiddushin* at his wedding.

He was *mesader kiddushin* at Rav Elyashiv's *and* Rav Shlomo Zalman Auerbach's wedding. They looked toward him as the leader, and as far as I know, Rav Elyashiv never changed his view of Rav Kook. I'm not saying he agreed with everything he stood for, but Rav Elyashiv's family was in Rav Kook's camp at the time of the great dispute, as was Rav Shlomo Zalman Auerbach's family.

In light of the Torah's admonition to "stay far away from falsehood," what do you make of all these examples of censorship? Isn't it dishonest to rewrite history or remove passages in books that one dislikes or finds uncomfortable?

Truth is a value, but there are other values as well. We know that if a bride is not beautiful, the Gemara rules you can say she's beautiful because there are other values more important than absolute truth.

But this opens up the door to censors. So, for example, if you're worried that Rav Kook's *haskamot* will lead people to conclude that he's a great sage and therefore it's okay to be a Zionist, [you will give yourself] a green light to alter the truth. That's part of the problem because I don't think anyone wants truth to be absolute. We agree with Hillel that you don't hurt people's feelings and if someone gives you a present you don't like, you still tell the person, "I like it very much." However, since truth is not absolute, it does open the door for all sorts of individuals to say, "We can cover this up."

Would you prefer that editors at least tell readers they've removed material? For example, in *Changing the Immutable* you have a picture of a page of Rabbi Moses Hyamson's translation of the Rambam's *Mishneh Torah* in which the words "Translation omitted" appear in place of two *halachos*.

Yeah, that's interesting because he tells us. Clearly if people leave things out, they should let the reader know. But I don't think they should leave things out. I don't see what the problem is. It's Torah. Torah deals with all matters, and there's nothing to be embarrassed about.

Some people argue that many rabbis would censor their own works if they were alive today. For example, in one of your posts on The Seforim Blog you note that the translator of a recent biography of Rav Elyashiv omitted the fact that he apparently didn't know his own children's names due to his deep involvement in Torah study. But wouldn't Rav Elyashiv himself have given the okay for the translator to omit this fact if told that American Jews wouldn't appreciate this facet of his character?

You're probably correct. But the person who wrote the book on Rav Elyashiv is alive and was involved with the translation. He can do what he wants with his own book. That's very different than taking a book from 100 years ago and deciding to cut something out.

But what if the material you take out is completely incidental to the author's life and philosophy and will do nothing except decrease the number of people who will read the author and respect him?

I understand that argument, but I don't accept it for the simple reason that who are you to decide what's important? I personally do not believe that anyone has the right to tamper with someone else's writings.

Last question: Your critics argue that many of your books make one cynical and disillusioned with Judaism. What's your response?

If that's what they feel, they shouldn't read them. But I'm not writing as a yeshivish-type person or spiritual leader putting forth a vision. I'm writing historical books. If certain people find them troubling, that's fine; they shouldn't read them. I don't take any offense at that. Not every book is for every person.

— originally published July 15, 2015

Postscript: *Marc Shapiro is currently writing a book on the recently-published writings of Rav Avraham Yitzchak Kook.*

Professor Gil Troy

Revisiting the UN's "Zionism Is Racism" Resolution

On November 10, 1975, the United Nations General Assembly passed Resolution 3379, declaring Zionism a form of racism. In reaction, Daniel Patrick Moynihan, the United States ambassador to the UN, rose and proclaimed, "The United States...will never acquiesce in this infamous act."

Moynihan's fight against Resolution 3379 is the subject of a new book by historian Gil Troy. Titled *Moynihan's Moment: America's Fight Against Zionism and Racism* (Oxford University Press), the book also traces the resolution's impact on American foreign policy and Moynihan's subsequent 24-year career as a New York senator.

The author of eight previous books, Troy is a professor at McGill University, a fellow at the Hartman Institute, and a columnist for The Jerusalem Post. He is also the brother of Tevi Troy, a fellow at the Hudson Institute and an adviser to Mitt Romney during the 2012 presidential campaign.

The Jewish Press: Why did you write this book?

Troy: When I was growing up, Daniel Patrick Moynihan was my hero and I remembered the moment he stood up for Israel in the UN. But as an American historian, I was surprised that this moment – which to me was a critical turning point in America's relationship to the UN and the world – was barely mentioned in books about the 1970s.

When the General Assembly passed this infamous act, it was six months after the fall of South Vietnam. It was a moment of tremendous American demoralization, and Moynihan spoke a language that inspired Americans. In fact, it inspired Ronald Reagan, who quoted Moynihan in his speeches on the campaign trail in 1976.

Why did the UN proclaim Zionism a form of racism? Was it already so anti-Israel in 1975?

The UN had started turning anti-Israel in the 1960s. I interviewed George Will for the book, and he said Israel made a tremendous mistake in 1967: It dared to win at a time when the Left was falling in love with victims.

The interesting thing about Resolution 3379 is that it was a fallback. The original idea was to kick Israel out of the UN. But that ran into the opposition of Henry Kissinger and many Asian and African countries that were new members of the United Nations and didn't want to start making membership in the UN something that was debatable.

You write in the book that Moynihan fought Resolution 3379, not out of love for Israel, but America. Please explain.

Moynihan came in as UN ambassador in 1975 saying, "Israel is not my religion." But he saw that the new way of humiliating the United States was Israel, and it offended his sensibilities. It played into his fears of where the Third World and the UN were going, so he said, "This is unacceptable."

You also write that while the UN was debating whether Zionism was racism, a genocide was under way in Cambodia which the UN ignored.

Absolutely, and that's part of the reason why I call November 10, 1975 the day the UN died.

Although Henry Kissinger, secretary of state at the time, opposed Resolution 3379, he also didn't fully support Moynihan's campaign against it. Why?

Kissinger was more from the realist school than the idealist school Moynihan was from. He wanted a quieter, softer diplomacy, so he found Moynihan a bit of the bull in the diplomatic china shop. I found transcripts where Kissinger literally says to one of his foreign aides, "We're conducting foreign policy here. This isn't a synagogue."

In fairness to Kissinger, though, the Americans [believed] Egypt was in the process of leaving the Soviet orbit after the 1973 war. Kissinger – and the Israelis – saw Resolution 3379 as a line in the sand that the Palestinians, Libyans, and Syrians were drawing to force Egypt to vote with them and thus keep Egypt alienated from the West. So Kissinger and the Israelis didn't want to overreact because they thought, from a geo-strategic global perspective, that it was better to have Egypt come into the American camp.

Kissinger also wanted to make friends with the Third World, so he was annoyed by this "Zionism is racism" thing. He wanted to be fighting on other fronts.

Finally, Kissinger had established himself as a German-American intellectual and was uncomfortable with his Jewish identity. Like so many of us in the 1960s and '70s, he understood that the best way to get ahead was by not emphasizing his Jewishness. He didn't want to be the *Jewish* secretary of state. He wanted to be the *American* secretary of state. So this whole thing stirred a hornet's nest of discomfort.

Among the surprises in this book is Betty Friedan. Most people know her as a feminist, but you write that she actually was something of a Zionist too.

In July 1975, the International Women's Year Conference came out against Zionism and, given the discourse among many feminists today about Zionism, I had assumed before writing this book that Betty Freidan had rolled over and embraced that idea.

I'm very happy to say, though, that I discovered this whole story of Betty Freidan, Letty Cottin Pogrebin, and Bella Abzug – joined by non-Jewish American feminists – opposing the conference's resolution against

Zionism. And on November 11, 1975 when [Jewish groups organized] a huge rally in midtown Manhattan against Resolution 3379, Betty Friedan was the surprise guest speaker. She got up and said for the first time publicly: "I am a Zionist." This is something that really affected her soul and shook her up.

Going back to the UN: Many people today take it for granted that the UN is anti-West. In your book, though, you write that Americans were actually in love with the UN when it was first founded.

It's like a messy divorce where people forget they were once in love. The UN in 1945 was supposed to be the mechanism that was going to bring peace and world order. There was this redemptive, almost messianic quality of the conversation about the UN in 1945. I remember people in my neighborhood would trick-or-treat for UNICEF.

So what happened?

First, by getting involved in Vietnam, the United States lost its credibility with much of the world. But the two more important things are the growth in UN membership and the Soviet ascendancy. The UN grew from 40 or so nations in 1945 to 142 in 1975. These new members included many Third World countries with dictators who started using the very democratic rights and procedures that most of them didn't give their own people to assert themselves in the UN. And the people who [took advantage of] this were the Soviets who started realizing that the UN could become a new arena in which to fight the West.

In the first 20 years of the UN's existence, the Soviets were actually known as the veto people. Andrei Gromyko, who was the Soviet ambassador to the UN, was known as "Mr. Nyet." But by the 1970s, you start seeing the U.S. for the first time using its veto in the Security Council and being outvoted in the General Assembly.

What did the Third World have against America? Why would it vote against it in the UN?

It's complicated. If you look at the Kennedy administration, the Third

World was in love with America. But things changed due to Soviet manipulation, America's involvement in Vietnam, and, ironically enough, America's own internal rebellion in the 1960s and 1970s. Elite Americans, especially on the far left, started trashing America. And if America itself has voices saying that America is an evil, imperialist, racist, colonialist country, then the Third Worlders – manipulated by Soviet propagandists – say the same thing.

Moynihan saw this turn against the United States in the UN and said, "Let's acknowledge it. Rather than appeasing, let's start doing something. Let's link our foreign aid to voting records in the UN. What kind of people have we become that we continue to pump money into countries that disrespect and betray us in the UN?"

For many liberals today, bashing America is something of a fad. Moynihan, interestingly, was a liberal and yet decried this practice. You quote him saying, "It is past time we ceased to apologize for an imperfect democracy. Find its equal."

Right, that's one of his classic lines. Moynihan was fighting a double fight. On the one hand, he was fighting the Third World, the Soviets, and American diplomats who were appeasing them. But he was also fighting the Left. He was a man of deep liberal principles, and he saw the New Left breaking away from core liberal values of universal ideals and human rights. It's one of the things that scared him about the 1960s.

On December 16, 1991, the UN reversed itself and repudiated resolution 3379. What led the UN to change its mind?

This is a great and important story today when we so often get discouraged. Everyone told the Jewish community that the General Assembly does not repeal resolutions. The General Assembly had never gone back on any of its resolutions. But Moynihan, Israeli President Chaim Herzog, Ronald Reagan, Bibi Netanyahu, and the American Jewish community pushed. They didn't succeed, but they kept on trying.

And then under George H. W. Bush, in a remarkable moment of

bipartisanship, the resolution was repealed. The Soviet Union was weeks away from falling, and the Jewish community cleverly framed it as a declaration of independence of Soviet influence. They made it a moment of healing, and it worked.

Resolution 3379 was passed 37 years ago and repealed 21 years ago. Why should anyone care about these events today?

Three reasons. First, it's an inspirational moment. It teaches us that activism counts and that we can win this fight. Second, unfortunately the great big lie that Zionism is racism lives, and we have a responsibility to understand it. And third, we have to learn that the fight against the delegitimization of Israel must be a core value that unites Left and Right. It should not be a right-wing issue. It must be a Left-Right issue.

— originally published January 30, 2013

Postscript: *In 2015, Professor Troy published "The Age of Clinton: America in the 1990s." His next book, to be published in the spring of 2018 with a foreword by Natan Sharansky, is called "The Zionist Ideas: An Update of Arthur Hertzberg's Classic Zionist Reader."*

Professor William Helmreich

Walking New York – All of It

For his latest book, City College's William Helmreich walked nearly every block of New York City – 120,960 blocks in total. It took him four years and nine pairs of shoes, but the result is *The New York Nobody Knows: Walking 6,000 Miles in the City* – the first sociological study of America's "greatest city," as New Yorkers like to call it.

In a recent interview, Professor Helmreich spoke about his new book, as well as two earlier ones: *The Yeshiva World* and *Against All Odds*.

The Jewish Press: Despite covering 6,000 miles, you actually did not walk New York City in its entirety. Which unfortunate blocks missed your attention?

Helmreich: Out of 6,350 miles, I walked 6,000. I'm working on the other 350 now. There are a couple of areas in Staten Island that missed my attention, like Bay Terrace and New Dorp. There were also a couple of little pockets in Marine Park.... I guess you can say 98 percent of the city was walked.

Walking 6,000 miles is not easy. What inspired such an endeavor?

My father was much the inspiration because when I was a kid he devised this game called "Last Stop." We would take a subway to the last stop and then walk around the neighborhood. It was a cheap way of entertainment and it also taught me what a fascinating place New York City is.

In addition, my area [of expertise] is urban sociology, and I realized that no sociologist had ever done a study of New York – or any large city for that matter. There's a book about Canarsie, about the Upper West Side, about 10 blocks in Greenwich Village, but apprehending a large city is much more complicated.

When I decided to write about New York, I thought I would find 20 blocks or so that represented the city – say, 13th Ave. in Boro Park or Broadway in Manhattan. But I soon realized that in a city of 120,000 blocks, I wouldn't be able to justify or explain why 20 streets really accurately represent all of New York. So I concluded that I would have to do the entire city.

You write that your father was a walker as well.

He walked 7-8 miles a day well into his 80s, and he lived to be 101. He died three weeks shy of his 102nd birthday in his apartment with his brain intact, so I guess it was a good idea.

What are some of the most interesting things you learned about New York while writing this book?

For one, I found that the city is a lot friendlier than people think. I rarely found anyone who refused to talk to me. People were uniformly friendly.

It's interesting you say that because people sometimes tag New Yorkers as sharp-edged and brusque.

They have that sharp-edge, wise-guy sense of humor, but at the same time, once you get beyond that, which takes about a minute, they will be friendly. They'll make a wisecrack, but that's the way New Yorkers are. In another city, if a person responded that way you would think they were rude, but here it's sort of the New York attitude.

When older Jews reminisce about New York, they sometimes fondly recall such old Jewish neighborhoods as Brownsville and Pelham Parkway. What happened to these areas?

It's a complicated question. Brownsville started out as a Jewish neighborhood. It was built up at the turn of the century when the Lower East Side became too crowded. Speculators came out and built housing, but these apartments were never built very well.

And then, in the 1950s, there was a tremendous migration of blacks from the Deep South, plus hundreds of thousands of Puerto Ricans came here. The city was overwhelmed. It couldn't care for these people. They had lousy apartments, no jobs, few libraries, very poor schools, and ultimately, because of unemployment, families broke up and a lot of children grew up with one parent in the home. Crime developed as a natural outgrowth and Jews started running away.

How about other areas that have long had bad reputations – Crown Heights or Washington Heights, for example – but which have been yuppifying and gentrifying in recent years?

It's all part of crime reduction, ethnic outreach, ethnic understanding, and various other social and economic factors. And you hit the right neighborhoods. When you talk about Crown Heights, it's not just the traditionally Lubavitch side of Crown Heights, but the other side – the side north of Eastern Parkway – that's gentrifying.

And Washington Heights… look what they did. A lot of this is about image. Washington Heights is now renamed Hudson Heights and gentrification is taking place not only above 181st Street but below it as well. When people have the opportunity to live in a neighborhood 20 minutes away from work in midtown Manhattan, they're not going to turn that down. In fact, my understanding is that apartments in Washington Heights now cost more than apartments in Riverdale.

I believe the next area ripe for gentrification, by the way, is the Bronx, and you're seeing the birth pangs right now in areas like the Grand Concourse below 161st Street.

Thirty years ago, you wrote a book called *The World of the Yeshiva*. As part of your research you interviewed many of the famous *rashei yeshiva* of yesteryear, such as Rav Moshe Feinstein, Rav Yaakov Kamenetsky, and

Rav Shneur Kotler. Many people would probably be fascinated to listen to those interviews. Do you still have the recordings?

At one time I thought I did, but it seems that all I have are the transcripts. It's possible that Yeshiva University, to which I donated all the transcripts, has them. In fact, I received a letter two weeks ago from someone – a grandson of Rav Shneur Kotler – who read the interviews.

Any chance they will one day see a wider audience?

It's interesting you mention that because the fellow I was talking to told me that if I put the interviews together in the form of a pamphlet, it would probably be widely distributed in the yeshiva world. So when all this dies down – this book is only out four weeks and is already going into a second printing – I'm going to turn my attention to that because I really feel these interviews should find a wider audience, especially because there's so much revisionism that goes on in the Orthodox community.

For example, in the second chapter of *The World of the Yeshiva,* I write about the attempt to start a college in the mid-1940s. I got hold of documents from the Board of Ed from New York State that indicated that Chaim Berlin and Torah Vodaath – Rabbi Hutner and Rabbi Mendlowitz – wanted to start a college to counter Yeshiva University's influence on their community. They got together a charter and spent $150,000 on it and a year later in 1946 they got approval for this college called the American Hebrew Theological University.

I have a lot of information about this that I did not put in the book. I probably want to attach that as an addendum. There's a lot of stuff that I didn't put in the book. When it was published, Rabbi Moshe Sherer, who was the head of Agudah for a long time, said to me, "We thank you for what you wrote; we thank you even more for what you didn't write."

In addition to writing the first in-depth work on American *yeshivos*, you also wrote *Against All Odds*, the first sociological study of Holocaust survivors in America. The book's subject matter is arguably very important due to the common phenomenon today of people blaming their past for their problems in life. If there ever were a population,

though, that could have justifiably blamed circumstances for not being able to function, Holocaust survivors would be it. But for the most part, they didn't. They bit their lips and rebuilt their lives.

We don't always have a lot of control over what happens to us but we do have control over how we deal with it. A lot of the survivors were damaged. My statistical study based on a random sample of survivors indicates that 15,000 of the 140,000 survivors who came here were seriously damaged. Now, that's not small potatoes, but it's also important to understand that 125,000 managed to go on with their lives.

It has to do with a fundamental attitude. I think today, as our society has grown more comfortable materially, we don't make the same demands nor do we have the same expectations of people that we had then. The truth of the matter is we have so much therapy available that it's almost like we have too much therapy. It's almost like we're always trying to find an excuse for somebody who does something wrong rather than hold him accountable for it. And there's a natural tendency if you have a choice between being made to pay for what you did wrong and not having to pay, you would rather not. And if you're given the opportunity to blame other forces, you will.

Survivors didn't have that kind of opportunity.... And it's also not clear that talking about your suffering really clears your head. People say, "Oh, you're just repressing." Well, maybe it's better to repress. You go through your whole life, you repress, you don't think about it too much, you die, and you've lived a relatively satisfying life. Or, you wallow in self-pity and you can't go on. I think today people are much more self-indulgent.

— originally published December 4, 2013

Postscript: *Professor Helmreich is currently working on a five-volume walking guide series – one volume per New York borough. The first, "The Brooklyn Nobody Knows: An Urban Walking Guide," came out in October 2016.*

The interviews he conducted with famous rashei yeshiva three decades ago are now available for free on the Internet.

John Rosengren

Telling the Hank Greenberg Story

To his parents' friends, he was "Mrs. Greenberg's disgrace," but to sports fans, he is arguably the greatest Jewish baseball player of all time.

Long before Sandy Koufax came on the scene, Hank Greenberg excited Jewish sports fans with his prowess on the baseball diamond. Playing in the 1930s during the most anti-Semitic period in U.S. history, Greenberg served as daily proof that Jews were neither foreign nor inferior, and could excel even in that most American of all sports: baseball.

The Jewish Press recently spoke with John Rosengren, author of *Hank Greenberg: The Hero of Heroes*.

The Jewish Press: Hank Greenberg is one of the greatest baseball players of all time. Yet, fans in his day routinely taunted him, as you note in your book. Why?

Rosengren: Things were different back in the '30s and '40s. First off, ethnic identification was much stronger. Also, anti-Semitism was much more widely practiced and socially acceptable. So Greenberg was singled out as a Jew and frequently derided with ethnic slurs and insults.

You write that many Jewish ballplayers at the time changed their last names to ones that sounded less Jewish. Greenberg didn't. Why not?

Well, it wasn't just ballplayers who changed their names. People in Hollywood and other professions changed their names too so they could become more socially acceptable.

But Greenberg didn't. He was proud to be a Jew. He was raised in an Orthodox household by his parents, and his heritage was very important to him as a young man. He'd go to temple on high holy days, and when he was in the minor leagues he lived in an Orthodox boarding house so he could eat the Seder meal on Passover. He didn't want to deny who he was.

It's interesting that of all cities to play in, Greenberg chose Detroit, home to one of America's most notorious anti-Semites at the time, Henry Ford.

It was certainly a hostile city. Ford was the arch anti-Semite of America and his screeds against Jews in his newspaper, the Dearborn Independent, were quite frequent. At the same time, the Roman Catholic priest Charles Coughlin was also in Detroit and he had a radio show with an audience of 10 million that eagerly listened to his rants against Jews.

Jews represented only five percent of Detroit's population at the time, so there were many people in Detroit who had never met a Jew and didn't have a point of reference to challenge these stereotypes until Hank Greenberg came along. He was 6' 4", 220 lbs., and as soon as he stepped on the field, he shattered any stereotype of Jews being weak or unathletic. Later on, he proved himself to be an intelligent, charming, and charismatic guy and won over a lot of fans.

You write that Greenberg served as a tremendous source of pride to Jews. How so?

The '30s and '40s were very difficult times for Jews – not just in Europe but also here in the United States. Jews couldn't practice at many law firms, couldn't be treated at certain hospitals, and couldn't attend the college of their choice. Greenberg actually had a scholarship to Princeton but wasn't allowed to attend because the university had already fulfilled its Jewish quota, which was two percent. Additionally, there were ads in newspapers that said "gentiles only" and there were restricted communities where Jews could not live. The climate was very much against Jews.

And so at a time like this, Greenberg became a rallying point for Jews. They felt an affinity with Greenberg as one of their own and took a special pride in his accomplishments. If someone today tells you a certain baseball player is Jewish, you say, "Oh, nice," but back then the fact that Greenberg was Jewish meant so much to people. Ethnic identification was much stronger then. The other night, I was in New York doing a book event and an elderly woman said to me, "We looked to him as such a hero."

Interestingly, Greenberg wasn't really comfortable at first in his role as a representative Jew, especially in 1934 when he was forced to decide whether or not to play on Rosh Hashanah.

Well, he was a young man. He promised his parents he wouldn't play and yet his team was in a pennant race against the Yankees and needed him. He was a very private man and it was a personal decision, yet it got thrust into the public spotlight. People around the country were sending him telegrams or letters with advice. Rabbis were telling him to play or not to play while the owner of the Detroit Tigers called him and said, "We really need you."

He ended up playing on Rosh Hashanah and hit two home runs, carrying the team to a 2-1 victory. But afterwards he went back to his hotel and received phone calls from people complaining about him playing and telegrams from rabbis saying his decision was going to make it hard for kids who want to observe their faith.

He was 23 years old, and that's a lot of pressure to carry. He just wanted to be an American and to be able to do this thing that he was good at. Instead he became a *Jewish* ballplayer and representative of the Jews. He knew that was a big load to carry but he grew into it, came to accept it, and I think in the end did the Jewish people very proud as their standard-bearer.

Jews apparently were especially proud of his decision to quit baseball and enlist in the U.S. Army in 1941.

Greenberg was the first major leaguer to re-enlist after Pearl Harbor was attacked, even though he had just been honorably discharged two days earlier, on December 5. Jews took a special pride in his patriotism. He also really won over the admiration of all Americans for his willingness to set aside his personal career to fulfill his patriotic duty. Greenberg was baseball's best player at the time. He was the American League's Most Valuable Player in 1940 and the highest paid player too.

Nowadays, a great many parents encourage their children to pursue sports. Greenberg's parents did not. Why not?

His parents came over trying to escape persecution and economic hardship in Europe. They came to America, the land of opportunity, wanting to have a better life for their children, and they saw college as the gateway for that. So they wanted Hank to go to college, become a professional, and have a good life. They saw baseball as a "bum's game." He was considered "Mrs. Greenberg's disgrace" for playing baseball. They didn't understand the game. It's like, "Why are all these grown men chasing this ball around a field?"

As someone who's not Jewish, what made you decide to devote so much time to writing a book about Greenberg?

It was this story of an American hero, a cultural icon, that attracted me. As an author, I'm always looking for stories of substance and social significance, and in Greenberg's story I found that. He transformed the way gentiles viewed Jews, and transformed the way Jews viewed themselves.

You've called Greenberg the greatest Jewish baseball player of all time. What about Sandy Koufax?

Sandy Koufax played once every four days. Hank Greenberg played every day. Also, Greenberg was consistently good throughout his career while Koufax had six years when he wasn't very good.

— *originally published May 22, 2013*

Postscript: *In 2015, Rosengren published another baseball book, "The Fight of Their Lives: How Juan Marichal and John Roseboro Turned Baseball's Ugliest Brawl into a Story of Forgiveness and Redemption." In 2016, an article he wrote for The Atlantic was nominated for a Pulitzer.*

Professor Jess Olson

Explicating an Unusual Prayer

Last week, Maggid Books released *Mitokh Ha-Ohel: The Shabbat Prayers* – the fourth volume of an ongoing series featuring essays from Yeshiva University rabbis and professors. To get a taste of the book, The Jewish Press spoke with Professor Jess Olson about his chapter, "The Prayer for the Welfare of the Government."

Olson is an associate professor of Jewish history at Yeshiva University and the author of *Nathan Birnbaum and Jewish Modernity: Architect of Zionism, Yiddishism and Orthodoxy*.

The Jewish Press: For centuries, Jews have recited a prayer for the welfare of government leaders. Among these leaders were many Jew-haters including Czar Nicholas II. Why would Jews pray for anti-Semites?

Olson: You have to think about this prayer outside the context of *tefillah* where there are rules and reasons why you do x, y, and z that make sense within *halacha*. The prayer for the government is different. It reflects Jews being a dependent minority in very complicated social contexts where they have to find ways to accommodate their position in line with what the external world thinks of them.

So the personality of the leader is really a moot question. It's never said with the idea of, "Oh, this is a particularly good king, so we say the prayer for him, and if it were a bad king we wouldn't." The idea is we, as a minority in a kind of precarious situation at all times, have to find political ways to make life a little bit less fraught. It's a way of putting on a good face to the outside world.

You write that this prayer began to change in America in the 1840s. How so?

Very early, the prayer took on a standard form that begins with the words "*HaNotein teshuah* – He who grants salvation to kings and dominion to rulers…may He bless…" But in *Tefillot Yisrael*, published in the late 1840s in the United States, it is a much more poetic prayer with expansive references to the United States, the government, and ideas of freedom. It takes on this very American quality.

So whereas the traditional version [is based on Jews being] a minority, seeing themselves outside the larger structure, this new version reflects a vision of Jews seeing themselves as Americans, as being part of the scene.

Black-hat Jews are often thought of as upholders of tradition while Modern Orthodox Jews are thought of as more open to adapting to changing times. Interestingly, though, this traditional prayer for the government is much more likely to be said nowadays in Modern Orthodox shuls than in black-hat shuls.

I think that's a symbol of the triumph of exactly what the new 1840s prayer was saying. It was saying, "We've arrived in America. Here's a place where we can be who we are and pursue what we want without fear of repercussion."

So the charedi disuse of the prayer – and I'm sorry for generalizing, I know it's not all charedim – is reflective of this new reality. [They're implicitly arguing,] "If our reason for saying the prayer was, 'We're worried what the *goyim* are thinking of us,' and 'We're concerned about our safety' – well, we're not afraid of those things anymore. We've accepted the promise of America that we can practice our religion as we see fit." So I actually see the disuse of the prayer as a really positive sign.

To be clear, all *frum* Jews in pre-World War II Europe said this prayer?

Let me be very specific. We're talking about proper *kehillot*. *Chassidim* in the 19th century really destabilized and decentralized the old *kehillot*, so you could have variation. There are probably *chassidim* who did not say the prayer since they didn't view themselves as being in the limelight. But in the real *kehillot* where you had to be concerned about the government, this prayer was pretty much said universally.

Let's turn to Nathan Birnbaum (1864-1937), the subject of your dissertation and first book. Birnbaum coined the term "Zionism" in 1890 but later became an anti-Zionist, an Agudath Israel activist, and a *baal teshuvah* to boot, which was very unusual at the time. How do you explain his transformation?

First of all, he had a very early receptivity to an idea about Jewish peoplehood – he believed that we have a deep, authentic, integral culture. He viewed it almost in terms of 19th-century organic nationalism. Over the course of his career, though, he found Zionism as it became expressed in its political form increasingly unrepresentative of that authentic culture.

He became a *baal teshuvah* in his late 40s, early 50s. We don't know how that happened, but I would say as a historian that he was fixated on this idea of an authentic Jewish identity and moved closer and closer with time to the notion that this identity is rooted in Torah and the historical religious experience of the Jewish people.

Why did Birnbaum later turn on Zionism?

His connection to the Orthodox world was primarily through Vizhnitz, and Vizhnitz was very active in the early days of the Agudah, which was culturally anti-Zionist. Now, when I say anti-Zionist, I don't mean Neturei Karta. The Agudah was functionally anti-Zionist because it saw Zionism, as it was being practiced, as being really antagonistic to religion. But Agudah didn't have a problem with people moving to Israel, and they didn't even have a problem with some kind of organized settlement in Israel. In fact, in the late 1920s and into the '30s, the Agudah was very instrumental in helping people get out of Europe and into Israel.

In a political context, most contemporary Jews associate the name "Birnbaum" with Nathan's grandson, Jacob (Yaakov) Birnbaum, founder of the Student Struggle for Soviet Jewry. Would Nathan Birnbaum have been proud of his grandson?

I think Yaakov Birnbaum is in so many ways a real heir to his grandfather's legacy. His spirit, the depth of his conviction.... I mean, the man really sacrificed everything with the Student Struggle for Soviet Jewry. That's what Nathan Birnbaum was like. So I think he would've looked at Yaakov and applauded him as a kindred spirit.

I should add that in an article in the early 1930s, Nathan Birnbaum wrote that his biggest concern was the threat of communism facing *frum* Jews in Russia. He was afraid that communism would spread to Germany and the rest of Europe and that *frum* Jews would be in the crosshairs. So this concern for the Jews of Russia is a thread that runs from Nosson to Yaakov.

— originally published February 17, 2016

Israel Mizrahi

Selling *Sefarim* in 50 Languages

For some, he evokes a bygone age – when *sefarim* store owners lived and breathed books and could direct customers to, and discuss, a rare Yiddish work just as easily as the latest Feldheim classic.

Israel Mizrahi, though, is a young man of 29. And, unlike *sefarim* store owners of yore, he earns half his profits online where patrons can view and buy any one of 36,000 volumes, ranging in price from $2.99 to $3,299.99. (He carries a total of 150,000 works in his Flatbush store.)

The scion of several rabbinic families (he is named after the Baba Sali, his grandfather's uncle), Mizrahi lives with his wife and three children in Brooklyn.

The Jewish Press: Where did you grow up?

Mizrahi: I grew up locally in Brooklyn, went to community schools, learned in Yeshivat Chevron in Yerushalayim for three years, and got married while I was in Israel. Six days later, I was back in the United States and soon found myself with some bills to pay. I owned a lot of books, so I sold a few. But it's always easier to buy than to sell and, before I knew it, I had 20,000 books. So I was stuck.

Can you talk a bit about your rabbinic family background?

My mother is part of the Abuhatzeira family, and my father comes from rabbinic families in Syria and Yerushalayim.

It's a bit of a conflicting background in the sense that my mother's side was more of the kabbalistic, pious type and my father's side was more of the rationalist, Maimonidean type. My great-great-grandfather, for example, wrote a classic book called *Kenesiya L'Shem Shamayim,* which is a treatise against belief in superstition, magic, *sheidim* – things like that. Jews in Syria at the time were following Muslim practices and basically *makrivim* to *avodah zarah,* so the book is a very strong attack against any such beliefs.

How many languages are represented by the books in your store?

Probably around 50, but I try to focus on about 10 of them: Hebrew, English, Yiddish, German, French, Spanish, Russian, Ladino, and Judeo-Arabic.

I also have a very large collection of books in Judeo-Marathi, which is the language of the Bnei Israel community in India; I have quite a few books in Judeo-Persian; and I even have a book in Judeo-Tatar, which is the language the Jews of Crimea spoke.

What are some of the most interesting books you've sold over the years?

Books that interest me the most are ones that tell a story. So, for example, I have an old *selichos* volume printed in Germany in which somebody handwrote a very long *kinah* about a pogrom that happened in Poland in the 1620s. He describes in detail how the children were killed, the women raped, etc. If you look in the history books, there's no record of this specific pogrom. The only source we have for it is this *sefer,* which happened to survive and end up in my hands.

You apparently used to also carry the Koran in Hebrew.

[Israeli President] Ruvi Rivlin's grandfather did the first translation. There are seven translations in total. You also have a fellow, Professor Abraham Katsch, who did a translation. He was a grandson of the *Maskil L'Eitan,* and his father was Rav Reuven Katz, the *rav* of Petach Tikva. They both came from rabbinic backgrounds and ended up professors.

What other interesting books do you carry?

When you acquire 100,000 books a year, everything shows up eventually. I just acquired an old yearbook from the Rabbi Jacob Joseph School and found among the students a smiling Sheldon Silver.

Other items of interest include a popular explanation of Albert Einstein's theory of relativity in Yiddish; two leaves of a manuscript of *Pirke Merkabah* written in Spain in the 14th century; and a volume from the Bomberg Talmud. You may recall that a full set of this Talmud recently sold for nine million dollars.

A few weeks ago I also supplied two first editions of the Abarbanel that were presented by an organization to Benjamin Netanyahu whose father wrote the definitive work on this famous rabbinic figure.

Where do you find all these works?

Well, I get phone calls if somebody has a library and is moving or if someone who owned a lot of books passed away. There are also rare book collections that are occasionally sold for one reason or another. And then there are many synagogues in small towns in the United States that are closing. They all had libraries, and somebody has to take care of them, so I'm often the one to do it.

You also recently acquired the Toronto Jewish library, correct?

That was quite a sad situation. Toronto had a very fine library of about 50,000 books. It was around since the 1930s but the community, I guess, just didn't support it. The library of the Central Queens Y, which had about 8,000 books, just closed this month as well. I also picked up the library of the Jewish Center in Fairlawn. Nobody was using it.

It's a different world today. People don't go to their little shul anymore to hang out and read books. If they do read, they're reading at home. It's just the way things are.

What kinds of customers enter your store?

Rabbis, book collectors, people who have family interests. Many people, for example, discover their grandfather wrote a *sefer* and want a copy. And then there are learned people who have specific interests. I have a few *mohelim,* for example, who want good libraries on *milah.* One of them has 500-600 books on *milah.* I sold him probably half of them.

The general idea is, whatever interest you may have, chances are I can supply you with reading material for a lifetime.

Do you have non-Jewish customers too?

Yes. There are quite a few evangelical Christians in the U.S. who are very pro-Israel and pro-Jewish. There's also some interest in Asia. The Japanese are known to have quite an interest in Jewish studies. In Tokyo, for example, you have Yiddish courses in Tokyo University, and I've sold them a lot of Yiddish books. I've also sold a complete ArtScroll *Shas* that went to South Korea.

I also have someone from Qatar who has been buying anti-Zionist works from me for a few years already. I generally send him an extra book or two that's more balanced so hopefully he can read those as well and not end up hating us as much.

Is it true that old chassidic *sefarim* are often more expensive than regular *sefarim*?

Yes, because many chassidic groups were small pre-World War II. Take Satmar, for example. Before the war, the Satmar Rebbe just barely had a *minyan* and 200-300 *chassidim* at most. Today there are tens of thousands, and everyone wants a piece of that history. There are only so many books published and only so many letters he wrote, so if everybody wants them, there's going to be a bidding war – and that's what happens.

Other expensive chassidic *sefarim* include ones published by the Shapiro family in Slavita and Zhitomir in Europe. They were grandchildren of Rav Pinchas of Koretz, and the Skverer Rebbe prefers to use only these *sefarim.* But the Shapiros only published so much and time and the Holocaust did their own too, so the market has risen quite a bit for them.

On your blog you write, "Come and experience an Authentic bookstore before they cease to exist." Please explain.

Well, Judaica stores will always be here. But if you go back 50 years on the Lower East Side, there were 50 stores just like mine. Today it's a harder world. People are busy with their lives, they're reading less, and there's nothing you can do about it. Maybe it's the price of a better life. A hundred years ago people were more aware of anti-Semitism. They were more Jewish in many ways, and so they had more of an interest.

Another thing is the price of maintaining a store has risen very fast. Today on the Lower East Side it's prohibitive to rent a store. Used books sell for only so much, and it's very hard to make a proper living from it. The story of bookstores in the U.S. in general – not just Jewish bookstores – is a pretty bad one.

How do you survive? Through Internet sales?

There's no way I could do it without the Internet. Also, it's sort of two parallel businesses at this point with the rare books paying for the other books.

Many people with your interest in *sefarim* become rabbis or librarians. What led you to become the owner of an old-style *sefarim* store?

I don't know. God leads in funny ways. I don't know if it was a conscious decision. It just was something I always wanted to do. And once you're in, it's hard to leave, because what am I going to do with 150,000 books? So I don't know if I can ever retire. Maybe they'll bury me with the books.

— originally published August 10, 2016

Postscript: *Since this interview, Israel Mizrahi has acquired, among other works, a Tanach printed in Amsterdam in 1701, which is said to be the edition needed to conduct a "Goral HaGra."*

The copyright to all photos in this book belong either to the interviewees or the organizations and institutions they are associated with. Specific permission to use the Ben Zion Shenker and Shimon Mercer-Wood photos were obtained from the Milken Archive of Jewish Music and Toby Tabachnick of the Pittsburgh Jewish Chronicle, respectively.

Made in the USA
Middletown, DE
18 April 2022